Memory, Migration and (De)Colonisation in the Caribbean and Beyond

edited by Jack Webb, Rod Westmaas,
Maria del Pilar Kaladeen and William Tantam

University of London Press
Institute of Latin American Studies, School of Advanced Study,
University of London, 2020

British Library Cataloguing-in-Publication Data
A catalogue record for this book is available from the British Library

This book is published under a Creative Commons Attribution-NonCommercial-NoDerivatives 4.0 International (CC BY-NC-ND 4.0) license. More information regarding CC licenses is available at https://creativecommons.org/licenses/.

This book is also available online at http://humanities-digital-library.org.

ISBN:
978-1-908857-65-1 (paperback edition)
978-1-908857-66-8 (.epub edition)
978-1-908857-67-5 (.mobi edition)
978-1-908857-76-7 (PDF edition)

DOI: 10.14296/220.9781908857767 (PDF edition)

Institute of Latin American Studies
School of Advanced Study
University of London
Senate House
London WC1E 7HU

Telephone: 020 7862 8844

Email: ilas@sas.ac.uk
Web: http://ilas.sas.ac.uk

Cover image: The Bronze Woman, Stockwell. Photograph by Cecile Nobrega.

This book is dedicated to the Bronze Woman Charity, who with the OLMEC Charity work tirelessly for the Children of the Windrush.

The Bronze Woman Statue, located in Stockwell Gardens, and depicted on the cover of this book, was the brainchild of Cecile Nobrega, a poetess, who was relentless in her pursuit to honour Caribbean womanhood. With a symbolic statue of Bronze for her toughness, Uplifting her Child, Shaping the next generation.

Contents

	Notes on contributors	vii
	Prologue *Rod Westmaas*	xi
	Introduction *Jack Webb, Maria del Pilar Kaladeen and William Tantam*	1
1.	Loving and leaving the new Jamaica: reckoning with the 1960s *Matthew J. Smith*	19
2.	Why did we come? *B. M. Nobrega*	31
3.	History to heritage: an assessment of Tarpum Bay, Eleuthera, the Bahamas *Kelly Delancy*	37
4.	'While nuff ah right and rahbit; we write and arrange': deejay lyricism and the transcendental use of the voice in alternative public spaces in the UK *William 'Lez' Henry*	57
5.	Journeying through the 'motherland' *Peter Ramrayka*	79
6.	De Zie Contre Menti Kaba – when two eyes meet the lie ends. A Caribbean meditation on decolonising academic methodologies *Nadine King Chambers*	85
7.	Organising for the Caribbean *Anne Braithwaite*	107
8.	The consular Caribbean: consuls as agents of colonialism and decolonisation in the revolutionary Caribbean (1795–1848) *Simeon Simeonov*	117

9. To 'stay where you are' as a decolonial gesture: Glissant's philosophy of Antillean space in the context of Césaire and Fanon   133
    Miguel Gualdrón Ramírez

10. Finding the Anancyesque in Shakespeare's *Julius Caesar* and the decolonisation project in Jamaica from 1938 to the present   153
    Ruth Minott Egglestone

11. Maybe one day I'll go home   173
    Rod Westmaas

    Index   183

Notes on contributors

Matthew J. Smith is professor of Caribbean history at the University of the West Indies, Mona in Jamaica. His research interests include Caribbean migration, and popular culture and politics in the 19th and 20th centuries with special emphasis on Haiti and Jamaica. He is the author of *Liberty, Fraternity, Exile: Haiti and Jamaica After Emancipation* (UNC Press, 2014), and *Red and Black in Haiti: Radicalism, Conflict, and Political Change, 1934–1957* (UNC Press, 2009). He is co-editor with Diana Paton of *The Jamaica Reader: History, Culture, Politics* (Duke University Press, forthcoming).

Ruth Minott Egglestone grew up in Jamaica but has spent most of her teaching career in England and Scotland. She has a background in literature (English and Spanish), education, drama and cultural studies. Her seminal doctoral thesis mapped the development of the Jamaican Pantomime tradition as a model of national identity and a new theatrical form. She is currently working with children in the field of inclusive education, refining a manuscript about teaching with a reggae sensibility in Britain, and collaborating on a biography of Roger Mais. At present, there are also two Shakespeare-based writing projects in the pipeline.

Peter Ramrayka, MBA, CIHM, FIHM, FRSPH, FIHEEM, is author of the acclaimed monograph *Recycling a Son of the British Raj* (Hansib, 2015), which highlights the cultural transformational changes and challenges he went through in his early life as an Indo-Guyanese migrant to the UK. He was an officer in the RAF, and rose to a senior management position in the National Health Service. His career was interspersed with national, international and voluntary consultancies in the UK (including being appointed a Justice of the Peace), Botswana, Pakistan and Tanzania.

Miguel Gualdrón Ramírez is visiting professor of philosophy at Oxford College of Emory. His work focuses on the interconnection between history, politics, and aesthetics in Latin America and the Caribbean, and a philosophical attempt at approaching these topics collectively. He is particularly interested in aesthetic theories and practices (such as literature and film) of this world region that critique colonial forms of self-understanding and self-expression, and contribute to new epistemologies of resistance. His work investigates a

European philosophical tradition of history and aesthetics as challenged by the existence of the Americas.

Bruce Nobrega was born in Guyana and attended Queens College. He came to England for the second time in 1969, and settled, just in time to be included in what is now termed the Windrush Generation. He studied quantity surveying and up to his retirement worked on various projects including social housing. He is a long-standing treasurer of a BAME housing association, originally formed for women; he is a committee member on various organisations connected with the community; and he has been involved with the Adult Literacy Programme. He is an activist whose travels have enhanced his knowledge and understanding of black history, and the nuanced effects that the various western colonising powers have had on their subject–citizens.

Kelly Delancy is from Nassau, Bahamas. She graduated in 2011 with a BA in anthropology from the State University of New York and in 2015 with an MA in anthropology from the University of Florida. She hopes the information generated during her studies will be of value to future generations of Bahamians and others interested in the history of south Eleuthera and the Bahamas. Delancy currently assists researchers tracing Bahamian histories and continues to share information collected on community histories through the 'From Dat Time': Oral and Public History Institute of the University of the Bahamas, and through the Finding Home Bahamas project, which can be found on Facebook and Instagram.

Simeon Simeonov is a PhD student at Brown University interested in the history of extraterritoriality and its relationship to diasporas, empires, states, colonialism and decolonisation. His work historicises the creation of the modern nation state as a process shaped as much by 'external' as by 'internal' agents and institutions. Methodologically, his scholarship aims at transcending the inner-disciplinary boundaries separating cultural, social, political and diplomatic history. It is only by elucidating the role of marginalised groups as political and diplomatic agents that we can fully understand the stakes of creating colonial and post-colonial polities and the political-economic system of global capitalism.

William 'Lez' Henry, born in Lewisham, London to Jamaican parents, is the British reggae deejay Lezlee Lyrix. He is an associate professor at the University of West London and is renowned as a first-class public speaker. He has lectured nationally and internationally and featured in numerous documentaries and current affairs television and radio programmes. He also writes about many of the concerns of the African diaspora in the UK, and is a keen martial artist.

Jack Webb is a research associate in the School of English, Newcastle University, whose work focuses on the cultural history of the Caribbean and the British Empire. He is the author of *Haiti in the British Imagination, 1847–1904* (Liverpool University Press, 2020), and has published in the *Journal of Caribbean History* and *Small Axe: A Caribbean Journal of Criticism*.

William Tantam is postdoctoral fellow in Caribbean Studies, Institute of Latin American Studies, University of London, and directs the Centre for Integrated Caribbean Research. His work focuses on embodiment and agency in relation to class, gender and power in the Caribbean. His forthcoming publications include *An Ethnography of Class and Masculinities in Jamaica: Letting the Football Talk* (Bloomsbury, 2019).

Maria del Pilar Kaladeen is an associate fellow at the Institute of Commonwealth Studies. She works on the colonial history of the system of Indian indenture in Guyana (1838–1917). Maria is co-editor of *We Mark Your Memory: Writing from the Descendants of Indenture* (School of Advanced Study, 2018) and a contributor to *Mother Country: Real Stories of the Windrush Children* (Headline, 2018). Her monograph on indenture in Guyana is forthcoming with Liverpool University Press.

Anne Braithwaite is a Guyanese living in London for almost 50 years, who has worked extensively with Guyanese, Caribbean and Pan-African political activists. Additionally, she has had an accounting and finance career in industry, commerce and education, then later worked with the Race Equality Foundation's 'Strengthening Families, Strengthening Communities' programme. These experiences propelled Anne's rethinking of her own miseducation about Guyana's race-based politics, [neo]colonialism, class and white supremacy. Anne's trips to Haiti and Cuba strengthened further her understanding of culturally based history, Pan-Africanism and reparations. She remains available to support work towards these ends, alongside volunteering as associate hospital manager with South West London and St George's Mental Health Trust.

Nadine King Chambers is an Afro-Caribbean raised by working-class grandparents and a librarian in Jamaica. Since 1991 she has been dividing her time between the semi-rural and urban Pacific west coast of Canada and Jamaica. Her formal studies have primarily been to hunt out the influence of colonisation in the areas of gender/law/resource management, literature and Indigenous studies. She has recently returned to academia to undertake a PhD at the University of Central Lancashire. She is grateful for acknowledgement of her unlettered support on multiple dissertations in social and applied sciences. Since 2015 she has been visiting archives in Jamaica, Canada and England.

Rod Westmaas was born in Georgetown, Guyana in 1957. He has since lived in the United Kingdom, the United States and Guyana. He has performed independent research into the history of Guyana in archives situated in Guyana and at The National Archives (Kew) and has spoken about his findings at academic and public events, and his experiences of migration and sense of national identity. Now based in London, Westmaas has become a prominent member of the Guyanese community. In 2016 he, along with Juanita Cox Westmaas, established the organisation Guyana SPEAKS which brings together Guyanese people based in London to discuss issues relating to the social, economic and political condition of Guyana, as well as the concerns of members of its diaspora. These monthly meetings bring together a delegation of some 80 people, and are televised in Guyana, garnering an audience of around 10,000. In his most recent endeavours, Westmaas has been carrying out oral history interviews with Caribbean migrants to the UK with the view of publishing a book.

Prologue

Rod Westmaas

We are here because you were there.
Stuart Hall

To say goodbye to 'home' was an extremely perplexing request made by the motherland to its colonial citizens. That is exactly what was confronting tens of thousands of men, women and children who were contemplating the journey to 'their' England. With grip (suitcase) in hand, wearing their 'Sunday best', fedora donned at a slight angle, a gleaming smile with an ample supply of smokes for the long voyage, kisses were blown and hankies waved. It was goodbye, land of my birth, and hello to England.

When asked what were they going to miss most when they left home the responses were varied, such as: the sounds of rain beating hard on the zinc roof; the smell of cow dung early in the morning; the weekends spent at the sweetwater creeks; shouts of 'Argosy, Chronicle and Graphic' from the newspaper vendors; a juicy mango and a fleshy ginip [Spanish lime]. Most of all it was the people being left behind: uncles, aunts, mothers, fathers, sons and daughters. The distance would be hard to bridge yet each knew this fresh opportunity to carve out a new life was theirs for the taking.

Getting jobs was not the problem. The employment exchanges were advertising; and factory workers, dishwashers, welders, stockroom attendants, street sweepers and nurses were a few of the positions being advertised. My father Patrick, a manager at one of the many sawmills in Guyana's interior, was one of those newly arrived citizens thumbing through the job cards. At 37, Patrick's managerial options were few to non-existent. No sawmills in London! His reflection to me many years later on his decision to apply for a job as a stockroom attendant at the John Lewis department store on London's Oxford Street was that it had not been an easy one: 'What would my father think? He was a prominent civil servant all his life in Georgetown. He was even awarded an ISO [Imperial Service Order]'. Status back home was no longer a consideration. Making a living, finding a home and sending money back for the family to join him were his priority.

R. Westmaas, 'Prologue', in J.D. Webb, R. Westmaas, M. del Pilar Kaladeen and W. Tantam (eds.), *Memory, migration and (de)colonisation in the Caribbean and beyond* (London: University of London Press, 2019), pp. xi–xii. License: CC-BY-NC-ND 4.0.

John Lewis gave him the start he needed. His job description was simple: sweep the floor, take out the rubbish and pack the shelves. After a year of loyal service, management recognised his dedication and hard work by awarding him a guinea (£1.05p) raise in his wage packet. Like many of his Windrush generation, Patrick was willing to accept whatever viable offer came his way. Black and brown faces were rapidly becoming commonplace on the streets of London. The bus drivers and conductors, train-ticket collectors and porters, nurses and orderlies were all positions proudly filled by the newly arrived citizens of the Empire.

As a young family from British Guiana each day something new was being discovered. The ugly side of the English was gradually emerging. The next-door neighbours were not for mixing, often describing us as the coloureds upstairs cooking all that smelly food. The odd names we were given, 'wog', 'chalky', 'Nig Nog' or simply 'the black bastards', became commonplace.

The voices from back home had become a faded memory for many. Phone calls were expensive and a rarity, mainly Christmas or the occasional family announcement. When they did happen, it was a major production. A phone call to the overseas operator to book the call back home was the necessary first step. The crackly reception a couple of hours later would often consist of small talk: 'How's Granny?'; 'The government did what?'; 'We miss the wiri wiri pepper and some cassareep'; 'She married who?'; 'No I haven't seen the Queen yet'.

The English lifestyle was gradually blending into our unique British Guiana memories. In fact, the new life, in spite of the many challenges, had its positive side: television, seaside trips, grapes and apples, double-decker buses, ice cream setting on a cold, winter window sill, and the friendships of Guianese and other West Indians that, for better or worse, made the motherland more tolerable.

'Maybe one day I will go home … or maybe not'.

Introduction

Jack Webb, Maria del Pilar Kaladeen and William Tantam

Throughout the history of colonialism in the Caribbean, there have been processes of decolonisation. Caribbean peoples have adopted (and adopt) various techniques – from advocating imperial reform to employing strategic military resistance – to challenge, change and in many cases overturn the political structures of colonialism. This dynamic has not only taken place within the region itself. As people migrated from the Caribbean to North America and Europe during, for instance, the era of formal decolonisation in the mid to late twentieth century, they confronted new 'colonised' contexts across the West and in particular in Britain. By challenging ideas of racial superiority and British exceptionalism that were prevalent in the 'motherland', Caribbean migrants worked to decolonise these new contexts. As the ensuing chapters illustrate, these acts of decolonisation become clear in the memories of members of the Caribbean diaspora now based in Britain. Academic and personal accounts are placed in conversation through the inclusion of critical reflections of Caribbean migrants and academic works that detail and critique broader contexts of Caribbean migration and decolonisation. In reading these chapters together, a complex vision of Caribbean decolonisation(s) emerges, a process that takes place as much in the personal context as in that of the transnational.

This volume provides a nuanced understanding of decolonisation, an understanding which is rooted in community knowledge and heritage as much as it is in scholarly pronouncements. We understand decolonisation to be a negotiated *process* rather than any fixed event. Conceiving of it in this way stresses the actions of, and interplay between, people in the Caribbean and the broader Atlantic, and moves us away from a binary notion of colonisers and colonised. Through perceiving decolonisation as processual, rather than as an event, we are necessarily paying particular attention to the ranging forms that such processes can take and their varying outcomes. As many of the contributors to this book point out, processes of decolonisation coincide with, or indeed involve, acts of colonialism.[1] Our use of the term (de)colonisation is thus a

---

1 See ch. 6 by Nadine Chambers and ch. 8 by Simeon Simeonov for two widely differing examples. Chambers deals with the expropriation of resources from Jamaican communities

J. Webb, M. del Pilar Kaladeen and W. Tantam, 'Introduction', in J.D. Webb, R. Westmaas, M. del Pilar Kaladeen and W. Tantam (eds.), *Memory, migration and (de)colonisation in the Caribbean and beyond* (London: University of London Press, 2019), pp. 1–18. License: CC-BY-NC-ND 4.0.

means through which to stress the multiplicity of processes of colonisation that are advancing and receding simultaneously across various contexts.

Rather than an event, too often identified by scholars as the formal 'transfer of power' from imperial authorities to national political elites, processes of decolonisation have occurred throughout histories of colonialism as acts of negotiation between colonised and colonising peoples. In this sense, decolonisation can be seen to have occurred across historical and cultural contexts, both before and after the formal decolonisation acts of the mid to late 20th century. To some extent, this understanding of decolonisation has been made possible by critiques of colonialism offered by scholars such as Frantz Fanon (1967) and Ashis Nandy (1983). Respectively working on the Caribbean and South Asian contexts, both these critics highlight the effects of colonisation on the cultures and world views of people within colonised regions. More than just territorial annexations, Nandy explains, there is a 'second colonialism': 'This colonialism colonizes minds in addition to bodies and it releases forces within the colonized societies to alter their cultural priorities once and for all ... The West is now everywhere, within the West and outside; in structures and in minds' (1983, p. xi). This move towards an understanding of colonialism in personal, intellectual and cultural terms brings into question the multiple power struggles of and against imperialism beyond the diplomatic sphere. Jordana Bailkin emphasises the need for a turn towards a more pluralistic conception of decolonisation when she writes that 'the extraordinarily diverse challenges to European empire cannot be reduced to a singular process' (2015, p. 885). Decolonisation, then, needs to be recognised as a set of processes that could take place in the everyday as much as an event that occurred with the formal transfer of power.

The chapters that follow demonstrate the multiple processes of decolonisation that have taken place throughout the history of the Caribbean, from personal acts of challenging and correcting racialised discourse to efforts to prevent multinational corporations expropriating resources from Caribbean communities. This more diffuse treatment of decolonisation, as something that could be enacted personally as much as on the state level, is illustrated most effectively in the chapters that reflect on the actions of Caribbean migrants to Britain. Such individuals worked, both wittingly and unwittingly, to challenge ideologies of colonialism, such as forms of racism and nationalism, within the 'motherland'. Caribbean decolonisation was not, then, a process that applied only to the Caribbean: it also occurred across the Atlantic World. This phenomenon was proliferated and made more expedient by the fifty thousand Caribbean people who arrived in Britain during the Windrush generation. Decolonisation is not something that was brokered solely by colonial governments and local

---

by multinational companies in our contemporary era, while Simeonov discusses how consuls aided in the advance of colonisation while undermining colonial rivals in the 18th and 19th centuries.

political elites but is a negotiated process that involved many, if not all, of these Caribbean migrants, as well as those that stayed at home.

By moving away from decolonisation as a fixed event and paying attention to the constant negotiation of colonisation and decolonisation in the history of the Caribbean, we necessarily acknowledge the agency of 'colonised' Caribbean peoples in dismantling not only colonial political structures and institutions but also the knowledges and cultures of imperialism. This emphasis on personal interaction and negotiation highlights further the extent to which both colonisation and decolonisation were not inevitable effects so much as multifaceted processes which could simultaneously advance or recede in any particular historical moment. Just as colonisation did not follow a simple path of annexation and control, decolonisation has not simply progressed in the wake of colonisation. Historically, the two processes are inextricably entwined and in constant conversation.

Decolonisation in histories of the Caribbean

By moving away from the conceptualisation of decolonisation as a formal event, it becomes clear that aspects of imperialism, and resistance to it, have – to use Ann Laura Stoler's term – endured (2016). It also illustrates the fact that acts of decolonisation have a long history that precedes the withdrawal of colonial forces. The substantial resistance to European settlement by Amerindian communities in the Lesser Antilles has seen one historian refer to the area as the 'Poison Arrow Curtain' (Burnett, 2000, p. 19). In his assessment of 18th-century Dutch colonialism in Guyana, historian Alvin Thompson has argued persuasively that much of the Dutch portrayal of 'ownership' of Guyana was illusory and emphasised the extent to which the Dutch relied upon the assistance of the indigenous communities of the region (1987, p. 199). And during the English invasion of Jamaica (1655), to illustrate the point further, a group of resident African men and women enslaved by the Spanish on the island seized the opportunity not only to escape and form their own communities, but also to resist and harass the English army (Pestana, 2017; chapter 8 by Simeonov in this volume). These communities would go on to form the Maroon settlements that took in the enslaved who had escaped from the plantation system. The rejection of colonial rule by a population of self-emancipated African people thus occurred at the very beginning of the British colonisation of the Caribbean.

The meaning of decolonisation has evolved throughout the history of the Caribbean. Nowhere is the shifting significance of decolonisation clearer than in the Haitian context. In the Haitian revolution (1791–1804), the armies of enslaved and 'free' people of mixed ethnicity defeated the colonial forces of France, Spain and Britain. Enslavement was abolished, reinstated and abolished again. And, on 1 January 1804, the revolutionaries declared independence from French colonial rule.² Despite such radical assertions of emancipation and liberation, the effort to decolonise the territory in a formal sense was not omnipresent throughout the revolution. The painstaking research of scholars such as Carolyn Fick (1990; 1998) has laid out the complex ideological motivations behind the actions of the enslaved, illustrating that many would-be revolutionaries were, at the outset, compelled to violence through the desire for improved working conditions rather than any notion of Haitian independence. It became clear to the leaders of the rebelling armies, however, that to maintain their self-emancipated status and permanently to destroy the plantation system, it was necessary to declare independence from the enslaving forces of France. What made this gesture especially radical in the context of the Atlantic world was not necessarily the declaration of independence, as this had a precedent in the United States, but the assertion of what this country was to become: a nation state governed by people of African descent, with the ex-enslaved predominant among its ranks. This statement of 'black' independence and statehood ended the violence of military procedures in Haiti, but also set the nascent nation on a trajectory of ideological conflict with the world's colonising powers. In a sense, the formal declaration of the independence of Haiti in 1804 marked the *beginning* of struggles to decolonise, to assert the legitimacy of Haitian independence, and to have this recognised by the Atlantic's imperial powers.

The decolonisation of Haiti was, and continues to be, a negotiated process, a negotiation that took place over the course of the 19th and 20th centuries. Since 1804 Haitian leaders have issued clear statements of their right and ability to govern over the independent nation in a language designed to be understood by European and American audiences.³ Some of the earliest examples of these include the writings of Boisrand-Tonnerre and the Baron de Vastey (Daut, 2017, 2009).⁴ These early Haitian authors, as Marlene Daut makes clear, asserted the legitimacy of the Haitian nation. Vastey observes that '[t]he majority of historians who have written about the colonies were whites, colonists even ... [N]ow that we have Haitian printing presses ... we can reveal the crimes of the colonists and respond to the most absurd calumnies, invented by the prejudice and greed of our oppressors' (in Daut, 2009, p. 3). The military engagements of the Haitian Revolution were over and independence had been declared but, as Vastey realised, Haitians were now faced with a new project of decolonisation.

It is clear that varying projects of decolonisation had taken place within the Haitian and the wider Caribbean contexts long before any discussions

---

2   For general histories of the Haitian Revolution, see James (1938), Dubois (2004) and Geggus (2001).

3   On the adoption of European symbolism by Haitian leaders see Aravamudan (1999).

4   Aravamudan also makes clear that such tactics were deployed by revolutionaries such as Toussaint Louverture during the revolution.

concerning the formal transference of power occurred among amongst colonial elites. These histories of decolonisation have, though, been neglected within the academy. This is not least because evidence of the involvement of Caribbean peoples in these negotiations is not readily available in the archives. Archival records overwhelmingly represent decolonisation as the formal 'transfer of power' (Mir, 2015). This situation is the outcome of the very practice of archivisation. As Jacques Derrida makes clear, the act of archivisation determines what is to be accessible and inaccessible to the future; it 'produces as much as it records the event' (1996, p. 17). As the colonial authorities constructed archives, they also created a narrative of imperialism for future researchers. Commenting on the condition of the records pertaining to decolonisation at the National Archives in London, Caroline Elkins, for instance, observes '[f] rom the carefully managed files, a sense of a coherent decolonisation process, and one that adhered to and imparted the rule of law, just as the colonial administration and archivists in London adhered, and still adhere, to the rule of document preservation' (2015, p. 852). For Caribbeanists, then, the archive can be a dangerous place as it offers versions of the past that reflect the concerns of the imperial authorities rather than a more democratic record of the voices and actions of the 'colonised' peoples. This archival bias is part of what Michel-Rolph Trouillot has referred to as the 'silencing' of certain Caribbean pasts (1995).

To generate histories that encompass 'colonised' Caribbean voices, it is necessary to reconsider what constitutes the archive. One means through which to create a more democratic collection of data, and thus to generate inclusive histories of decolonisation, is the use of oral histories. Perhaps in part because of the lack of archival material pertaining to Caribbean life outside imperial accounts, oral testimony has proved particularly fruitful for scholars of the region (Besson, 2002; Chamberlain, 2005). This volume adds to this tradition by considering the importance of oral accounts in creating a more pluralistic understanding of decolonisation. The memories of Caribbean peoples serve to construct a particular archive that provides alternative visions of decolonisation. Without such memories and the experiences that they recall, the history of decolonisation remains limited and, indeed, dominated by imperial narratives. The act of recording life histories thus aids in the decolonisation of the archive. This is not necessarily to isolate the experiences of Caribbean peoples and place them at the 'centre of scholarship', so much as to move towards a multifaceted history of the Caribbean in which the overwhelming significance of the actions of Caribbean peoples is recognised.[5]

---

5 On the complicated process of recognising 'colonised' peoples in scholarship, see Creary (2012).

Personal acts of decolonisation

As Caribbean people migrated within and across national contexts, they reckoned with multiple forms of colonisation and the attending imperial logics. Examining personal testimonies of such Caribbean migrants enriches any understanding of decolonisation as a democratic venture that takes place in locales across the Atlantic. Christer Petley describes the need to recognise historical relations between the Caribbean and the wider Atlantic as akin to islands in relation to one another, rather than as 'metropoles' (centres) and 'colonies' (peripheries) (2011). Examining the movements and experiences of peoples between these 'islands' challenges notions of a centre/periphery divide. Histories of decolonisation also emerge as decentred ventures. As the Guyanese schoolteacher and all-round educator Joyce Trotman once exclaimed, amidst an oral history interview to her 'British' interviewee: 'So this is your history too? People always see the Caribbean as a different place to Britain, as if Caribbean people are not British. We've all got British grandfathers and family. My grandfather was Scottish. What you're asking about is British history too, it's not just Caribbean'.[6] Trotman here provides a powerful reminder that the history of the Caribbean involves a set of personal entanglements with the wider world and in particular with imperial powers.

Oral histories help to emphasise the rich tapestry of Caribbean lives as opposed to an imposed colonial narrative. The chapters in this book which are based on memoir (Nobrega, Ramrayka, Braithwaite and to some extent Egglestone, Chambers and Henry) and its analysis (Westmaas) all highlight the various and specific struggles for, and encounters with, decolonisation. Westmaas, for instance, examines the experiences of two Guyanese migrants (Joyce Trotman and Eric Huntley) to Britain during the period of formal decolonisation in their country of birth. Leaving one decolonising context, they were met in Britain with a set of colonial world views that worked to deny their status as British citizens and instead emphasised a racial inferiority. Their experiences were not, though, wholly equivalent to one another as each set about challenging the colonial mindsets with which they were confronted. Faced with racism in the classrooms of London's East End in the 1960s, Trotman worked to educate her pupils with astonishing effect on the absurdity of the concept of racial hierarchy. Trotman decolonised both institution and community as she fronted down child racists-in-progress and challenged them to critique the prejudicial stories they heard at home.[7] Eric and Jessica Huntley strove for the decolonisation of their native Guyana, by organising on behalf of the British Guyana Freedom Association and of the British context, by establishing the

---

6   Joyce Trotman in an interview with Rod Westmaas and Jack Webb. Trotman was addressing Webb in this exchange.

7   See also the biography of Beryl Gilroy, *Black Teacher*, which was published by the Huntleys' press.

radical anti-racist, anti-colonial bookshop and publishers, Bogle-L'Ouverture Publications. This publisher formed a nodal point in decolonising networks, producing and disseminating anti-colonial ideas from its base in London.[8]

In many of the essays and testimonies of Windrush-era migrants we can see that they inadvertently found themselves taking on the burden of decolonising the metropole. In Peter Ramrayka's case, this took place through his work in institutions like the RAF and the NHS (chapter 5). From Bruce Nobrega's powerful act of confronting his boss with the fact of the company's discriminatory pay policy (chapter 2) to the time Joyce Trotman, as a student, confronted the uncharitable behaviour of 'Christians' at her hostel (chapter 11), it is clear that while Guyana was literally in the process of decolonising, its migrants to the UK were performing a role in decolonising the minds of the British people they encountered every day. Sometimes these acts of resistance were subtle challenges to invisible colour bars, for example Peter Ramrayka's ascendance to a senior management role in the NHS when there was a seemingly unwritten rule that people of colour could not occupy management positions; at other times it is clear that Windrush migrants were literally putting their lives on the line.[9]

Through these same contributors we are able to understand, at firsthand, the power of the colonial structures that dominated their lives in the Caribbean. Joyce Trotman, for example, references the sense of belonging to a collective empire that was fuelled by the singing of 'Land of Hope and Glory'. Poignantly, she notes that at the same time Indian indentured labourers were present outside the church, passengers of empire notoriously poorly treated in colonial Guyana, awaiting a portion of land or return voyage to India. Bruce Nobrega also highlights the propaganda of empire as he reminisces on the extent to which Guyanese of the colonial era felt a sense of British identity through the process of 'indoctrination' that formed part of their experiences in church and in school. He references the face of Queen Elizabeth on his exercise books – only one element of his daily life that served to send him a message of 'belonging' to the 'mother country'.[10] This experience intercedes with that of Anne Braithwaite, who describes how she learned to see her compatriots through a racialised lens under colonial tutoring.

While migrants were involuntarily burdened with decolonising the minds of the people and institutions they encountered in the UK, some were also

---

8   The lives of Eric and Jessica Huntley were recently part of the exhibition 'No Colour Bar' that ran at London's Guildhall in 2016.

9   See, for example, the racist attacks on the Huntleys' bookshop documented in Andrews (2014).

10 The placement of the monarch's image on colonial Guyanese exercise books fuelled the early work of the British-Guyanese artist Hew Locke. See I. Khanna, 'The artistic imagination of Hew Locke' (https://www.stabroeknews.com/2012/features/in-the-diaspora/08/06/the-artistic-imagination-of-hew-locke/ [accessed 4 Feb. 2019]).

coming to terms with the myths of colonial benevolence that had been peddled by the British at home. These stories are more than descriptive: they challenge how we define activism and resistance. For it is evident in each of these chapters that the individual lives of Windrush-era migrants were records of continual fights against prejudice and racism. Whether or not they were teachers like Joyce Trotman, they were forced into the role of educators. Crucially, Guyana's Windrush women had an important part to play in this story and Bruce Nobrega's dedication to his mother Cécile Nobrega, the remarkable woman responsible for Britain's first public statue of a black woman, depicted on the cover of this volume, is indicative of the knowledge, at community level, of the vast contribution made by these women. The extent to which the contribution of Windrush women has been devalued or ignored is seen in the lack of attention paid to their output. While many of us know the memoir *To Sir With Love* by Guyana-born E. R. Brathwaite, few have read or are aware of his fellow Guyanese Beryl Gilroy's biographical novel *Black Teacher* and her pioneering work in schools in the 1950s.

The primary focus of this volume is to place in conversation academic knowledges of (de)colonisation with those of the Caribbean community and in particular members of the Windrush generation. Its aims are perhaps best summed up by one of the contributors, Kelly Delancey, whose piece was motivated by her desire to understand how the 'residents and descendants of Tarpum Bay define their heritage and themselves'. Her determination to rectify the situation of top-down heritage creation and prioritise a community's right to share their history in their own words is the very essence of the editors' intention to disrupt and challenge academic power by giving voice to the lived experience and authority of British Windrush-era migrants.[11] Through placing academia in conversation with individual self-reflections of decolonisation, we are able to consider in new ways how academics have traditionally accepted and enforced colonial structures rather than critiqued and confronted them. Such analysis forms an important part of the work of Henry, Chambers and Egglestone (chapters 4, 6 and 10 respectively) as they reference their own experiences, directly disturbing the lie of the academic as an impartial observer. Henry shows how problematic the assumption of 'Eurocentric' academic authority over the lives and experiences of black youth has been by exposing the 'hidden' history of references to decolonisation in the deejay performance. Such references have been completely missed by theorists who were confined by their own negative preconceptions. Chambers's important assessment of the transnational lives and after-lives of colonialism begins with a call to activism to 'join a decolonisation quest to re-navigate history'. Chambers, however, is not only concerned with the reassessment of history but urges a movement towards 'the sacred work of decolonising what we remember', unsettling binaries of

---

11 See ch. 3 in this volume: Kelly Delancy, 'History to heritage: an assessment of Tarpum Bay, Eleuthera, The Bahamas'.

black/white and colonised/coloniser as she questions the meaning of Black History Month when it is observed in the unceded territory of Vancouver, for example.

While the chapter by Chambers highlights the continual and dynamic process of decolonisation and the transnational capitalist networks of exploitation, both Matthew Smith (chapter 1) and Anne Braithwaite (chapter 7) reference how the shadows of colonialism operate to detrimental effect in contemporary Guyana and Jamaica. Brathwaite, for example, highlights the fact that many of the Guyanese elite, helped to power by the US and Britain in 1966, feature in positions of power in today's government. The divisive racism the British promoted between Indian-Guyanese and African-Guyanese when the country was a colony still 'stymies' the country, she observes. In both Brathwaite's 'old' and 'new' contexts, forms of colonialism threaten to return: capitalist interests loom like parasites in the distance as oil companies prepare to begin work in Guyana; and as Brexit prompts British politicians to consider new trading opportunities, the Commonwealth is increasingly returning as a viable sphere of influence in the British imagination. With these threats, Brathwaite is rightly able to say that the work of decolonisation is ongoing.

Practising decolonisation

This volume attempts not only to reflect on processes of decolonisation but also, as Braithwaite urges us, to participate in its practice. This commitment comes out of early conversations among the editors when convening the conference 'Memory, Migration and (De)colonisation in the Caribbean and Beyond' (University of London, 2017) from which this volume proceeds. There is, of course, a major problem in that academia has a long tradition of producing knowledge to service colonial ventures. Indeed, although the academy has become much more self-reflective in the past 50 years and various scholarly works published since the civil-rights movement have sought to critique and dismantle colonial knowledge, more work remains to be done to decolonise the academy. Various universities have also been highlighted as continuing to extol and honour imperial traditions, sparking counter-movements seeking to decolonise the university. The pioneering work of the campaign 'Rhodes Must Fall' provides one example of the attempt to challenge colonial cultures in the academy. In 2015 this movement recognised the statue of Cecil Rhodes – the late-19th-century British prime minister of the Cape – on the campus of the University of Cape Town as a clear example of the ongoing extolling of imperial figures, knowledges and narratives within the university setting. After significant protest, in particular by students, the university removed the statue in recognition of the need to decolonise academia more broadly. This movement has since gained momentum and inspired parallel campaigns across Europe and the United States. While planning our own conference, we were keen to think of how to decolonise the space of the event and consistently to challenge established boundaries between those attending from inside and outside the academy. Indeed, our starting point was that decolonisation was not only a series of historical moments, with the Haitian Revolution as a key point in this trajectory, but that it also held meanings in the present in terms of challenging the boundaries that continue to centre the privileged view of those within the academy (most often white and male). Concomitantly, we were committed to ensuring that 'terms on which [academics] start debates about decolonisation and decoloniality are determined by those on the margins' (Esson et. al, 2017). We wanted to challenge consistently the emergence of boundaries between academic and non-academic participants and to find means to democratise participants' contributions. In this section, we think through the different methods by which we attempted to decolonise the conference and its outputs.

Through the close relationships of the organisers, and particularly Roderick Westmaas, to the Guyanese community in London, we were privileged to receive their support in organising the event and participating in it, and in producing this publication. Following the maxim 'nothing about us, without us, is for us' (with its own history particularly aligned with disability-rights activism), we were committed to including the experiences of those who had moved from the Caribbean to the United Kingdom and had their own views on memory, migration and decolonisation. While it was easy to provide a space in which to speak, we wanted to assume the responsibility to go further by facilitating their inclusion in discussions throughout the conference and not only in the sections dealing with 'Caribbean migrants' experiences'.

At the same time, while wanting to be ambitious in our attempts to break down boundaries between knowledges, each of the organisers was also constrained by his or her junior status within the academy and its concomitant precarity. It can be a challenge to be ambitious and to try to alter established formats without being a little anxious about the outcomes. We knew that we wanted to encourage different forms of participation and the submissions reflected this. We received more typically 'academic' submissions from disciplines including criminology, literature, history, sociology and anthropology. We received the community involvement of a range of Caribbean migrants' voices. We were also fortunate to have submissions that challenged the boundaries between formal and informal knowledges, including community practitioners, independent researchers and popular authors.

Further, while trying to emphasise the interconnectedness of people and knowledges from different disciplines and backgrounds we also did not want participants to feel as though they were having to sacrifice depth of analysis or insight in order to make their input transferable. We were concerned that community participants should not gain the impression that their contributions were viewed as entertainment or addenda rather than equally valid insights into the discussions. Conversely, we were aware that some academics can feel threatened by questions raised about their research and wanted to maintain an openness to discussion and a willingness to learn from the unique opportunities offered by the conference's mixture of knowledges.

Decolonising the space of the conference also consisted in encouraging innovative ways of contributing. Our invitation of guest speakers Professor Tina K. Ramnarine and Dr Lez Henry was inspired by their commitment to challenging traditional forms of academic knowledge and production, and their continued dedication to engaging with communities outside the university. Alongside those working within the academy and the voices of Caribbean migrants we were fortunate to receive presentations from independent researchers working from outside the academy. Indeed, Nadine Chambers' engagement with the organisers has been invaluable in pushing us to think further about how to maintain the commitment to decolonisation in the process of producing this publication. For instance, the fact that it is to be made open-access and thus available to those without university privileges was key in our decision to approach ILAS/University of London Press. The conference also included the contribution of the artist Rubén Dávila, who gave a performance of his work 'El Vuelo del Golondrino' on the experience of Caribbean and Andean migrants to New York.

We therefore decided to organise the community voices as the opening plenary session and elicited ideas for skills workshops, to be interspersed between panels, that would provide tools which might enable the community members to communicate their experiences further. These workshops consisted of 'Creating memoirs and recording experience: how to produce podcasts and write memoirs'; and 'Organising for the Caribbean: how to campaign for change in the Caribbean'. Each offered practice-based discussions for how to transmit the experiences of Caribbean communities to wider audiences. Importantly, we wanted to make sure that the conference might offer means through which contributors might be empowered with new skills for disseminating or further mining their experiences, or for organising events around themes emerging from their histories. We felt that community members were often encouraged to attend conferences as though their attendance at these events or introduction into these spaces was enough to justify their gift of time and knowledge. In contrast, we felt responsible for making sure that the conference was meaningful and useful for all those presenting. The workshops were one means through which we attempted to deliver concrete contributions to non-academic participants who might want to develop their studies and their organisations further.

These community experiences and workshops also enhanced the more formal academic contributions by elucidating the challenges of life-history research and community organising and helped to place the discussions within a wider political and social context. One consistent theme to emerge was the highly politicised legacy of the Haitian Revolution, particularly for Haitians living abroad but also for the Caribbean diaspora more generally. The mixture of viewpoints on the issues underscored the recognition that history is both lived and living and has a dramatic impact on people and communities. The heterogeneous contributions demonstrated the continuities of racisms and placed them in wider historical and global contexts.

Moreover, the conference unearthed and sought to recognise the processes of marginalisation, often overlooked, that continue to exclude people from educational institutions. This thread began in the Caribbean migrants' session in which contributors spoke of their experiences of school in the Caribbean and how these school networks allowed some to travel and achieve social mobility. It continued through Joyce Trotman's experience of racism working as a school teacher in the UK, as well as those of a participant who was the first black police officer in his area. A number of contributions approached these themes in terms of higher education and how certain forms of knowledge and researchers are privileged. Marginalisation can work in myriad ways and can easily emerge in forms of academic discussion and event-planning through a lack of care and attention given to thinking about how best to engage with participants who might find the traditional conference format exclusionary.

We have tried to carry these sentiments through into the production of this volume. Similar to our thoughts about how best to integrate personal experiences of migration into the conference, we also wanted to think about how best to intersperse these contributions through the book. We decided that rather than having a section for migrants' experiences and a separate one for 'academic' contributions, it would be more in keeping with our commitment to decolonisation to intersperse each type of submission. Bruce Nobrega's 'Why did we come?', Peter Ramrayka's 'Journeying through the motherland', Anne Braithwaite's 'Organising for the Caribbean' and Roderick Westmaas's 'Maybe one day I'll go home' use personal testimony as a way into thoughts about aspects of memory, migration and decolonisation in people's contemporary lives. Thus they serve as a consistent reminder that these discussions have real-world implications and effects felt beyond the academy. While the Haitian Revolution was a particular historical moment, its legacy as a symbol for the overturning of established hierarchies and the democratisation of knowledge practices lives long.

Fortunately, the organisers were blessed by the openness and generosity of all the participants. In the lead up to the conference, all the organisers were taken aback by the support we received from them. Putting the event together became exciting for what it might produce and what we might learn if we critically reflect on the academic practices we take for granted and begin to challenge them. Similarly, as editors we have been more fortunate to have the continued support and input of the contributors, which has not only included their own chapter submissions but also their ideas for how to make the volume meaningful and useful.

However, while we were extremely grateful for and excited about the conference and its productions, we also recognise that much further work remains to be done and more improvements need to be made. London as a venue for knowledge- exchange is steeped in colonial and historical associations. For centuries the city has been enriched and, indeed, made rich by the labour of Caribbean populations, often with little or no remuneration. One significant difficulty for the organisers was the lack of funds available to include more participants from the Caribbean. Although we attempted to mitigate these issues by drawing on the wealth of experience among the Caribbean community in the UK, we were aware of the power imbalances that allowed us to hold a discussion of the Haitian Revolution in London. Nevertheless, we were fortunate to have the contributions of Clara Rachel Eybalin and Marie Lily Cerat, who are active members of Haitian communities in Europe and America. It is our feeling that future conferences might be able to make better use of internet technologies to bypass the prohibitive economic and climate costs of long-distance travel to conferences, and the better to include Caribbean practitioners within discussions.

This volume and the conference constitute our modest attempts to decolonise academic practices through recognising and challenging the boundaries imposed between different forms of knowledge. Recognition of the existence of hierarchies of understanding that emerge between those generated within the 'academy' and those emerging from outside constituted a starting point for how we might think about attempting to democratise knowledges. The question to which we consistently returned might be summarised as 'how to integrate different approaches to decolonisation and reflect that in our practices and the spaces we create'. Decolonisation is always a collaborative act. While the chapters that follow emerge from a variety of disciplines, each has something valuable to contribute to understandings of decolonisation in the Caribbean. Moreover, the efforts made to discuss and learn across disciplinary boundaries themselves constitute a significant act of academic decolonisation. These chapters demonstrate that attempts to dismantle established hierarchies of knowledge have occurred throughout different fields and stages of research. Indeed, decolonisation requires systematic critical reflection on all aspects of practice, from research planning to methods, writing and teaching. What follows is our contribution to this broad global movement currently changing the way we think about the relationship of the academy to other forms of knowledge and cultural production.

The contributions

The chapters are organised so that academic analyses of questions of migration and decolonisation are punctuated by 'community voices'. Chapter 1, by Matthew Smith, opens our book by detailing emigration from Jamaica in the wake of formal decolonisation in the 1960s. The island's leaders and ruling elite packaged full self-government as a leap towards modernity in which the challenges of the past would be overcome, and yet Smith illustrates that for many this era was characterised by economic hardship leading to an outflow of people. Indeed, it was a paradox of 1960s Jamaica that in the early years of nationhood the country experienced its highest rates of migration up to that time. This chapter offers a fresh perspective on 1960s Jamaica by examining the hopes and losses of the young nation coming into its own in an unravelling world. Bruce Nobrega, in chapter 2, offers a counterpoint to Smith's focus on emigration through his reflections on leaving his native Guyana for London. He charts both the effect of 'indoctrination' by imperial propaganda when growing up in British Guiana as it instilled a tentative admiration for Britain; and the everyday challenges – once in Britain – of finding a new home and work in the face of an often racist, hostile host population. What becomes palpable is the protagonist's double movement of disenchantment with the empire and the motherland and yet a growing sense of affection for his new surroundings as he made them 'home' through establishing community.

Chapter 3 picks up on and discusses the themes of community and memory through the context of heritage in Tarpum Bay, Bahamas. Here Kelly Delancy illustrates the power of oral-history interviews in tracking the passing of intangible heritage – in this case the knowledges, traditions and values – between generations and the construction of local identities. In the absence of official commemorations of local histories or memories, Delancy shows how the recent past, specifically relating to processes of decolonisation, is related through elders to the benefit of their descendants. In particular, Delancy provides a forceful analysis of how national narratives concerning decolonisation, independence and nationalism are received and mediated within the local context. Chapter 4 by Lez Henry sustains a focus on community in relation to the international, or what Henry terms the 'outernational', through the discussion of a community of Caribbean deejays and lyricists based in London in the 1980s. In particular, Henry examines the lyrics and linguistic styles of these artists to argue that these types of lyricism were far more than types of resistance but were, in fact, postcolonial forms of linguistic, cultural antagonism couched in Rastafarian and Garveyite sensibilities. Through such expression, and with the creation of alternative public arenas in which it was consumed, an autonomous sociocultural self that unified members of the Caribbean was created within the UK. Reaching across the 'Black Atlantic' these musical cultures combated, and still combat, the imposition of a Eurocentric 'alien' worldview on African peoples on an outernational level.

Peter Ramrayka, in chapter 5, illustrates how Caribbean migrants shaped British culture in ways very different to those discussed by Henry, as he considers his experience of moving from the Caribbean and working within two key British institutions: the National Health Service and the Royal Air

Force. These two organisations would attract many Caribbean workers. Ramrayka's chapter is a powerful meditation on a particular experience of career progression in a national context that was so often unwelcoming to Caribbean arrivals. Ramrayka reflects that racism was not so great an obstacle to him as to many of his travelling countrymen, reminding us of the wide variation in the experiences of Caribbean migrants. More to the point, his chapter, especially when read next to Henry's, demonstrates the multifaceted impact that Caribbean migrants had on shaping Britain's greatest of institutions, the NHS, and indeed on the British cultural landscape.

Chapter 6, by Nadine Chambers, merges personal reflection with scholarship to create a stimulating, 'decolonised' critique of the activity of multinational companies in the (de)colonial Caribbean and Canada. In particular, Chambers' chapter highlights the little-documented impact on the Jamaican rural community of Kitimaat of capitalist transnational corporations which have developed smelters to process ore. Through her compelling exploration of the relations between notions of indigeneity and decolonisation, Chambers emphasises the urgent need for scholarship to be driven by ethics that centre the concerns of the communities affected and hold multinational companies to account. Anne Braithwaite's ensuing essay in chapter 7 proffers techniques through which to organise against such ongoing acts of colonialism, as discussed by Chambers. As a young migrant to Britain, Braithwaite successfully campaigned against the expropriation of resources from her native Guyana by multinational companies. To some extent, Braithwaite comments, this realisation of continuing colonialism in Guyana and the Guyanese government's lack of action against it were made possible by her vantage point from Britain. For Braithwaite this struggle for Guyanese decolonisation was a self-reflective journey. As she relates: 'At the heart of my quest was a desire to understand Guyana's position in the world, but mainly my place in it here – and there'.

The chapters by Chambers and Braithwaite both provide a strong sense of the continuation of colonial narratives and practices into our present. Chapter 8, by Simeon Simeonov, historicises the modes of colonisation in the transnational, or rather transcolonial, by interrogating the creation and proliferation of consulates across the Caribbean. These institutions formed nodal points in colonial networks and were key in creating and transmitting knowledges for the purposes of trade, diplomacy, policy, migration and citizenship. However, consulates in the Caribbean were not straightforward forces of colonialism but, as Simeonov elaborates, while working to enforce the colonialism of the empire they represented, they could also undermine colonial rivals. Consulates could effect modes of decolonisation just as they promoted a rival form of colonialism. Miguel Gualdrón Ramírez, in chapter 9, provides a more theoretical analysis of Caribbean pasts and, indeed, how such pasts have been defined and thought about by the key Caribbean thinkers

Édouard Glissant, Aimé Césaire and Frantz Fanon. Notions of any sort of linear history in the Caribbean are made problematic by the fact that for so many of its current inhabitants the first experience of their ancestors in the Caribbean was marked by a 'brutal dislocation', a historical 'abyss'. Gualdrón carefully teases out the different responses of the three Caribbean thinkers to this problem. Whereas Fanon demands a break with history (in particular with the concept of black, or blackness) in order to decolonise and liberate, Glissant does not want to break completely with the identity that was created through an apparatus of enslavement, transportation, colonisation and exploitation. In a move that is radically anti-colonial, Gualdrón argues, Glissant thus links emancipation to the history of those same devices employed in the creation of 'blackness' and the resistance to them: this, Gualdrón proffers, is the history of a *productive* abyss.

In chapter 10 Ruth Minnot Egglestone blurs the lines between the personal and the academic once again to offer a forceful reading of Shakespeare's *Julius Caesar* to reflect on decolonisation. Egglestone thinks deeply about her personal act of reading *Julius Caesar* at a time when Jamaica was still creating a national identity under Michael Manley. In this play Egglestone finds allegorical reference points with which to understand processes of decolonisation in the Caribbean. In Cassius, Egglestone perceives a 'hungry thinker', a patriot who emphasises dignity and self-respect over blind loyalty to 'the state'. As a young reader Egglestone identified with this character and used him to understand the formal transference of power from Britain to the Jamaican people. More than this, for Egglestone *Julius Caesar* – recently translated into Jamaican Patwa and Rastafari vernacular – should be considered alongside Jamaican folk stories and pantomime, such as the figure of Anancy, who acts as a warning against both credulity and one-upmanship. Read side-by-side, Egglestone explains, these stories pose many uncomfortable questions relating to Caribbean politics and power.

In the final chapter of this book, aptly entitled 'Maybe one day I'll go home', Rod Westmaas considers the notion of a return, a return not to Africa as thought about by so many descendants of transatlantic enslavement, but to 'home' in the Caribbean. Rod Westmaas discusses this theme by relating the stories of two Guyanese Windrush migrants to Britain, Joyce Trotman and Eric Huntley. As noted above, both the protagonists worked to decolonise – wittingly and unwittingly – the Guyanese and British contexts. Based on oral interviews with these elders, Westmaas provides their stories with detail and care to work through their personal experiences and motivations in migrating and decolonising. Huntley, along with his partner Jessica, established the radical anti-racist and anti-colonial bookshop Bogle-L'Ouverture Publications, which would go on to publish works by eminent Caribbean anti-colonialists such as Walter Rodney. Trotman, who incidentally published her work on Guyanese proverbs with Bogle-L'Ouverture, became a formidable educator in both Britain and Guyana. She did not punish those students who aimed racist abuse at her in the schools of the East End of London but instead remained committed to their education. Trotman dealt with these pupils by educating them on the absurdity of their racialised thoughts. The stories of these two individuals and their acts of decolonisation provide forceful illustrations of the productive responses of Caribbean migrants to imperialism and its afterlives.

Taken together, what these chapters demonstrate is that decolonisation should not necessarily be conceived of as a simple opposition to colonisation. The act of migration between the Caribbean and Britain is itself an illustration of the productive consequences of old colonial ties. Decolonisation is not the simple division of deeply entwined histories into two, colonial and non-colonial, blocs. Instead, to understand decolonisation in its multiplicity, it is imperative to understand the aims and desires of colonised peoples in any particular moment. What these chapters offer is not only an intervention into academic scholarship, a simple refinement of our concepts for understanding decolonisation, but also a demonstration of the value of bringing together academic and community voices – many of which belong to people once considered 'colonised subjects' – to show the varying, yet related experiences and versions of (de)colonisation.

Bibliography

Andrews, M. (2014), *Doing Nothing Is Not an Option: The Radical Lives of Eric & Jessica Huntley* (Middlesex: Krik Krak, 2014).

Aravamudan, S. (1999) *Tropicopolitans: Colonialism and Agency, 1688–1804* (Durham, NC and London: Duke University Press).

Bailkin, J. (2015) 'Where did the empire go? Archives and decolonization in Britain', *The American Historical Review*, 120: 884–99.

Besson, J. (2002) *Martha Brae's Two Histories: European Expansion and Caribbean Culture-Building in Jamaica* (Chapel Hill, NC: University of North Carolina Press).

Burnett, G.D. (2000) *Masters of All They Surveyed: Exploration, Geography and a British El Dorado* (Chicago, IL and London: University of Chicago Press).

Chamberlain, M. (2005) *Narratives of Exile and Return* (New Brunswick, NJ: Transaction Publishers).

Creary, N. (2012) *African Intellectuals and Decolonization* (Athens, OH: Ohio University Press).

Daut, M. (2009) 'Un-silencing the past: Boisrond-Tonnerre, Vastey and the re-writing of the Haitian Revolution', *South Atlantic Review*, 74: 35–64.

— (2017) *Baron de Vastey and the Origins of Black Atlantic Humanism* (New York: Palgrave Macmillan).

Derrida, J. (1996) *Archive Fever: A Freudian Impression*, trans. by E. Prenowitz (Chicago, IL: University of Chicago Press).

Dubois, L. (2004) *Avengers of the New World: The Story of the Haitian Revolution* (Cambridge, MA: Harvard University Press).

Elkins, C. (2015) 'Looking beyond Mau Mau: archiving violence in the era of decolonization', *The American Historical Review*, 120: 851–68.

Esson, J. et al. (2017) 'The 2017 RGS-IBG chair's theme: decolonising geographical knowledges or reproducing coloniality?', *Area*, 49: 384–8, https://onlinelibrary.wiley.com/doi/full/10.1111/area.12371 [accessed 4 Feb. 2019].

Fanon, F. (1967) *Black Skin, White Masks*, trans. by C. Markmann (New York: Grove Press).

Fick, C. (1990) *The Making of Haiti: The Saint Domingue Revolution* (Knoxville, TN: University of Tennessee Press).

— (1998) 'Dilemmas of emancipation: from the Saint Domingue insurrections of 1791 to the emerging Haitian state', *History Workshop Journal*, 46: 1–15.

Geggus, D. (2001) *The Impact of the Haitian Revolution in the Atlantic World* (Columbia, SC: University of South Carolina Press).

James, C. L. R. (1938) *The Black Jacobins: Toussaint L'Ouverture and the San Domingo Revolution* (London: Secker and Warburg).

Mir, F. (2015) 'The archives of decolonization', *The American Historical Review*, 120: 844–51.

Nandy, A. (1983) *The Intimate Enemy: Loss and Recovery of Self Under Colonialism* (Oxford: Oxford University Press).

Pestana, C. G. (2017) *The English Conquest of Jamaica: Cromwell's Bid for Empire* (Cambridge, MA: Harvard University Press).

Petley, C. (2011) 'New perspectives on slavery and emancipation in the British Caribbean', *The Historical Journal*, 54: 855–80.

Stoler, A. L. (2016) *Duress: Imperial Durabilities in Our Times* (Durham, NC and London: Duke University Press).

Thompson, A. O. (1987) *Colonialism and Underdevelopment in Guyana, 1580–1803* (Bridgetown: Carib Research & Publications).

Trouillot, M.-R. (1995) *Silencing the Past: Power and the Production of History* (Boston, MA: Beacon Press).

1. Loving and leaving the new Jamaica: reckoning with the 1960s

Matthew J. Smith

The young are the conveyors of a nation's history. Small wonder that new governments claim the youth as the principal beneficiaries of their plans for 'a better tomorrow'. It is widely appreciated that an administration's successes and failures are best measured by the legacies it leaves for the citizens who inherit that tomorrow. Jamaica's first decade as a new nation may be reflected in the stories of three young girls: Sybil, Ioni and Maureen.

Two days to go before Independence Day. Jamaica's children wake up on 4 August 1962 with more visible excitement than the adults. Sybil, not yet ten, joined 1,000 children from Kingston's schools for a fun day at State Theatre in Cross Roads. The promoter, Dudley McMillan, in a show of festive charity, opened the doors to the country's future, the city's youth, for free films and entertainment. Sybil sipped her free Kelly's flavoured soda and laughed with the other children at the Three Stooges. In the intermission in the morning's double bill she and her friend Carol performed the English nursery rhyme 'Two Little Blackbirds' in an impromptu talent contest. They came second. In the afternoon Sybil and the other children made their way to the national stadium for the youth rally. There she beamed even more brightly as she and a stadium of peers waved their small Jamaican flags affixed to a narrow piece of wood. Some sat on their parents' shoulders so as to raise the flag higher. Sybil radiated when she got a glimpse of Princess Margaret – so pretty – in the stands beside Prime Minister Bustamante, the Governor-General Sir Kenneth Blackburne and Lady Blackburne. A field of little girls like her in their peasant blouses and bandanas, singing the National Pledge, more moving than the anthem, more committed on that day, hours before Monday's flag ceremony, hours before they would be referred to as Jamaicans and not 'subjects'. 'Linstead Market' and 'Sly Mongoose' followed – all the children singing in unison. They sang for the princess, 'our princess by our own choice', said the minister of education;

M.J. Smith, 'Loving and leaving the new Jamaica: reckoning with the 1960s', in J.D. Webb, R. Westmaas, M. del Pilar Kaladeen and W. Tantam (eds.), *Memory, migration and (de)colonisation in the Caribbean and beyond* (London: University of London Press, 2019), pp. 19–30. License: CC-BY-NC-ND 4.0.

they sang for Jamaica, 20,000 young voices belting out 'Hip Hip, HOORAY!' They sang for the future of their island, which was now fused with their own.[1]

1964. Two years later to the day, 11-year-old Ioni put on her best dress, nervously getting ready to leave her house. The excitement for the independence anniversary had been building outside her narrow room window on Slipe Pen Road. She heard the noise, the roving cars advertising Independence Day sales at King's Street stores, Millie Small's 'My Boy Lollipop' blaring over and over again, Prime Minister Bustamante's independence message filtering through nearby radio sets. All Jamaicans, said the prime minister, must be proud of the progress that has been made in just two short years. It was all out of reach for her, out of mind. Closer were the area boys who sat all day, shirtless, on the road outside her shanty, who seemed to do nothing else but stare out to Maxfield Avenue and chat, chat, chat. The cemetery was not far away and its stillness insinuated the distance from the loud cheers at the stadium. Independence was not marked on Slipe Pen Road. It belonged to another part of Kingston, other people.

Ioni's mother helped her with her suitcase and she walked out of the front door for the last time, crossing the zinc fences, stopping momentarily on the dirt track to respond to one of the boys:

Ioni, is today you going?

– Yes

Den you glad?

– No mus'

You mus' learn education yah. Even if when you come back you nuh talk to bwoy like we, learn education an' better you'self.

– Me fadda say we not coming back. It too hard and cruel out here fi some people. If you put yuh head to you book it pay you more ah England dan out here.

She took off one of her shoes and showed them to the boys. Quoting her father, a mechanic before he left for England and a known preacher in the community, Ioni looked them in the eye and said, 'Im say we must shake the dust off we foot when we coming'. Unhurriedly she slipped her shoe back on, took one glance, turned around, then took her mother's hand towards the vehicle waiting to take them to the Palisadoes airport, then to London.[2]

Two more years passed. Independence 1966 was meant to bring what was now routine parading, the festival song competition, speeches, fireworks, flags: the requisite fanfare. It was nothing but woe for Maureen Ellis. Maureen was

---

1 This account is inspired by information in 'Princess opens the stadium', *Daily Gleaner*, 5 Aug. 1962, 1; 'Dancing and singing at youth rally', *Daily Gleaner*, 8 Aug. 1962, 3; 'Children's treat at State', *Daily Gleaner*, 8 Aug. 1962, 7.

2 This account is inspired by information in George Thurst, 'The dust under her feet', *Public Opinion*, 14 Aug. 1964, 11.

barely three years old when the government bulldozed the shack she and her mother were living in on Foreshore Road that July. The world around her, the only one she knew – a galaxy of decrepit lean-tos – was flat. Foreshore Road and Industrial Terrace were long regarded as the worst eyesores of Kingston's extensive slums. 'Den of iniquity', 'shantytown', 'deprived', 'depraved', 'embarrassment' were all words that seemed to follow the very name Foreshore Road. It was also home to hundreds of children like Maureen, the largest proportion of its residents.

When Maureen and her mother were forced out they had nowhere else to go. With other children she made her way to the May Pen cemetery, within view of the home where Ioni used to live. Maureen never visited the stadium and never left Jamaica. Her mother's suitcase was used only for local travel. After the destruction of their house it was one of the few possessions they had left and whatever else they had was in it.

A photograph of Maureen has survived. It was taken in 1966 by a *Daily Gleaner* photographer and shows the lone survivor of a personal apocalypse, sat on that old suitcase of her mother's in the cemetery, forlorn and disconnected. Nothing around her but tombstones and nothing with her but what was below her in the case. Just behind her was an overturned table, perhaps a found item used for shelter from the cold night air. In her eyes a strain to make sense of this forced readjustment. The city's welfare agency would eventually take in Maureen and place her with other dispossessed children in a special home for children on Haining Road in New Kingston, a short-lived hope for a fresh start. On Christmas Day 1967 the home caught on fire and Maureen and five other children were burned to death.[3]

******

Sybil, Ioni and Maureen were children of independence, inheritors of what was popularly called the 'new Jamaica' who did not all experience its bright promise. They were like many other children and many other Jamaicans trying to make sense of the place they were given in post-colonial Jamaica. They were more than this, reflections of different realities of Jamaica's early years of decolonisation. These years, in which they experienced joy, resignation and tragedy, were the foundation years of the island's political self-determination.

How do we remember Jamaica's 1960s? Whose reality is superimposed on the nation's history of Jamaica in these years? These three examples are elemental to the picture of these years but in their own ways are subsumed too often under the cloud of the violently divisive 1970s. To say that Jamaica in the 1960s was consumed with hope and unity destroyed by the ideological and turf

---

3   This account is inspired by information presented in 'The little girl who was bulldozed: death by fire', *Public Opinion*, 29 Dec. 1967, 1. See also, 'Six infants die in Christmas Day fire', *Daily Gleaner*, 27 Dec. 1967, 1.

battles of the following decade is to present an inadequate reflection of what life was truly like in those preceding years. Independence arrived with all the ingredients of disharmony intact.

Political scientist Louis Lindsay's influential essay 'The myth of independence' – dated but still relevant – suggests that the fall of the colonial order had only rearranged the power dynamics in a structure long predetermined by island elites and rulers. An 'Afro-Saxon' elite – Lindsay's term – had assumed power after a gradual transfer from British rule following universal adult suffrage in 1944. Its interests were vested in the continuity of a social order of privilege – colour and class being the most crucial determinants of access (Lindsay, 1975).

The state had crafted a vision of a 'new Jamaica' that was offered to the citizens of the island. 'Newness' was not only in the dismantling of the appearances of colonialism or the replacement of old ways with new symbols: for example, replacing 'God Save the Queen' with the Jamaican national anthem before film viewings in the cinemas. It was to be a consciousness, a mindset that all Jamaicans lived in a 'new' era in which they had a stake, rights and regard. Jamaicans had to see themselves as Jamaicans. A pamphlet issued by the government on the eve of independence announced that, 'Jamaica is one of the world's most beautiful islands. Jamaicans of all races and colours live together in harmony. Jamaica has produced some of the best athletes in the world'.[4] The pamphlet further asked the question: 'What does independence mean?'. It also provided the answer:

> In the first place, it means that for the first time in our history we will be on our own. We will be responsible for all our affairs, both at home and abroad. In the second place, it means that, also for the first time in our history, we will be citizens of **Jamaica** not citizens of the United Kingdom and colonies as is now the case. We will travel abroad on Jamaican passports under the protection of the Jamaican government. In the third place, it means that the future of each of us and the future of our country will lie in our own hands. Our Government will be responsible for us and to us alone.[5]

A Jamaican attitude was encouraged, a consciously Jamaican way of being, with all the uplifting rhetoric of nationalism. It was an idea long worn even by 1962. There was no cloaking the visible and sensed reality of disenfranchisement that threatened the virtue of the country's motto: 'Out of Many One People', the phrase that even its originator, Norman Manley, admitted (in a speech to his party in September 1962) was an ideal more than a reality (in Nettleford, 1971, p. 313).

Jamaica's independence came in the context of party divisions and the state and the elite's fledgling sense of its place and potential. There were multiple

---

4 The Government of Jamaica, 'Independence: what it means to us', 1962, Special Collections, University of the West Indies Mona, Library.

5 Ibid.

visions of the way in which Jamaica and Jamaicans were to face the challenge that lay ahead. A prominent columnist, Vere Johns, wrote facetiously that on 7 August, the day after independence, nothing had changed. All that he had experienced before remained the same and expectations of meaningful difference in the country waned within him.[6]

A contemporary put it more directly: 'There are very few people with the nerve to question seriously the promises on which we base our case for national existence'.[7] And in 1963 came another view: 'Who is to speak for Jamaica? Not the colonials no matter how important they seem, but the young men for whose children we are preparing the new world and the bright promise'.[8]

The party in power in 1962 was the Jamaica Labour Party (JLP), having won a general election in April. Its rivalry with the People's National Party (PNP), the party of Norman Manley, defined Jamaica's politics then as it does now. The stakes and expectations were different in the 1960s. Independence promises and improved social welfare were de rigueur in the campaign build-up. Whichever party – and leader – won, they would be monitored rigorously by their rival in the years following 1962. They were closely held to this by a politicised public rallied behind one leader or another. The PNP criticised the ruling party for its authoritarian tendencies, evidenced by its treatment of perceived dissent. Bustamante was called 'Chief' and his rule and that of his ministers were compared to Duvalier's Haiti, a democracy in name that was drifting towards abusive power.[9]

The Coral Gardens incident in western Jamaica in April 1963, in which Rastafarians were assaulted, arrested and their locks shorn, was held up as proof of the PNP's suspicions. This was politics and there was exaggeration in it. But it does give a sense of the volatility that existed on both sides. By the end of Jamaica's first year of independence, the government's rivals were delighted to argue that no signs of improvement were evident, that it had only deepened the challenges the poor island faced. Consider this 1964 poem by Sybil with humorous reference to the first verse of Jamaica's national anthem:

> Eternal Father Bless our land
> *(Need the P.M.'s permission)*
> Guide us by thy mighty hand
> *(For Cabinet decision)*
> Keep us free from evil powers
> *(Castro?)*
> To our leaders, Great Defender,

6 Johns (1962), 7.
7 *Public Opinion*, 2 March 1963, 1.
8 *Public Opinion*, 5 Jan. 1963, 1.
9 See, e.g., the poem by Sybil, 'Heil! Chief!', which takes a swipe against Bustamante's leadership style (*Public Opinion*, 7 Sept. 1963, 9).

(Is this my name, I wonder)
Grant true wisdom from above
(Sedition; Under our constitution, God, Holds no advisory position)
Justice, truth, be ours for ever,
Jamaica, Land we love
(These phrases have no legal meaning and do not bind the JLP).[10]

Political realities connected with the daily hardships faced by most Jamaicans, particularly those in the overcrowded capital. A demographic increase in the decade worried politicians and made the situation in Kingston tough. Migration into Kingston and St Andrew from rural parishes contributed to a ballooning population with few options for social improvement.

Government promises flowed. New Jamaica would benefit all Jamaicans and everyone would receive adequate housing – in time. But the old places, the squatter lands that spread wide in the west, were frequently referenced as proof of failure. The island's elite classes were embarrassed by them, denigrating them as ugly reminders that the country was not as modern as it proclaimed. In 1966 the government moved in and demolished the shacks on Foreshore Road. The shanties had housed children, hundreds of them, like little Maureen Ellis, forced to move out with their families.

By 1966 the intensity of the gangs in the tightly connected network of ghettoes had become a troubling concern. Political rivalries were to blame for pushing Jamaica's independent future, a future in construction for its children, to a new level of violence. In Denham Town, Trench Town, Foreshore Road and Back-O-Wall gangs, which once used to support politicians in their bids in the last election, were now unleashed, recruiting and executing their force on the young.

Vere Johns was incredulous in a commentary on the situation that emerged after the bulldozing and the beginning of a political battle in which the parties were building a cadre of enforcers: 'Who organized these "gangs" in the city's west?', he asked, continuing:

> The old gangs satisfied themselves with fists, sticks, stones, bottles and a few knives and weapons. The present ones are building arsenals of firearms, home-made bombs and dynamite. All for WHAT? POWER. Power to do to this country as they will ... Power to run the affairs of our young nation according to personal desires and party expediency. Power to deprive us of our rights as citizens of a democratic country.[11]

Elsewhere, he issued a call against the effect of this on the youth: 'What manner of citizens of the world these children make, but future inmates in the island's

---

10 Sybil, 'Eternal father', *Public Opinion*, 21 Dec. 1963.
11 'Vere Johns says', *The Star*, 3 Aug. 1966, 6.

prisons and mental asylum?'[12] Having earlier called Jamaica 'a motherless child', he here extended the metaphor further.[13]

The government responded to these tensions with a state of emergency, imposing a strictly enforced curfew in the west. The result of this, in the medium term, was a tenser situation in the island's capital. Social lines were drawn more starkly along geographical lines. These were not, as yet, the garrisons that they would become. But the seeds were sown. By 1966 Edward Seaga, who had earlier announced his entry into politics with an impassioned speech in parliament on the haves and have-nots, spoke on the radio about the situation unfolding in Kingston's heart:

> To understand West Kingston today one has to understand [its] past neglect … Covering the sore with the skin-coloured powder of police patrols is no more than a temporary measure. Until the gunmen are caught and guns seized there will be no real peace. Medical science, with all its skills and centuries of research, has found no other way to deal with a cancer than with a surgeon's knife, and this cancer in West Kingston has to be cut out with a surgeon's knife.[14]

Norman Manley was equally upset and worried about where the country might be headed. In his own radio address he stated: 'Jamaica is still two nations – the rich and the poor, the haves and the have-nots. The social structure is still dominated by the plantation big man system, is still governed by the master and servant plan for mankind. The gap gets wider not narrower'.[15]

The response to this situation was an increasing desire to leave. Migration has always been a part of Jamaica's reality. But in the 1960s those like Ioni and her family who left for England did so not only because of the promise that existed in other places but with the view that Jamaica was 'harsh and cruel', to use Ioni's father's words. Migration in previous decades had been, among other things, a safety valve for the island. Demand for Jamaican labour encouraged the massive movement to England before – and especially after – the arrival of the *SS Empire Windrush* in England in June 1948.[16] This remained steady in the 1950s.

The impact was beginning to dip as Jamaica readied for independence. The British Commonwealth Immigrants Act of 1962 imposed new regulations on Commonwealth citizens entering the UK in a manner that was criticised

12 'Vere Johns says', *The Star*, 18 July 1966, 10.
13 'Vere Johns says', *The Star*, 17 Aug. 1965, 9.
14 Edward Seaga, radio broadcast reprinted as 'West Kingston—to know it is to love it', in *The Star*, 30 Aug. 1966, 4.
15 Norman Manley radio broadcast reprinted as 'Jamaica in a mess', *Public Opinion*, 1 April 1966, 3.
16 There were 492 West Indian immigrants, mostly Jamaicans and Trinidadians on board. The arrival of the *Windrush* is often regarded as the symbolic beginning of the post-war Caribbean migration to the United Kingdom. On the importance of the 'Windrush generation' see, e.g., Phillips and Phillips (2009) and Francis (1998).

by opposition leader Hugh Gaitskell in the British parliament as 'cruel and brutal anti-colour legislation' (Woodspring, 2016, p. 30). The act limited the number of Jamaicans migrating to the UK to only those, like Ioni's father, who obtained an employment voucher. Jamaicans worried over the implications of this and also of losing their British passport status and the rights they believed it bestowed on them over the Jamaican one.

All of this produced a great deal of anxiety. In the very months that construction workers laboured overtime to make the stadium ready for the August independence celebrations, extraordinarily long lines formed daily in front of the passport office on Harbour Street, where Jamaicans sought to obtain British passports before the Curb Bill took effect in July. The 'Beat the ban' push was large. Hundreds made their voyages to London, so many in fact that extra BOAC flights were commissioned. More security was called in to assist with the ticketing.[17]

The subsequent enforcement of the act drew more attention to the United States, another receiver of large numbers of Jamaican immigrants and also a place with discriminatory migration laws. The McCarran Act (Internal Security Act) of 1950 imposed a quota system on migrants to the US, a move that affected Jamaicans.[18] The issue that Jamaica's leaders had to contemplate was how migration fitted in with the direction in which the new nation was heading. Both Bustamante and Manley understood that with the rising population there was a need for migration. The two of them travelled separately to the United States to plead the case for a repeal of the McCarran Act, which, they argued, discriminated against Jamaicans (and for that matter Trinidadians) unfairly.

Equally resonant was the view that migration was robbing the country of its professional sector – the women and men on whose shoulders the future of the country could be developed. One observer noted in 1963 that migration had cost the country much more than it gained. Calling the Curb Bill a 'very big blow to Jamaica', the observer nonetheless saw benefit for the country: 'We now need all the resources at our disposal: the doctors, lawyers, teachers, tradesmen … and in effect everyone who would contribute their various skills in the interest of a stronger and more abundant Jamaica'.[19]

There was also a cynical view. Some were upset at Jamaicans' willingness to seek migration overseas. They called it a colonial mentality. That Jamaicans did not believe in their country, seeking their opportunities elsewhere and giving of their skills to a place that would never be their own. One local writer

---

17 See, e.g., 'Airport barring of migrants for Minister's probe', *Daily Gleaner*, 9 Jan. 1962, 1; and 'Migrant-rush for UK', *The Star*, 23 March 1962, 21.
18 'The Internal Security Act of 1950', *Documents of American History II* (http://tucnak.fsv.cuni.cz/~calda/Documents/1950s/Inter_Security_50.html [accessed 17 Jan. 2018]). For Jamaican reactions, see, e.g., Colin Legum, 'The truth behind the Migrants Act', *Public Opinion*, 14 Dec. 1963, 7.
19 Legum, 'The truth behind the Migrants Act', 7.

stated that 'the notion that Jamaicans must migrate to find opportunity is a product of colonial mentality. Independent Jamaica must create opportunities for her people'.[20] Norman Manley, a patriotic Jamaican, rebutted the negative implication in this view vigorously: 'Is it the colonial mentality of England that sends more Englishmen abroad every year than all migrants who come to England?'[21]

This was a clearly complicated issue made even more so by the troubling events of 1966 already described. That year coincided with the eventual removal of the McCarran Act. President Lyndon Johnson, under civil-rights pressure, signed the Hart Cellar Act in 1965 – something he promised he would consider when he visited Jamaica during independence celebrations in 1962. The effect of this was astounding. Jamaican migration to the United States shot up dramatically and would remain high for the rest of the decade.

Worry remained that Jamaica was suffering a troubling brain drain. A nationalist consciousness in the mid to late 1960s, carried forward by radical youth, Rastafarians, critics of empire and leftist politicians, and, simultaneously, an expressive revulsion towards European and North American ideologies, in the context of civil rights and the Vietnam War, fuelled a deeper attachment to the country among some Jamaicans. Whatever its problems, Jamaica was their country and needed its people. One proposed solution to this was to encourage professional Jamaicans to return.

Some did return and their fortunes were mixed. In 1962 a Jamaican technician in England was sufficiently moved to go back home, following the example of African immigrants he knew who had done just that. His reality was harder than he had imagined it would be. Frustrated over employment conditions, he told his story to a local paper, vowing to go back to England at his first opportunity, to be 'anywhere but here'.[22]

This example may not have been typical. Others returned from abroad, weary of the anonymity of life in a foreign place, and likewise pulled by the rousing national spirit – enhanced by 1964, when Jamaican culture, particularly Ska music, began to mark its own space on the pop music scene. Figures for return migration in these years are hard to come by, but there is some indication that it was important. To this is added the flow of remittances into the island, already an important element by then. By 1963 more than three million pounds had been sent back to Jamaica by migrants in the UK.[23]

No condition made the desire to leave greater than the deepening political tribalism and violence which worsened after the 1967 election that returned the JLP to power. Following strikes by teachers, journalists, bus operators,

20 This view was quoted in Norman Manley, 'Colonial mentality', *Public Opinion*, 7 April 1966, 4.
21 Ibid.
22 George Thurst, 'Frustration begins at home', *Public Opinion*, 2 Nov. 1963, 11.
23 Paul Scully, 'Our losses from migration', *Public Opinion*, 14 Dec. 1963, 6.

nurses and students and most notably the October 1968 protest by students at the University of the West Indies in response to the government's banning of the lecturer Dr Walter Rodney, participants left in droves, signalling the tensions with which young Jamaica was dealing. As ever the situation was worst in Kingston. A newspaper commentary in 1969 had this to say:

> Kingston is fast becoming the most crime-infested city in the Caribbean … [W]hat is noticeable, what is significant and unquestionable is that most of the crimes are being committed by youths who were 9 to 15 years old in 1962, our independence year. Why? The answer is around for all to see. There has been a tremendous growth in our slums and the depressed areas.[24]

Taken together these circumstances did little to persuade Jamaicans abroad to return. In fact, it only strengthened the desire to leave. By 1970 Jamaicans were the largest number of migrants per capita entering the United States.

The new leader of the PNP, Michael Manley, in his 1969 New Year's address to the country said Jamaica was in a state of crisis. An escalating cost of living and growing fatigue with the JLP had created a bitterly divided society. The political tensions – more violent by then than ever before – and the crime problem had betrayed the ideals of independence, according to the younger Manley: 'The man who has not got the price of a plane ticket is no better off than the man who has not got a passport'.[25] He argued that new Jamaica 'needed something new'.

Michael Manley offered himself as that 'something new'. In a speech to students at the Wolmer's Boys School in May 1970 he pushed the same message, another call to the island's youth, another vow to change their world with their help: 'I am in no doubt in my own mind that the will of this country needs to be summoned to a great effort of reconstruction … [T]he younger generation are critical of the world that their fathers have made. My plea is to get involved … more than ever before this country needs the energy the enthusiasm and the new ideas of youth'.[26]

******

Manley's impassioned call for a transformation revolved around the word 'love'. His slogan, repeated then and ever more frequently in the early years of his administration in the early 1970s, was 'The word is love'. And what sort of love? One love? Love for one another and for country? Love for the children who will reap the world made by their forebears? The appeal of love as an ideal in Jamaica echoed a common Rastafari greeting, 'Love my brothers

24 'Jamaica is a dangerously sick and divided country', *Public Opinion*, 28 Nov. 1969, 1.

25 Michael Manley radio broadcast published as, 'We are in a state of national crisis', *Public Opinion*, 10 Jan. 1969, 6.

26 Michael Manley speech to Wolmer's Boys School, published as 'Jamaica needs the energy and new ideas of youth', *Public Opinion*, 22 May 1970, 6.

and sisters'. Manley's appropriation of it was a conscious gesture towards the influence of Rastafari consciousness – principally through reggae music – on a new generation of Jamaicans, like the students at Wolmer's School, whom he claimed to represent. Manley brought into the political sphere a popular notion of unity and togetherness as a rhetorical device to suggest an end to the violent political division that had come to define Jamaican electoral politics. But it never transcended the status of political device.

Ten years after independence Michael Manley became prime minister on 1 March 1972, promising to use love to reconstruct the nation. The promise he gave was a reversal of the losses of the past decade, the misplaced and departed hope of the 1960s, the creation of another 'new Jamaica'. Jamaica's 1960s ended that February night when he became the country's new leader. The details of the achievements and failures of Manley's Jamaica were carried by the young, those who lived it, loved it and left it. The seeds sown in the 1960s blossomed into full bloom in the 1970s. Crime and political violence worsened to frightening levels and in greater numbers Jamaicans left with no intention of ever returning. 'This is how our world ends', wrote a columnist in 1976, when hundreds took flight and the country was under its second state of emergency since independence, 'not with a bang but with a visa'.[27]

The title of this chapter is influenced by Roger Mais's classic reflection from 1950, 'Why I love and leave Jamaica'. Mais's work captured the conflict between attachment and departure that has long haunted Caribbean history and is pronounced in the Jamaican experience. In that text he offers these lines: 'Shall I have regrets about leaving Jamaica? No. ... If I should know regret it would be a betrayal and a denial of [my values] that have only met with sneering and contempt in this country of my birth, or have met with an odious kind of patronage, which is worst of all'.[28]

Mais's defence of his leaving touched on that perpetual ambivalence of intentions that has remained a constant in Jamaican life. Leaving does not bring about a resolution. Those who depart know well that their personal histories, tied so tightly with Jamaica's history, are a partial narrative in a larger story of the search for freedom. Migration cannot by itself satisfy the reckoning. Mais left for England, which for him, in the words of his friend George Lamming, turned out to be like 'stale porridge'. He would return to Jamaica, where he died in 1955.

The decision to stay also offers no lasting calm. The country's problems continued to multiply and with the passage of time these overwhelming circumstances have forced a reconsideration of the personal and national journey. Edward Baugh, a Jamaican poet, in his brilliant poem 'Choices', written decades after Mais, envisions a conversation between a Jamaican who

27 Malcolm Sharp, 'Styles of departure', *Daily Gleaner*, 12 Aug. 1976, 8.
28 Mais (1950).

left and one who stayed. Each has an unsettled sense of the virtue of their choice, made pellucid in the poem's final lines: 'I wouldn't say I would never leave, | but if that's what they calling ambition, | then for now I sticking with love'.[29] The 1960s were expected to change that tension between leaving and loving Jamaica, to tip the balance towards love. Independence was expected to deepen attachment to Jamaica and the island's commitment to its people. Perhaps that was expecting too much. Critics had said in 1962 that the country was not yet ready for independence – a comment that still echoes. Whatever the reasons why the 1960s did not achieve what it promised, their effects – love, loss and leaving – the stories of the children of the new Jamaica, must be told if today, half a century later, we are to understand what they truly meant.

Bibliography

Baugh, E. (2013) 'Choices', in E. Baugh, *Black Sand: New and Selected Poems* (Leeds: Peepal Tree Press), p. 58.

Francis, V. (1998) *With Hope in their Eyes* (London: Nia).

Government of Jamaica (1962) *Independence: What it Means to Us* (Special Collections, University of the West Indies Mona Library).

Johns, V. (1962) 'Vere Johns says', *The Star*, 8 Aug.

Lindsay, L. (2011 [1975]) 'The myth of independence: middle-class politics and non-mobilization in Jamaica', Sir Arthur Lewis Institute of Social and Economic Studies, University of the West Indies, Mona, Working Paper no. 6., https://papers.ssrn.com/sol3/papers.cfm?abstract_id=1822826 [accessed 5 Feb. 2019].

Mais, R. (1950) 'Why I love and leave Jamaica', typescript, Roger Mais Collection, University of the West Indies Mona, Special Collections, http://contentdm64-srv.uwimona.edu.jm/cdm/ref/collection/RogerMS/id/1626 [accessed July 2019].

Manley, N.W. (1971) 'Independence: the assets we have', in Rex Nettleford (ed.), *Manley and the New Jamaica: Selected Speeches and Writings, 1938–1968* (London: Longman), pp. 313–17.

Phillips, M. and T. Phillips (2009) *Windrush: The Irresistible Rise of Multi-Racial Britain* (London: Harper Collins).

Woodspring, N. (2016) *Baby Boomers: Time and Ageing Bodies* (Bristol: Policy Press).

---

29 Baugh (2013), p. 58.

2. Why did we come?

B. M. Nobrega

Many factors are involved in why we came. My story and experiences, though they may not be typical, still entwine many elements of the Caribbean migrant's experience. We came because we were coming to the mother country. Years of colonisation had indoctrinated us with a sense of belonging to England, loyalty to the Queen and country, a willingness to fight to defend this mother country and all the values of this mighty seat of empire. We learned of it in church and from our school system, our text books. Even our exercise books, which we handled daily in our classrooms, had the face of the beautiful Queen Elizabeth on the cover. We were not royalists and yet the Queen was wonderful (I love the Queen even now) and so we sang the national anthem. For us, the Queen was everything that was wonderful about England and about empire.

So, with the ending of World War Two, with the call and invitation to the colonies, particularly to the Caribbean, to help with the reconstruction of England, it was only natural that the Caribbean soldiers who had fought for their mother country should jump at the opportunity to leave their beautiful, sun-drenched islands, stifled by the colonial restrictions of colour, class and privilege. So, the *SS Windrush* came in 1948, with some of the returning soldiers who would inititally stay in the Clapham Common bunkers. Then followed many immigrating Caribbean subjects, flocking to the mother country for work, opportunity and accessible education, and to help to rebuild it. None of us planned to stay. Nearly everyone had a five-year plan: to earn enough money and to return home.

The magical fantasy land sold to us through images of the Queen was nowhere to be seen. There was very little sunshine, and there was smog. One went to work and school in the dark and returned home in the dark. To me it seemed like perpetual night. In those days the cultural revolution, with the Beatles and so forth, was only just beginning and so the whole sense of colour was changing. At that time you did not have all these blue shirts and pink shirts, it was always just black and white and grey. In the Caribbean there is colour, there is light, there is space. England was so dark and grey. The houses were all joined together and belched smoke like bakeries and they were cold:

B. M. Nobrega, 'Why did we come?', in J.D. Webb, R. Westmaas, M. del Pilar Kaladeen and W. Tantam (eds.), *Memory, migration and (de)colonisation in the Caribbean and beyond* (London: University of London Press, 2019), pp. 31–5. License: CC-BY-NC-ND 4.0.

paraffin heaters were the order of the day. Of course, the colonies had their own hierarchies and some workers in Guyana did not enjoy the luxuries of space – they, too, might live in a row of houses, all joined together. But when I came to England and saw that the majority of people were living in a house joined up to another one, I was shocked and confused.

Arrival brought a steep learning curve for Caribbean immigrants: we saw white people sweeping the streets and doing menial jobs, lacking education and speaking an incoherent language. I remember that on arrival we took a taxi to Wimbledon and the driver said – it was old money then – 'nanty naan'. We thought, 'What's he on about? I thought they spoke English'. It was 9s. 9d.[1] We could not understand many of the people, just as we could not understand where the motherland sold to us through images of the Queen had gone. The mystique of white superiority was totally dismantled. Seeing the realities of the mother country was a major factor in the emboldening of Caribbean peoples in our quest for decolonisation. And yet, there was still something about England that we loved.

For many in Britain the new arrivals were economic migrants, but for some Caribbean people this was the homecoming of an overseas citizenry. So why did we stay? This is an indomitable question which perpetually enters our thoughts. Was it just the audacity of hope? There was always the initial hope, dreams of upliftment and a better life.

Furthermore, there was a great investment, the investment of getting to the mother country, where things were so much better, perhaps with streets paved with gold, as we were forever told in movies and newsreels. As one Kitchener calypso said in 1948, 'London was the place for me'.[2] The investment was, for many working-class Caribbean people, simply tremendous. Goats had to be sold, sometimes cattle and other livestock, to raise the pounds required for the passage and costs on arrival. Another factor was the mass exodus of the young and strong from the villages and towns, thwarting the development of those places, in the hope that in a few years they would be able to return home with financial security and more knowledge and skills to help the brethren left behind. Others pledged their savings to come: not content with the 'secondary' education obtained at home and their clerical, administrative jobs, they took the leap in the hope that they would be able to work and study to enter one of those most lauded and respected professions like law or medicine.

One had to stay and persevere in spite of the shock of the weather and the lack of welcome. Returning without achieving anything would have inflicted such humiliation and shame on one's psyche. We would have earned the disrespect of all and sundry in the homelands and have been seen as just wasteful good-for-nothings. So staying was a must. This entailed getting a job,

---

1   Just under 50p in modern decimal currency.
2   See https://www.theguardian.com/music/2011/jun/16/lord-kitchener-empire-windrush [accessed 5 Feb. 2019].

finding housing, saving and coping with all the expenses and vicissitudes of daily living. These were all momentous tasks. Some were fortunate and were recruited directly from the Caribbean, especially for the transport services or the fledgling National Health Service. But most of us could spend all day at the job centre (then known as the labour exchange) and get no job and when a job was offered it was the most basic kind with the lowest pay, one that no Englishman would take up. Even the well-qualified struggled, perhaps more so. The ex-Forces folk were not welcome once the uniform of war was taken off. Jobs were largely low level; a position at Lyons tea rooms paying £7 per week plus meals was considered a blessed godsend.

I remember going to the job centre. I was asked, 'Well, what can you do?'. I said I was a surveyor. 'Right', he responded, 'I think I've got the exact job for you'. He rang up the employer and said, 'I've got this guy here and he did this and he did that', and so on and so on, adding, 'Oh and he's from Guyana'. And then he said, 'Oh no, no, no, you must meet him, he's a very nice guy!'. The boss decided to meet me. He liked me, found out what I could do and gave me a job in his surveying company on £10 a week. In this role I was teaching an apprentice, a young fellow not long out of school. His spelling was bad, his arithmetic was rubbish. I had to do everything because he and I were together in the estimates department. And one day his payslip falls out on the floor and he is getting £15 a week! I approached the boss and in his embarrassment he said that my alternative would have been to work 'in the field', on the M3, where I would get subsistence. My pay then increased from £10 to something like £20. It was all a struggle.

Rent had to be paid for accommodation that was in short supply, so scarce that we huddled together in rooms in shared houses under ruthless landlords for whom new words in the English dictum like 'Rachmanism' were invented.³ But out of all this, *savings* were to be made: there were 'Boxhands', 'Sou Sous', 'partners', all terms for ways of pooling and saving money. This was particularly so for the first generation, who would put money together and then would buy a house, an old rotten house, for a lot of us to inhabit. The bed was so cold and wet. You had to get these blankets and wrap up in them and just wait for your body warmth to warm you up. There were no duvets in those days! Indeed, I have seen this England come a long way. We dealt with the cold by using paraffin heaters with their blue and pink flames. We had to clean them out constantly or else the place would smell and you would get soot and smoke all over the place. And you had to wash your hair almost every day and your clothes smelled because of the condensation that caused. But we used our skill and energy collectively to repair these buildings and create homes. Then we would buy another one and another one. And slowly we began to own those houses. Fortunately, many of the second generation got jobs in housing offices.

3 Perec (or Peter) Rachman was a Polish-born London landlord notorious for exploiting and intimidating his tenants in the 1950s and early 1960s.

They would not, of course, discriminate against other Caribbean people and so council housing then also became more available to us.

Am I glad that I left the Caribbean? I wish I had not had to. In many aspects I am glad that I left. But I wish that I had not had to leave. I am glad I left because I was able to come and get an education. Not that I did not have an education, but I was unlikely to have obtained a tertiary education. And it was not all bad. There were some nice folks among the English, Welsh, Scottish and Irish who already resided here. Some were friendly, some were helpful, some were polite and not overtly prejudiced. Some socialising occurred. Not much at first, but the two groups were slowly growing together. We were learning and getting used to British ways, like queuing, fish and chips and the general pace of life, to the extent that on visits home the returnees were called 'British people'! We may have toned down our parties but, by some form of osmosis, our *joie de vie*, our sense of colour, style, dress and music were permeating and changing our host society. There were even interracial marriages and partnerships occurring, leading to mixed-race children. Such relationships were an anathema, a huge taboo for the native population, but in time tolerance occurred.

We took root. This is now our third coming or fourth, depending on the count. We bore offspring, we managed the cold and the damp, we managed the prejudice and discrimination, we fought our ground and fought for fair play. Things got better. The race laws were passed.[4] Our five-year plans became ten-year plans and later retirement plans. Things changed at home. Some returned there, some went back but returned to the UK to be with children and grandchildren. Some left for other shores like North America, some entered those lauded professions and either stayed or left. Some came back for health reasons and to make use of the National Health Service. Home is where one's family is. So we are here. We have integrated into and, indeed, made great contributions to this society. Now we pass the 'cricket test' – a test coined in 1990 by Conservative politician Norman Tebbit, which sees if one supports one's native land or the English team. The demise of West Indian test cricket may have contributed to this, but with so many of the children and grandchildren making the representative sports teams of the UK, the football and athletics teams, the British team is now our team. Other inroads that we have made into this land are in medicine, diplomacy, trade unionism and parliament. Such successes have helped to make us feel like we are here to stay.

I want to end this reflection by commenting on the Bronze Woman Monument, the brainchild of my mother, the poet Cécile Nobrega, which is in Stockwell Park, near where most of the Windrush settlers first resided. The statue is depicted on the cover of this book. It displays a Caribbean mother lifting her child as if to reach the limits of the British sky. It symbolises our hope and struggle. It was Cécile's vision that some monumental record should

---

4 The Race Relations Act in 1965, amended by the Race Relations Act in 1968 and repealed by the Race Relations Act in 1976.

be established, not merely to the Windrush settlers, our third coming and all loyal subjects of the British Empire, but to the strength of womanhood – particularly Caribbean womanhood. Her poem of the same name was penned in Guyana before she settled in the UK, the mother country. The statue embodied the reflections in her poem. In her life here she trailblazed as a teacher, campaigner for increasing adult literacy and against the government programme 'Educationally Subnormal Schooling' into which many Caribbean children were being dumped.[5] In her early 80s she tirelessly campaigned for this monumental statue to be built. Fairs, tea parties and numerous fundraising events were exhausting and largely financially unrewarding. But never giving up, the charity, Presentation Housing, with its section for Community Charitable Engagement (OLMEC), came to the rescue and provided all the remaining funding required. They are now the caretakers of the monument. The statue has been up for ten years and is a symbol of how …

Together we will all lift this land. We are here to stay, we can and must RISE.

---

5   For more on this, see B. Coard, *How the West Indian Child is Made Educationally Subnormal* (London: New Beacon Books, 1971).

3. History to heritage: an assessment of Tarpum Bay, Eleuthera, the Bahamas

Kelly Delancy

In his book *Silencing the Past* Michel-Rolph Trouillot observes that 'any historical narrative is a bundle of silences' (1995, p. 27). These are not merely absences, but the result of an active process in which 'one silences a fact as an individual silences a gun' (ibid., p. 48). All historical narratives contain silences, as any attribution of significance implies parallel attribution of insignificance. However, it is the actively manufactured absences in historical production as a result of power that have led to this study of history and heritage. Individuals, referred to as the 'historical guild', including academics, professional historians, journalists, political appointees and nations have often led in the privileging of certain histories over others in efforts to secure positions of dominance and legacies of majesty and colonialism. Heritage, being a past legacy in the present, has taken shape in much the same way as historical production. Persons in positions of power have attributed significance to tangible and intangible representations of narratives that privilege their position and establish hegemony. This authorised heritage discourse (AHD), as coined by Australian author and heritage worker Laurajane Smith (2006, p. 4), gives credence to epistemologies of dominant societies leading to top-down legacies. In counter to dominant narratives of the Bahamas derived from colonial records of Great Britain and influence from the nearby United States, this chapter seeks a history of the Bahamian community of Tarpum Bay from its members, with the overarching goal of ascertaining how the residents and descendants define their heritage and themselves. By assuming a bottom-up approach and giving the Tarpum Bay community a voice to share their unique history and values for themselves and in their own words, their history and heritage values may be preserved in a way that the present and future community can appreciate.

The significance of this work lies in its approach to the problem of representation in historical narratives and heritage-preservation activities. It is an example of how decolonisation methods can be applied in practice. This chapter is taken from a larger master's thesis project, completed in 2015,

K. Delancy, 'History to heritage: an assessment of Tarpum Bay, Eleuthera, the Bahamas', in J.D. Webb, R. Westmaas, M. del Pilar Kaladeen and W. Tantam (eds.), *Memory, migration and (de)colonisation in the Caribbean and beyond* (London: University of London Press, 2019), pp. 37–55. License: CC-BY-NC-ND 4.0.

that explores the idea of history and heritage at Tarpum Bay, Eleuthera, through memory to reveal cultural-heritage values. Within the field of heritage conservation, this is a living-heritage approach, the key concept of which is of continuity for the core community. It is specifically the continuity of the purpose for which the heritage was originally intended. It is for the community's enduring connection with the heritage, the care of heritage by the community as expressed by the community and the continuous process of embracing changing circumstances (Poulios, 2014, p. 22). The position of the 'professional' is to provide a framework of support and assistance to the core community to meet its own needs (ibid., p. 27). In conducting the heritage assessment of Tarpum Bay, this author applies the living-heritage approach by listening to and documenting the community's articulation of their history and their connection with heritage.

This approach is appropriate here because, like many settlements on the Bahamian Out Islands (all Bahamian islands outside the capital island of New Providence, also known as Family Islands), the Tarpum Bay settlement developed in relative isolation, thus the islands developed their own unique characteristics that may still be observed today, including distinct accents and some differences in food preparation. Unfortunately, narratives during the early period of Bahamian history, including the 19th and 20th centuries, focus heavily on Nassau and the island of New Providence at the expense of many outer islands, or generally group the outer-islands all together. Though the Bahama Islands may share a common history, it does not mean the people there share a common experience of that history, heritage values or a common connection to heritage. The living-heritage approach is therefore valuable here in challenging meta-narratives and understanding how the Out Island community of Tarpum Bay has experienced history and defines its their heritage and what the community's needs may be relating to it.

In some cases, there are gaps in archival records on Out Island settlements and in others the historical details have yet to be drawn out of archival records and presented in historical literature on the Bahamas. Documentary sources consulted for information on Tarpum Bay include unpublished records such as archived Out Island Resident Justice and commissioners' annual reports, registers of records and Votes of the House of Assembly located at the Bahamas National Archives at New Providence. The *Commissioner's Annual Reports*, compiled by Out Island commissioners, provide a more specific focus on the Bahamian Out Islands, though they can still be very general when it comes to the community level. The reports were a summation of a district's (a large portion of an island) economic activity and statistics, not necessarily values and experiences. At the Bahamas National Archives, Resident Justice Reports for Tarpum Bay begin in 1884. Later *Commissioner's Annual Reports* situate Tarpum Bay in the district of Rock Sound, begin in 1908 and continue up to 1974.

The settlement of Tarpum Bay is located on the south-western coast of the island of Eleuthera, approximately 67 miles east of the capital island of New Providence, and has an estimated population of 766 people (2010 census).[1] Using history as a proxy this research identifies, along with the community, the heritage and underlying heritage values of Tarpum Bay for effective cultural-resource management. At the same time, the study contributes documentation towards the development of a more accurate and inclusive picture of insular and national identity. This author uses a network sampling method known as the snowball technique to contact community members. This method is used to study populations that are scattered over a large area (Bernard, 2011, p. 147). A total of 33 recorded interviews were conducted over 11 months. They included 19 residents, ten descendants and two Eleutherans residing outside Tarpum Bay but familiar with the community. This chapter also draws on numerous informal conversations with many others. These individuals are members of the community directly and indirectly.[2] Residents offer information from experience on historical development and heritage. Descendants offer knowledge on their understanding of the history and their experience of heritage, while the Eleutherans residing outside Tarpum Bay offer yet another perspective on the place and people from their own observations and experiences.

It should be noted, however, that the oldest interviewee, Vera Carey, was born in 1917. Therefore, personal experiences and memories of interviewees date no earlier than the 1920s, with the exception of recounting narratives passed on from older family members, while the settlement of Tarpum Bay was in existence over a hundred years prior to this. As a result the history and heritage expressed here are of the early 20th century to the present and do not reflect earlier periods. This is important as, for example, memories reflect tomatoes being the chief export of the settlement. However, Resident Justice Reports from the 19th century show that pineapples were the chief export for the settlement during the late 19th century. In the 1880s and 1890s pineapples were the chief export of the Bahamas and the island of Eleuthera ranked first. The main pineapple-growing areas on the island are cited as Gregory Town, Hatchet Bay, Governor's Harbour, Tarpum Bay, Rock Sound and Wemyss Bight (Bahamas, Public Record Office, 1977). An 1886 Resident Justice Report for Tarpum Bay notes 'a number of commodious dwelling houses have

---

1   Bahamas Department of Statistics. South Eleuthera Population by Settlement and Total Number of Occupied Dwellings: 2010 Census. Nassau: Government Printing, p. 3. Available at: https://www.bahamas.gov.bs/wps/wcm/connect/a3b7140e-7992-42b2-9b21-73b81a0b8cad/SOUTH+ELEUTHERA+POPULATION+BY+SETTLEMENT_2010+CENSUS.pdf?MOD=AJPERES.

2   'Indirectly' in this context means that the individuals do not have a direct connection to Tarpum Bay as residents or descendants, but have a connection through other means, such as being married to someone from Tarpum Bay, having worked with people from Tarpum Bay or having observed or experienced them in another setting.

been recently erected; this, with the cheerfulness of the people generally, leads to the inference that the pine-apple industry is not retrograding. The majority seem to ignore every other industry and trust the cultivation of the pine-apple'. Tomatoes became the chief export from Tarpum Bay during the 20th century after the decline of pineapple exports, hence the present recollection of tomatoes being more prevalent than pineapple growing.

A community history of Tarpum Bay

Present residents and descendants alike agree that within their memories the main industry was farming and tomatoes constituted the main farm produce for export in Tarpum Bay, followed by pineapples. Boats came to Tarpum Bay from England for pineapples and from the United States for tomatoes (Mingo, 2015). Qurina Mingo (b. 1941) remembers the boats that anchored directly behind the rocks at the bay because the water was too shallow to enter it. He recalls 'black spots [in the water] with black stones are ballast. When they left, they would throw those out because they would carry loads of pineapples and tomatoes back. They say if you had a good breeze it would take three weeks to sail to England' (2015).

Tomatoes grew into the chief export of the district as early as 1911 (*Commissioner's Annual Report*, 1911). William McCartney (2014) recalls that his grandfather on his mother's side, William Wilkerson Allen (also known as Willie Butcher Allen) (b. 1875), was a tomato farmer. His grandfather on his father's side, William Ashwer McCartney, was captain of one of the fast sailboats on Eleuthera. His grandfather's boat was named *The Imperial* and used to transport tomatoes from Tarpum Bay to Florida.

Willie Butcher Allen also had a packing house at Tarpum Bay, as did 'Boy' [William Albert] Carey, John Hilton, Henry McCartney with Edwin Allen and John Louie (Johnson, 2015). Newton Carey ran a government-associated tomato packing house (Herbert Carey, 2015). The government supplied this with fertiliser and seed (*Commissioner's Annual Report*, 1940; Herbert Carey, 2015). The others were independent packing houses where the farmers bought their own fertiliser and seed. Herbert Carey (2015) remembers tomatoes being packed according to size and exported during the 1930s through to the mid 1950s:

> They graded them. A big one was five sixes. A very small one was like a seven eights. They had to build these crates to put them in then wrap these tomatoes, put them in there, then put the cover on them, then take them out on the dock, then a barge would come in. They used to export them then to Nassau and shipped to Canada. If it was a good season, they would start the first of November to the last of February.

It is said that Willie Butcher then went to the settlement of Wemyss Bight and had a packing house there. Samuel Johnson's (2015) three brothers and father worked for Willie Butcher, who eventually migrated from Tarpum Bay to Nassau:

> After Uncle Willie, and Kyle Nottage and Big John, those old fellows, Johnny Louie, Boy Carey all those old fellows died out, we tried to do the best we could, but nobody really was into farming ... Because the government started their own packinghouse in Greencastle and then the lazy farmer like me, we took up carrying our stuff to Greencastle because wasn't any other packinghouses here to do it. We spoke about it, but nobody ever went into it. In those days you could've grown anything and there was always a packinghouse there open.

The mass movement of people from Tarpum Bay in the 1930s was economically driven. Dorothy Moncur (granddaughter of Willie Butcher Allen) recalls that when her father moved from Tarpum Bay to New Providence, 'it was because of a depression and people were not able to make a living'. This is community knowledge rooted in memory. Dorothy Moncur (2014) has been told that her father, Alfred Arnold McCartney, owned a shop, 'but after a while people didn't have any money to buy anything, so he had to close the shop out'. She and her family subsequently moved to New Providence in 1933. In addition to New Providence, people of Tarpum Bay relocated to Key West and Miami. Steven Carey (2015) said that after having travelled back and forth to Florida with produce:

> A lot of 'em decided well I'm going to stay in Key West. So a lot of 'em came here and took their houses apart, you know the house right here by the shop, the wooden houses, they weren't put together with nails, they were put together with wood and pins, so they just come and they take it down and put it on the boat and took 'em to Key West. See now, my great grandma, she had seven brothers and she was the oldest one what stayed here ... Susan Allen. She was the oldest one out of all to stay here, but all of 'em went to Key West, but that's how they ended up in Key West. That's how they chose Key West because they was running on the boats, and they decided to stop off and stay there, that's how they get there. They bought property there or squatted on property there, say well this piece here is mine 'cause nobody was living there in Key West in 'dem days. Most people there ... was Bahamians because a lot of 'em went from here and most was Tarpum Bay people. And that's how we get that big old crew in Key West.

Those who remained at Tarpum Bay continued to farm and supplemented farming with available opportunities such as fishing, sponging, construction of boats and buildings, teaching and small businesses. According to Herbert Carey, the tomato industry began to decline in the early 1950s because Mexico was able to produce tomatoes at a cheaper rate than the Bahamas. People continued growing tomatoes, however, on a smaller scale. This is significant because the people of south Eleuthera, including Tarpum Bay, identify with tomato production (in the past and present), yet today the entire island of

Eleuthera is ascribed an identity linked to pineapple production as a result of the modern tourism industry. This may be seen as another example of lack of representation leading to misrepresentation.

Samuel Johnson (b. 1924) also recalls the downturn in the economy. He says (2015): 'Things all over the island were bad. Things were not good here … all we knew then was farming. We lived off the farm. With the little money we had, we had to travel then to look for a livelihood'. Samuel Davis (b. 1926) remembers the Contract as the first in a series of events that brought prosperity to Eleuthera and the Bahamas. The Contract, also called the Project, was a negotiated agreement between the government of Great Britain, as the Bahamas were a British colony, and the government of the United States for the recruitment of Bahamian labourers to fill shortages created by World War II. Bahamian workers in the United States began sending more modern items to their families in the Bahamas. At Tarpum Bay during this time Samuel Davis (2015) remembers wompers [locally made shoes from recycled rubber] transitioning out and into tennis shoes and then various other types of footwear. He saw thatch roofs transition into 'sheets' and shingled roofs become concrete roofs.

In the 1950s and 1960s investors began developing the island of Eleuthera. Tourism became a major industry for the Bahamas and Tarpum Bay felt its effects. Investors included Arthur Vining Davis, who served as president and later chairman of the Aluminium Company of America (ALCOA), and Juan Trippe, founder of Pan American Airways. According to Henry Allen (2015):

> An investor came into Nassau, which built Union Dock … and he was invited to come to Eleuthera and have a look at Eleuthera and see if he wanted to invest in Eleuthera. His name was Arthur Vining Davis. So, when Arthur Vining Davis came, I understand that he carried on farming just like Levy carried on farming. So, he done farming but on a larger scale. It was exported into Florida. At that time World War II was going on. When Arthur Vining Davis came along with his investment things began to change from farming to week work, receiving a pay roll. With farming you didn't receive a pay roll until the crop … People around Rock Sound and Tarpum Bay in particular were able to then start getting salaries and that caused life to be better … Then he moved from farming, he went into tourism and the houses that he used to house the people who worked for him he turned those houses into apartments where tourists rented and then the name came Rock Sound Club … as he transitioned from farming, the persons he had working for him had to melt into the community. He bought out a lot of the people in Rock Sound houses and property and the people he had working for him were mostly white people and strangers as well, lived in Rock Sound.

During the 1940s, Davis established South Eleuthera Properties Limited, acquired approximately 35,000 acres on Eleuthera and set the island's tourist industry in motion (Cleare, 2007, p. 120). South Eleuthera Properties would come to operate the Rock Sound Club, the Cotton Bay Club, the Winding Bay Club, the Eleuthera Beach Inn and Three Bay Farms. Davis also operated the Davis Harbour Marina near Wemyss Bight, sport-fishing boats for hire, a hardware store, supermarket and a machine shop where the company's vehicles, boats and equipment were serviced. Juan Trippe built the Cotton Bay Club in 1959 with an 18-hole golf course. He also bought the Rock Sound Club from Davis and expanded the Rock Sound airport: 'It was just a little short airport. I helped to work on it when it was extended. When the first jet came here, I think it was 16 shillings. You took that ticket and spend a day or two in Miami and came to Nassau and spend a day or two and come back to Rock Sound on that same ticket on that jet … When Trippe came here it was like glory' (Johnson, 2015). Similarly, Steven Carey (2015) remembers Juan Trippe's influence in the district as a positive one. He recalls: 'That's the first time that Pan American used to fly here, 747 used to fly here twice a day, you went to Miami for $27, I used to work for that company'.

Pan American Airways began a jet service between Rock Sound and the US in 1964 with two Boeing 707 aircrafts. By 1966 Pan American Airways had two daily flights between New York and Rock Sound via Nassau (*Commissioner's Annual Report*, 1966). Some 20 years earlier a modern schoolroom was erected at Rock Sound, replacing the old buildings and sites owned by the Board of Education (*Commissioner's Annual Report*, 1940). Improvements were made to the road between Tarpum Bay and Bannerman Town; buildings were constructed for housing machinery, storing stocks of lumber and cement and for housing workers. Other buildings were renovated. Davis introduced electricity to Rock Sound in 1944 as well as internal plumbing for the modern convenience of running water. The power plant was supplying electricity and Eleuthera Water Supply water to the Rock Sound community, and later all of Eleuthera, under government supervision. With the exception of a few American employees, the entire staff were Bahamian. Several thousand pounds were paid in wages during the year.

Contributing to the agricultural development at Eleuthera was the American, Austin Levy. He established a dairy and poultry farm in north Eleuthera, became the largest employer in the area, and was responsible for much of the infrastructure that developed at Hatchet Bay/Alice Town. George Baker was another individual who benefited south Eleuthera in more ways than one. As a representative for Eleuthera in the House of Assembly, he promoted the interests of the people. He ensured that public roads were improved at Tarpum Bay, had the government build a sea wall after the devastating effects of hurricanes, and personally assisted poor constituents whenever possible. George Baker's business interests also benefited the district economically. His canning factory at Rock Sound provided employment for the people of south Eleuthera, and he also hired boats to buy, can and sell peas produced by the people at Acklins Island in the southern Bahamas (Johnson, 2015):

> He [George Baker] came here to work under Arthur Vining Davis' portfolio. After he served here a little while, George Baker went into farming. Then he opened his factory, then he went for himself, then he went to join politics, went into parliament, but through that he had his factory open. He worked from Bannerman Town to Gregory Town. Had a pine field, tomato field in Bannerman Town, in Rock Sound, hired people all from all Eleuthera. Everybody was hired. Who wasn't in the farm, worked in the packinghouse. Who wasn't in the packinghouse, they worked in the factory. Who didn't work in the factory worked on the field, labour. People who grew pineapples, can 'em up. You grow tomatoes, you can 'em up. You grow pigeon peas, you can 'em up. Whatever you produce, carry them to the factory, you can 'em up … Before he [Arthur Vining Davis] came we knew nothing about fridge and electric and things like that. But after Arthur Vining Davis came [to] South Eleuthera [the] first thing he did [was] he bought land. Rock Sound Club was the first club on the island. It belonged to him. Most of the work was done by hand … clean the yard, the hole you dig, the foundation, 'most everything then was done by hand. Where the house is now, that used to be the office, machine shop down in that area. And then from there to Cotton Bay, then to Winding Bay. Where Winding Bay Club is, that was Arthur Vining Davis' house. So, he built Eleuthera.

Henry Allen (2015) speaks of the continuing legacy of Arthur Vining Davis:

> After Davis passed on, they turned his house into a club … Some of the money from these investments it trickled down to Tarpum Bay … between us [my brother and me] growing up and my third brother being born because of the Rock Sound Club in Mr. Davis' era, my father was able to build a house … They were able to buy better shoes, better clothes, better stores … were able to put more stuff in the stores because they were able to sell it. It made a difference. Then through him we were able to get electricity … As I understand it, Eleuthera was the first Family Island in the Bahamas to have electricity.

Foreign investment had ushered in a new way of life for the Tarpum Bay community and Eleuthera at large. It improved infrastructure, expanded resources for education and improved the economy. During this period, many gave up farming in favour of serving a new clientele, receiving new training and a weekly wage.

The events that led to the closure of these major developments on Eleuthera are rarely discussed and interviewees often seemed reluctant to talk about them. Responses often began with 'I know, but I hate to say it …' and 'Gee, I'm telling you this, I shouldn't tell you that'. Others rejoiced at the opportunity finally to share what they believe to be the truth of what caused the demise of the best thing ever to happen to Eleuthera. The change is attributed to a change in government. The social effects of that change, specific to Tarpum Bay, are not detailed in historical accounts. Therefore it is only through accessing the memories of residents that the social experience can be understood. It is necessary to describe the change as the meta-narrative constructed during the struggle for national independence (approximately 1950–73) and visions of a postcolonial Bahamian future by and for 'true' Bahamians, being black Bahamians, permeated from the capital through to the outer islands of the Bahamas with momentous impact.

A white mercantile elite, based in Nassau, had dominated the House of Assembly for generations, from the era of slavery to emancipation and beyond (Craton and Saunders, 1998). Though all forms of slavery were abolished in British Caribbean colonies on 1 August 1838, there had been little change in the relationship between former slave owners and former slaves in the post-emancipation era (Lee, 2012, p. 17). The white elite continued to use legislative, economic and property requirements to bar the majority class of darker-skinned Bahamians from participation in national life and control of the country (ibid., p. 13). Members of this ruling white oligarchy owned all the businesses along the main street in downtown Nassau, called Bay Street, and came to be known simply as the 'Bay Street Boys'. They maintained control of the country and promoted their interests through legislative and economic monopoly well into the 20th century.

The Progressive Liberal Party (PLP) was formed in 1953 to challenge the white oligarchy. It was modelled on the Jamaica's People's National Party (PNP) with its activist philosophy and call for democratic socialism (Dodge, 2005, p. 110). The PLP sought to represent the majority of Bahamians and gain equality for black Bahamians. With the PLP success in the 1956 general elections (they won six of the 29 seats in parliament) the Bay Street Boys formed the United Bahamian Party (UBP) in 1958. The white oligarchy sometimes functioned as benevolent overlords. For example, George Baker was elected as a representative for Eleuthera in 1949. His business investments in Eleuthera benefited his personal fortune but also brought greater prosperity to the labouring class in south Eleuthera. George Baker, being white, however, became a member of the UBP.

After being defeated in the 1962 general election, the PLP rallied and won by a slim margin in 1967 with the help of a white, independent candidate, Alvin Braynen, who represented Harbour Island (a tiny island just north of Eleuthera). The party sought to create a sense of Bahamian national identity with a strong emphasis on the black majority, separating themselves from the British identity. Their goal was to establish the country as an independent nation. As Bahamian anthropologist Nicolette Bethel expresses, Bahamian independence became 'more the outcome of racially-based competition than the result of some universal, nationalist uprising' (2000, p. 16). National symbols emerged with rhetoric similar to that of the Black Power movement in the United States: 'the darker one's skin, the purer one's status as a "true" Bahamian' (ibid., p. 17). Through the PLP's work an African heritage was emphasised at the expense of others as the Bahamian national identity. The imagery and symbolism of slavery, combined with slogans like 'Remember your chains', became propaganda used to remind black Bahamians of the struggles of their ancestors and their continued servitude to white masters (Lee, 2012, pp. 64–96). This was used to stir emotion and invoke the masses to continue voting for the majority black political party. This use of black Bahamian history to create ideas of heritage for purposes of political propaganda also had a great effect on Eleuthera. The propaganda cultivated divisions between white and black, employer and employee. One resident remembers:

> After the PLP came around ... it made a big mess. The PLP says that they can take the factory 'we have the keys in our pocket for the factory' ... He [George Baker] got a little upset about it so he just closed it down and that made a big mess because we wasn't able to grow any tomatoes no more ... not like that. Just a few and just sell them around. So that's why that closed. The PLP got biggity (Anonymous, 2015).[3]

Samuel Johnson (2015) recalls an atmosphere of animosity. He remembers this period and expresses a relationship between the change in government from the UBP to the PLP and the downturn in the economy of south Eleuthera:

> After government changed, I don't know what they done, but it seemed like something happened that all the jobs they just got against the Bay Street people ... When Pan Am used to fly from here, I saw some of my own people on the airport saying 'let Trippe and let this one go, let George Baker go'. And they all got contrary and everything on the island closed down because [of] the hatred. We had a place near the Rock Sound Club with livestock, by the factory. In between Rock Sound and Tarpum Bay you had two hotels. You had livestock and a packinghouse between Rock Sound and Tarpum Bay ... Airport singing 'let them go'. That hatred ... they took the same thing and brought it to Eleuthera what they took on Bay Street against the Bay Street Boys. They brought that same teaching or that same hatred on the island of Eleuthera. 'Race the Bay Street Boys out. We don't need 'em'. That's what happened, but ain't nobody want to speak the truth.

As for the resorts, it is said that the staff began stealing many of the items, possibly as a form of rebellion. Brenda McCartney (b. 1951) commented (2015) that the 'biggest blow was when Cape Eleuthera closed down. Eleuthera has really gone backward from where it was to now. Even though people were poorer then'. Cape Eleuthera closed around 1978.

The above accounts evidence how the silencing of certain perspectives in historical retellings have contributed to the strength of meta-narratives constructed during the struggle for national independence (approximately 1950–73) and visions of a post-colonial Bahamian future of black power and prosperity. This time in Bahamian history is remembered differently by different groups of people. The meta-narrative of its being a time of power and

---

3   Interview which forms part of a collection held at the Samuel Proctor Oral History Program at the University of Florida.

prosperity for black Bahamians differs from that at Tarpum Bay, where it is remembered as a time of division, hatred and economic downturn.

Tarpum Bay's community heritage

The overarching goal of this research was to ascertain how residents and descendants of Tarpum Bay define their heritage and themselves. Initially the common response to the question of heritage was, 'Heritage … exactly what do you mean?' (for example, Priscilla Clarke, W. McCartney and Vashti Simmons). This response suggested the potentially limited value of the concept of heritage for these people in contrast to academic understanding of the concept. Though the word 'heritage' is often used locally, it is used synonymously with history. Knowing I was conducting a study for academic credit, these interviewees would seek clarity on my definition of heritage. To avoid leading interviewees towards a certain belief system, I would instead ask about anything that might be unique to the place or people of Tarpum Bay; or what was valuable in their opinion. Interviewees found it difficult to articulate heritage or ascribe value to anything tangible. In reference to older or historic buildings, elder Priscilla Clarke (2014) recalls a beautiful wooden house that has been present in the community for as long as she can remember. However, she states that 'lots of them could be demolished to make something else. A lot of them could be built up and something nice made out of them'. To the contrary, Ruby Knowles and Samuel Davis lament the loss of certain buildings and evidence of key people who helped to make the community what it is today. For Knowles this is the loss of a building on the waterfront used to house principals of the old prep school.

Having listened to these different people expressing their feelings on the subject of identity and heritage, common threads that emerge are Christianity, civic engagement and accomplishment, expressed through an incomparable work ethic. Within the collective memory these three pillars characterise the people of the community and are associated with the place being their home. This results in a feeling of pride that many cannot trace to any tangible thing because the value is within the people themselves. Henry Allen (2015) refers to J. W. Culmer's[4] house as a historical home, valuable to the community and worthy of being kept by virtue of the man himself being 'an historical man'. Culmer's significance can be attributed to his contribution to the community as a developer (for example, the drainage system), as an employer and as a House of Assembly representative. Residents' respect for Culmer is demonstrated by their referring to him as the governor of the Tarpum Bay settlement. He embodies civic engagement and accomplishment. This reiterates the sentiment that it is the members of the community that give its places value, not the materials themselves that are of value or have valuable attributes. In other

---

4   J.W. Culmer was a community leader in the 1800s but his dates are not known.

words, the value is intangible. Without knowledge of the man and what he did for the community, the home has no value for these interviewees. Architectural style, material and date of construction are irrelevant to them.

Heritage is most often expressed as a feeling of pride. Among the responses to the question of what Tarpum Bay heritage is, 'It's about who I am' (A. Carey, 2014); 'I'm proud of it … It's a feeling I get whenever I hear the name or even if I meet someone from there' (D. Moncur, 2014). Similarly, William McCartney (2014) finds his value of heritage in the way the community has developed: 'Most of the citizens, the residents of Tarpum Bay and each person is a really, very business-like, very hard working, very … well, in other words, most of the Tarpum Bay people do own their own business. They like to be in charge of their own destiny financially'. Similarly, Henry Allen (2015) expresses the view that Tarpum Bay and the island of Eleuthera have been able to sustain themselves up to this point due to foresight and making provision for the future:

> Out of all of the people, Eleuthera people were one set of people in the Bahamas that invested their money into businesses and because they invested their money into businesses, they were able to weather the storm. I made couple dollars, I invested my money into repairs and parts. The other man, he made his money, he invested into hardware. This other gentleman over here he invested into hardware and other things … In Wemyss Bight, same thing … by people investing, they are able to make something sometimes and they didn't have to depend wholly and solely on their job. If you want to buy nails, I don't have to wait for nails to come out of Nassau. I could go to anywhere on Eleuthera and buy nails. I don't have to wait for cement to come out of Nassau … that kept Eleuthera. A lot of Family Islands didn't operate like that. They had no vision for that. They didn't see that future. My father said, stay here and work and you'll be able to sleep and make money. They were right. The other fellow, he saw the future in taxi driving. He went and bought his taxis. He went from growing tomatoes to driving taxis [to] self-drive cars. His children still drive the taxis and self-drive cars. So, what happens is the sacrifices that our forefathers made we can still feel the effects of that great sacrifice and we're so thankful we were able to make those sacrifices.

Steven Carey (2015) shares this sentiment and adds that:

> After south Eleuthera phased out then, the island was more or less developed then and just saying Dwight right there he worked for South Eleuthera Properties until he was able to build his first grocery store. Mr. Wallace down the road, he worked for South Eleuthera Properties until he could have built his first store, after he built his store then he quit working for South Eleuthera Properties. A lot of people learned [a] trade by South Eleuthera, so when they was able to go on their own or do a little something then they left South Eleuthera because South Eleuthera was paying but it wasn't paying no big money so if some of them home owners start to build a house, the carpenter get a job there and leave South

Eleuthera and go to work for the home owners. And that's how the island got going with carpenters and masons and stuff like that.

Among residents, descendants and extended members there is also constant mention of the prime minister of the Bahamas at the time, the Right Honourable Perry G. Christie, and the then deputy governor general of the Bahamas, the Right Honourable Oswald Ingraham, respectively descendant and resident of Tarpum Bay. The constant mentioning of these individuals in conversation about heritage not only indicates that they are a source of pride but also confirms the intangibility of heritage at Tarpum Bay. The heritage values are indwelling character traits.

All interviewees agree that Tarpum Bay heritage should be preserved. When they are asked how, their responses involve making any kind of positive contribution to the development of the community and the country, practising the heritage of Tarpum Bay by placing faith in God, being hard-working, striving toward self-sufficiency, financial independence and excellence, and documenting community history. The descendant William McCartney (2014) asserts that documenting the history of Tarpum Bay is important because 'if some of the younger people read the history and monitor the activity of the original people, that would help them to develop an appreciation for their settlement, appreciation for their family name, appreciation for their educational endeavours. I believe it would be very important'. Ownership of heritage, according to the community, belongs not only to residents and descendants but also to all who are willing to uphold and contribute to the hardworking and positive legacy of the Tarpum Bay people. This indicates, again, that heritage, to this group of people, is intangible and is the reason many of them live according to certain principles. This also indicates that heritage not only has the power to affect lives but has a potential use as a motivating force for future generations to create positive legacies. Preservation of knowledge of the past is therefore of utmost importance.

A museum does not exist in the traditional sense of materials or artefacts being displayed all year round. An attempt at building a museum was made in recent years by the Eleuthera Arts and Cultural Centre aiming to fulfil a shared vision developed by Friends of Lighthouse Point and later the One Eleuthera Foundation. The venture failed due to lack of attendance. Audrey Carey, director of the centre, said, 'The stuff sits there and collects dust' (2014). She expresses the need for a different sort of museum and an alternative way of commemorating the past at Tarpum Bay. Instead, the facility is promoted as a cultural centre. She describes it as a mini-museum where the building itself is on exhibit with additional components being exhibited on the exterior. She alludes to participation, programming or activities as being an engaging and essential component of the museum/cultural experience at the centre: 'If we have an exhibit it's located out[side]. You have activities that take place here in the centre. So, it's not just you coming in and walking in. The building itself, we have the outdoor surfaces, the patios steps were done by a local artist by recycled glass bottles, conch shells so it's … not the usual, traditional museum where you walk in and we showcase a few different exhibits'.

To the question of museum activities and preservation of Tarpum Bay legacies, Samuel Davis (2015) responds:

> Show me something outstanding what Oswald Ingraham done for south Eleuthera. Show me what Jimmy Moultrie done. Show me what the other guy from Green Castle done … It hurt me to know that moving up and down there's nothing you see about George Baker and you see these roads and things. This same road what you looking at, George Baker pushed that through. You couldn't pass by the waterfront because the water was beating up, the road was completely washed out. They built two walls around the graveyard and it was washed away … And finally, they come up, I believe George Baker was still there, they built a wall from what you call the Sanhedrin straight up to the grave yard during George Baker time and nothing you could see … They had a packinghouse in Rock Sound that was George Baker. They knocked that down and all. I mean nothing you could say for the young generation … Like myself, I know what he done in south Eleuthera but there's nothing. Even Arthur Vining Davis … I mean nothing outstanding no more. Me, of course, I could say he built the Rock Sound Club, I could say he brought light in Tarpum Bay, he brought water in Tarpum Bay and that's about it.

In relation to Trouillot's thesis, silences have occurred in the process of historical production concerning Tarpum Bay at these four moments: the moment of fact creation (making of sources); the moment of fact assembly (making of archives); that of fact retrieval (making of narratives); and that of retrospective significance (making of history in the final instance) (Trouillot, 1995, p. 26). Previously, the people of Tarpum Bay had little to no input into the making of sources, as most of the early generations were not educated to read or write beyond sixth-grade level. There was no input into the making of archives, as the National Archive is mainly a repository of government documents. Residents also had no input into the making of narratives due to a lack of opportunity and the lack of value the community ascribed to such tangible heritage assets as books written by locals. Finally, residents had little to no involvement in the making of the national history that is generally presented.

By assuming a bottom up-approach to this research, it was possible to gain access to local histories and values that could not have been obtained at the National Archive within Colonial Office records. But this was only through actively engaging with the local community. This project brings light to the overlap between sociohistorical processes (facts/that which has happened) and the narrative (knowledge of that process/that which is said to have happened), which Trouillot terms 'historicity 1' and 'historicity 2' respectively (1995, p. 29). Having used history as a proxy to understanding heritage at Tarpum Bay, this author finds that residents and descendants remember it as more than the maritime community it is passively identified as in literature. Instead, Tarpum Bay is remembered as a community of hardworking farmers, entrepreneurs and tradesmen. Also, contrary to the current branding of the entire island as pineapple producers, Tarpum Bay's chief produce in the early to mid 20th century was the tomato, and much of south Eleuthera is identified as a tomato-producing area by inhabitants. Older residents still engage in the growth and bottling of tomatoes today.

The community's heritage is largely intangible. Passed from one generation to the next has been a belief in God, a hardworking ethic that contributes to an entrepreneurial zeal and community leadership and farsightedness. The pride of Tarpum Bay is in the work of its residents and the achievements of its descendants. These people are notable business owners, wide-ranging professionals, upstanding citizens and civic-minded individuals dispersed across the Bahamas and the United States. Family and extended community values constitute heritage values in this settlement and keep it united. In discussing tangible heritage specifically, the subjects that are brought to the fore are those structures and materials relating to the arts, music and the annual Junkanoo street parade on Boxing Day and New Year's Day;[5] the tomato industry, packing, bottling and canning; religious life and education.

Conclusion

The community of Tarpum Bay on the island of Eleuthera has identified its heritage as the people who have come before them and the residents and descendants who continue to advance the community and the country. A sense of pride in the past and present emanates from these sources. This chapter applies lessons from past heritage work to the preservation of a community's heritage for a more accurate and inclusive picture of insular and national identity. These lessons include embracing new ontologies, which require long-term contextual study; the privileging of local epistemologies; inclusion of constituent voices; and the creation of an atmosphere of awareness within the community for the establishment of mechanisms for the community to represent itself. The fact that many Tarpum Bay inhabitants are concerned about heritage loss reflects a threat to that heritage and heritage preservation as a means for enabling ontological security in an uncertain present and in consideration of the future. It is evident that the community would like to preserve heritage, but they have been tentative about how to do so.

In an interesting contrast to uses of social memory, the social memory at Tarpum Bay is not associated with space or the built environment as in recent

---

5   Junkanoo is a street cultural parade that takes place on many islands of the Bahamas during the Christmas season. The origins of the parade are debated. It has been taking place for centuries and widely believed to be of African origin.

archaeology (Colwell-Chanthaphonh and Ferguson, 2006; Kearney, 2010), but rather with familial bonds and a connection to a community of people. This chapter demonstrates the need to decolonise the heritage sector in the Bahamas to account for differing relations to the past, because at Tarpum Bay heritage loss is not the losing of material or necessarily a change in landscape but is a loss of knowledge regarding the past and in relation to people. In his book *Archaeology That Matters: Action in the Modern World* (2008) Jeremy Sabloff expresses the view that in today's modern world heritage is important in strengthening cultural identity, pride in one's past and an ethic of stewardship. This research reveals how true this statement is. Empowerment of cultural identity and pride in one's past, as experienced by older residents and descendants, can be effectively reiterated and preserved, beginning with the documentation of this community's development and heritage. By documenting their heritage, community members hope that younger generations will learn about the past in order to learn from it. They wish for the preservation of their heritage to strengthen community and cultural identity, pride in their past and an ethic of stewardship for the future. Based on the information gathered through this history and heritage project, future directions may include the creation of a local history book; the revitalisation of the Tarpum Bay Historical and Heritage Society for the sustained collection and preservation of the community's history and heritage; the creation of an interactive community webpage where residents and descendants can learn about the community's history and interact; and the creation of heritage spaces that align with the values of the community.

Bibliography

Atalay, S. (2012) *Community-Based Archaeology: Research with, by, and for Indigenous and Local Communities* (Berkeley, CA: University of California Press).

Bahamas Public Records Office (1977) *The Pineapple Industry of the Bahamas: A Booklet of the Archives Exhibition held at the Art Gallery, Jumbey Village, 14 February–27 February, 1977* (Nassau: Public Records Office).

Bernard, H.R. (2011) *Research Methods in Anthropology: Qualitative and Quantitative Approaches* (Lanham, MD: AltaMira Press).

Bethel, N. (2000) 'Navigations: the fluidity of national identity in the postcolonial Bahamas' (unpublished doctoral thesis, University of Cambridge), http://ufdc.ufl.edu/AA00007511/00001 [accessed 5 Feb. 2019].

Cleare, A. (2007) *A History of Tourism in The Bahamas: A Global Perspective* (Philadelphia, PA: Xlibris).

Colwell-Chanthaphonh, C. and J. J. Ferguson (2006) 'Memory pieces and footprints: multivocality and the meanings of ancient times and ancestral places among the Zuni and Hopi', *American Anthropologist*, 108: 148–62.

Commissioner's Annual Report for the District of Rock Sound, 1911 (1911) Department of Archives, Nassau, Bahamas.

Commissioner's Annual Report for the District of Rock Sound, 1930 (1930) Department of Archives, Nassau, Bahamas.

Commissioner's Annual Report for the District of Rock Sound, 1940 (1940) Department of Archives, Nassau, Bahamas.

Commissioner's Annual Report for the District of Rock Sound, 1944 (1944) Department of Archives, Nassau, Bahamas.

Commissioner's Annual Report for the District of Rock Sound, 1945 (1945) Department of Archives, Nassau, Bahamas.

Commissioner's Annual Report for the District of Rock Sound, 1946 (1946) Department of Archives, Nassau, Bahamas.

Commissioner's Annual Report for the District of Rock Sound, 1953 (1953) Department of Archives, Nassau, Bahamas.

Commissioner's Annual Report for the District of Rock Sound, 1957 (1957) Department of Archives, Nassau, Bahamas.

Commissioner's Annual Report for the District of Rock Sound, 1962 (1962) Department of Archives, Nassau, Bahamas.

Commissioner's Annual Report for the District of Rock Sound, 1966 (1966) Department of Archives, Nassau, Bahamas.

Craton, M. and G. Saunders (1998) *Islanders in the Stream: A History of the Bahamian People. Volume Two: From the Ending of Slavery to the Twenty-First Century* (Athens, GA: University of Georgia Press).

D'Amico-Samuels, D. (2008) 'Undoing fieldwork: personal, theoretical and methodological implications', in F. V. Harrison (ed.), *Decolonizing Anthropology: Moving Further toward an Anthropology for Liberation* (Washington, D.C.: American Anthropological Association), pp. 68–87.

Delancy, K. (2015) 'History to heritage: a heritage assessment of Tarpum Bay, Eleuthera, The Bahamas' (unpublished master's thesis, University of Florida).

Denzin, N.K., Y.S. Lincoln and L.T. Smith (2008) *Handbook of Critical and Indigenous Methodologies* (Los Angeles, CA: SAGE).

Dodge, S. (2005) *Abaco: History of an Out Island and its Cays* (New Smyrna Beach, FL: White Sound Press).

Jordan, G.H. (2008) 'On ethnography in an intertextual situation: reading narratives or deconstructing discourse', in F. V. Harrison (ed.),

Decolonizing Anthropology: Moving Further toward an Anthropology for Liberation (Washington, DC: American Anthropological Association), pp. 42–67.

Kearney, A. (2010) 'An ethnoarchaeology of engagement: Yanyuwa llaces the lived cultural domain in Northern Australia', *Ethnoarchaeology*, 2: 99–119.

Lee, M.A. (2012) 'Black Bahamas: political constructions of Bahamian national identity' (unpublished honours thesis, University of Richmond, Virginia).

Poulios, I. (2014) 'Discussing strategy in heritage conservation: living heritage approach as an example of strategic innovation', *Journal of Cultural Heritage Management and Sustainable Development*, 4: 16–24.

Resident Justice Annual Report for Tarpum Bay, 1884, in *Votes of the House of Assembly 1885*, Department of Archives, Nassau, Bahamas.

Resident Justice Annual Report for Tarpum Bay, 1886, in *Votes of the House of Assembly 1887*, Department of Archives, Nassau, Bahamas.

Sabloff, J. (2008) *Archaeology that Matters: Action in the Modern World* (Walnut Creek, CA: Left Coast Press).

Smith, L. (2006) *Uses of Heritage* (London and New York: Routledge).

Trouillot, M.R. (1995) *Silencing the Past: Power and the Production of History* (Boston, MA: Beacon Press).

Interviews

Allen, Henry, interview by Kelly Delancy, Samuel Proctor Oral History Program Collection, University of Florida, 29 July 2015, call number HOEP 006B.

Allen, Hilda, interview by Kelly Delancy, Samuel Proctor Oral History Program Collection, University of Florida, July 2015.

Bethel, Philip, interview by Kelly Delancy, Nov. 2014.

Carey, Audrey, interview by Kelly Delancy, Nov. 2014.

Carey, Herbert, interview by Kelly Delancy, Samuel Proctor Oral History Program Collection, University of Florida, July 2015.

Carey, Steven, interview by Kelly Delancy, Samuel Proctor Oral History Program Collection, University of Florida, July 2015.

Carey, Vera, interview by Kelly Delancy, Samuel Proctor Oral History Program Collection, University of Florida, July 2015.

Clarke, Priscilla, interview by Kelly Delancy, Oct. 2014.

Davis, Samuel, interview by Kelly Delancy, Samuel Proctor Oral History Program Collection, University of Florida, July 2015.

Johnson, Samuel, interview by Kelly Delancy, Samuel Proctor Oral History Program Collection, University of Florida, July 2015.

Knowles, Ruby, interview by Kelly Delancy, Samuel Proctor Oral History Program Collection, University of Florida, July 2015. Call number HOEP 020.

McCartney, Brenda, interview by Kelly Delancy, Samuel Proctor Oral History Program Collection, University of Florida, July 2015.

McCartney, William, interview by Kelly Delancy, Nov. 2014.

Mingo, Qurina, interview by Kelly Delancy, Samuel Proctor Oral History Program Collection, University of Florida, July 2015.

Moncur, Dorothy, interview by Kelly Delancy, Oct. 2014.

Simmons, Vashti, interview by Kelly Delancy, Nov. 2014.

4. 'While nuff ah right and rahbit; we write and arrange': deejay lyricism and the transcendental use of the voice in alternative public spaces in the UK

William 'Lez' Henry

Man tell me bout Remington weh put man in ah grave,
the Remington me know my father use it fi shave,
at school the teachers taught me things like how to use a lathe,
couldah ask them any question bout when man live in ah cave,
if me ask them bout when black man down in ah slave,
them blush, turn red, them answer used to scathe,
I'll give you an example of the answer they gave,
bloody trouble maker, get out the class, until you learn to behave![1]

The above lyric became a focal point of discussion between myself and the Jamaican deejay Lone Ranger during the 'Reggae University' at the 16th Rototom Sunsplash in Italy in 2009, where we shared a panel with other commentators. It speaks to the manner in which deejay culture, created in Jamaica, profoundly impacted the consciousness of youth in the UK during the late 1970s to mid 1980s. Yet more importantly, one aspect of the discussion focused on 'yard-tapes',[2] which were the cassette recordings of Jamaican Sound System sessions that traversed the Black Atlantic (Gilroy, 1994) from around the mid 1970s. The suggestion was that a dependence on vinyl – on recorded releases – would never provide an accurate picture of the manner in which reggae music and Sound System culture impacted on communities far beyond the shores of Jamaica during this moment. For instance, I explained to Lone Ranger that the lyric was directly inspired by one of his performances on a Jamaican Sound System called 'Soul to Soul' in 1980, in which he dealt with the prevalence of gun crime in parts of Kingston, Jamaica. In his performance

---

1   Lezlee Lyrix, Diamonds The Girls Best Friend Sound System, Nettlefold Hall, London, 1984 (cited in Henry, 2012, p. 102).
2   See Henry (2006), ch. 3, for an in-depth analysis of yard-tape and the dissemination of the deejay voice.

W. Henry, '"While nuff ah right and rahbit; we write and arrange": deejay lyricism and the transcendental use of the voice in alternative public spaces in the UK', in J.D. Webb, R. Westmaas, M. del Pilar Kaladeen and W. Tantam (eds.), *Memory, migration and (de)colonisation in the Caribbean and beyond* (London: University of London Press, 2019), pp. 57–77. License: CC-BY-NC-ND 4.0.

he spoke to the popularity of the Remington hand gun and aspects of the lyric were later reworked into a track he released in 1982, on the Channel One label, called 'fist to fist days done'.

For us in the UK a Remington was an electric razor but in Jamaica it was the name of a popular handgun the 'bad-boys' would brandish in places such as dancehalls, so to use it in the context of a firearm in the UK would have been mere fantasy on my part. Therefore, my usage of this contrast in world-views from gun to electric razor, speaks to the difference between being inspired to create ('my father use it fi shave'), as opposed to merely pirating/copying another deejay's style. The lyric from which the extract is drawn is over three minutes long and I used to chat it 'non-stop' (see below); and while being inspired by Lone Ranger's take on 'gun-play', it enabled me to jump off in another direction. It therefore empowered me to write about and subsequently deal with some of the issues we were facing and still face within the UK that were and are equally 'destructive' from an educational perspective. Why this is important to this chapter is the fact that the contents of the yard-tapes became the template that was used to establish the performative aspect of Sound System culture in the UK. Moreover, British deejays would evolve from merely copying the yard-style in the first instance to creating a style and pattern that were uniquely their own, based on the reality of life in the UK.

Hence what follows is an argument that locates the British deejay contribution to black cultural politics within the broader framework of cultural antagonism across the African diaspora. The evolution of the British deejay narrative is considered in order to fill in some of the gaps in the literature with regard to how black youth, during this historical moment, used this alternative voice to challenge whiteness across a range of contexts (Henry, 2007). Consideration is given to how this particular and unique voice became known outernationally, eventually becoming a crucial part of Africentric[3] cultural exchanges with reggae music and Sound System culture at their core, as '[t]his is not a place for individual heroes or hierarchies; instead, we are deeply immersed into the sonic space of bass and beats – the vibe of reggae and dub. Such an ephemeral event, fuelled by post-colonial social marginalization, is intensely powerful in producing a sense of togetherness' (Rietveld, 2013, p. 83). Consequently, this sense of 'post-colonial social marginalization' underpinned the usage of what was known as 'island talk', which served to eliminate many of the inter-island rivalries that would play out in other arenas. This meant that the various takes on the English language by people from the Caribbean morphed with local vernaculars like London cockney to create a language that was owned and controlled by the partakers in the culture. Indeed, this form of 'directed

---

3   Paul Gilroy used the notion of an Afri-centric perspective in his book *The Black Atlantic* (1994); I first developed it in my undergraduate dissertation (1997) and then expanded upon it in my doctoral thesis (2002). I utilise this concept extensively in my book *What The Deejay Said; A Critique from the Street!* (2006).

defiance', which created a sense of togetherness, was aimed at white society, manifesting itself in the works of the conscious deejays who sought to write and arrange. Therefore, the accounts of black youth irrationally distancing themselves from the mainstream white society will be challenged using their lyricism and narratives to counter such claims. This approach can be linked to the metaphor of the seven-inch single I use as a framework (Henry, 1997, 2002, 2006), in which the A-side focuses on outsider arguments and the B-side presents the insider perspective. By doing so light will be shed on the importance of the black British contribution to the reggae world view, explaining how it had Rastafari, Garveyism and other forms of radical politics at its core, and perhaps represented the most pro-black voice ever to come out of the UK.

Overstanding alterity and outernational cultural antagonism

Every time a griot dies it's like a library burning down.
Tunde Jedege[4]

> Art as a product of consciousness is also permeated by ideology, although it is not reducible to the ideology. And to that extent, too, what the author or artist says in the work of art is actually (or perhaps one should say also) the statement of the social group and its world-view (Wolff, 1993, p. 119).

Combating the imposition of a Eurocentric 'alien' worldview on African peoples, by way of an analysis of British deejay culture in the late 1980s, is premised upon the fact that many subcultural and sociological accounts misrepresented the manner in which black youth countered, resisted and transcended racism through the medium of reggae music (Gilroy, 1987; Back, 1996; Henry, 2006).[5] These theorisations of what exactly motivated black youth to embrace many aspects of reggae-dancehall culture, especially the usage of patwa as a 'commonly agreed language' (Small, 1987), were largely inadequate as they failed to recognise the history behind these types of 'directed defiance', and thus lacked epistemological rigour and empirical depth. For example, the idea of black youth as a 'discrete social category' was given currency by suggestions like they were 'educated on words which they find irrelevant – and do not know how to spell anyway' (Cashmore and Troyna, 1982, p. 18). This type of thinking only makes sense because many social commentators had negative preconceptions regarding a highly visible black presence that obviously 'coloured' their 'findings' as these were a 'statement of the social group and its world-view' (Wolff, 1981, p. 119). For this reason there

---

4 Jedege, 'The modern-day griot,' BBC Radio 4, 5 June 2012. A 'griot' or 'jali' is the title of a West African genealogist who uses stories, songs, music and other forms of oration to inform their communities of their complete histories, in the context of oral tradition, including births, deaths and marriages.

5 See Bourne (1980) and Hall et al. (1978) for critiques of this perspective.

is a rigidity affixed to black cultures that does not reflect the lived experience of 'real people', who have a history of countering white racism across a range of contexts. Consequently, such analyses are unable to present a more complete understanding of the pragmatic nature of black countercultural forms, which actually represent historical sites of transcendence and resistance. One reason for this occurrence is that academic interpretation, explanation or expectation tries to rid itself of the problems associated with representation, questioning how it can more accurately represent the 'social reality' of 'the others', through a freeing of itself from the bias of 'ethnographic inscription'. Yet it cannot, for the social reality it ultimately portrays is subject to the epistemological biases of the interpreter/author: '[A]s a result, social facts no longer need to attain or demonstrate authenticity; their authority derives from their status as an emanation of assumed intellectual, and actual political, power' (Rigby 1996, pp. 89–90).

In line with Rigby's perspective, a focus on giving voice to the voiceless, as a means of contributing to the current debates on overstanding[6] the history of black communities in the UK, is timely and necessary. That is because of a grasp of the relevance of an outernational consciousness providing a means to think beyond social, racial and political constraints is central to this argument. Thus conversations about resistance are not enough as the expressive cultural forms, in this instance the recorded lyricism (on vinyl or cassettes) of the British-based deejays, are 'living' documents that enable the listener to experience a history that is premised on transcendence. In this way Jedege's thoughts on the passing of the *griot* are highly relevant when we consider that the deejay is a 'modern day griot' and the works in question here become the testimonies of those 'who mentally archived and disseminated traditional information to their respective audiences' (Webster-Prince, 2013, p. 80). If their words remain 'hidden' it is akin to a 'library burning down', forever losing the practical steps that are taken to maintain both one's liberty and one's sanity in a hostile environment. It is therefore incumbent upon the insider/interlocutor to make this history live on by constantly excavating these countercultural voices, which enable the downpressed to align themselves with discourses that are in a language they own and control. As the British deejay Bigga Monrose (Dr Kenneth Monrose) posits:

> Sound System and Sound System culture were everything for us in the early Eighties. Football or Sound System. The deejaying aspect of the Sound System enhanced our lives. My school books were covered in pictures of diagrams of pre-amps and speaker boxes. I had the names of the

---

6   The idea of 'overstanding' is taken from a Rastafari world-view within which the word 'understand' is taken to mean you 'stand under' the point you are discussing, and as such your view of it is limited by merely looking up. Consequently, Rastafari teaches us that to 'overstand' means to 'stand over' the point in question from the vantage point of seeing it from all possible angles. Therefore 'overstanding' is total awareness of the ramifications/permutations of a given situation.

more prominent and well-known artists scrawled over my school books, and it wasn't just black kids like me, white kids and some Asians gravitated toward it as well. The deejays spoke to and documented our condition. We all sailed in the same boat during Thatcher's Britain at the time. We were poor, voiceless and occupied fringe status in British society (Bigga Monrose, personal communication, 2016; recorded interview took place on 26 May 2016 in London).

Bigga's testimony speaks to how alternative viewpoints can be rendered/received as valid/authentic historical documents that not only resonated with the disaffected youth in 'Thatcher's Britain' but also unified them across racial and linguistic lines because 'we all sailed in the same boat'. This is a telling point as according to Roach (1996), anything that can be 'performed' can be regarded as a document which speaks to those who 'occupied fringe status' and whose personal narratives are largely missing from the 'recognised' historical accounts. Nevertheless, Roach's notion of the 'monstrous double' exposes the manner in which just as 'things living or dead, real or imagined' can become 'cultural artefacts', 'literature can be used to (make us) forget' (1996, p. 138). Consequently, in much the same way as the sounds of the performance are hidden once the lyrics become text, the more inclusive tales of 'real people' are hidden in many accounts of the black experience in Britain. Similarly, these accounts give little consideration to the value of a perspective which relocates the African as a conscious being 'in time and across time' (Gordon, 1998, p. 140) and also in place and across space, even more so when the British deejay voice is 'silenced' in many discussions of the history of reggae in the UK. These suggest: 'Last but not least, Jamaican reggae has obviously fathered British reggae whose emblematic figures remain Steel Pulse, Aswad, UB 40, Maxi Priest and Bitty McLean among others' (Dagnini, 2010, p. 5).

Dagnini's take on the 'emblematic' makes sense in the commercial world of reggae, for it is common knowledge that the bands mentioned appealed to, and were supported by, black and white audiences in line with what was known as the 'Two Tone' scene. However, for many African-centred youth during the late 1970s to early 1980s this scene represented a no-go area, as the main point for embracing was to use reggae music to distance oneself from white society. This means that Africentric subjectivities cannot be overlooked in these debates, as they often give rise to the 'self-generated concepts' (Lewis, cited in Henry, 2006) that allow the black downpressed to 'chant down Babylon' with no apology.[7] More importantly, while 'popularity' in an international sense explains who is known within the reggae world as emblematic, this in and of itself is symptomatic of a perspective that is ultimately flawed because it

7 In Jamaican culture to 'chant down Babylon' is to speak out unapologetically against the corrupt social, cultural and political system in which we are living, whether locally or globally. Its first usage was by early Rastafari and is biblical – as in 'Babylon', the place of great inequity – but also means the police, the authorities and any aspect of racist European/white domination and subjugation of African/black people, historically and contemporaneously.

does not represent the 'hidden voices' that dominated alternative public spaces during this moment. For instance, mention is made of Maxi Priest, who made his name on Lewisham's 'Saxon Sound System' in the 1980s, but what is not often stated is that the song that made him a household name in Jamaica, 'Sensi' (1984), was featured on a double-A-side with Papa Levi's 'Mi God, Mi King'. It was Levi's version (which had already reached the number one spot in the UK Reggae Chart on seven-inch vinyl), in which he unleashed the 'rapid rappin/fast style',[8] that arguably caught the imagination of the Jamaican public:

> Indeed 'Mi God Mi King' was so successful that it was snapped up by Sly & Robbie in JA, who released it on their own Taxi label. Levi then made history once again when the tune became the first by a UK deejay to reach number one in the JA charts. Imagine the feelings of elation that must have unleashed in the reggae community in the UK and London, who had looked to Jamaica for inspiration since the very beginning (Eden, 2012 [n.p.]).

The very title of Levi's track 'Mi God, Mi King' speaks to the influences of Rastafari and how their teachings offered a framework to challenge, and overcome, white supremacist thought and action across a range of contexts in the UK (Gilroy, 1987; Bradley, 2001; Henry, 2006). Indeed, Rastafari advocated a 'social gospel' based on knowing one's enemy, for it is not enough to pray to a transcendental being, who is generally portrayed as white, in one's hopes for salvation. That is why on the track Levi states:

> Mi God, Mi King, him name Jah-ov-yah,
> Him inspire me to be a mike chanter,
> Mi maas wid di mike round the amplifier,
> Mi fling way di slackness, cause now a culture,
> The conscious lyrics yuh a go hear me utter,
> ...
> Soh if you are an adult or a teenager,
> Seh every day you wake you fi read a chapter
> ...
> Not so long Jah walk pon di land,
> Di peaceful, righteous rastaman,
> Trod wid di Maccabee innah him hand,
> Preaching love to man an woman.

Levi's voice, coupled with the lyrical content of his track, demonstrates how for many reggae music was, and remains, a symbol of 'racial authenticity' that acknowledges a world beyond their peripheral placement in British society. The obvious mention of 'Jah' acknowledges the teachings of Rastafari, yet the fact that this track was so successful with a lyric that 'chants down Babylon' without apology needs consideration. A partial explanation runs in tandem

---

8   There has been much controversy around who originated the 'fast style' (Henry, 1997, 2002, 2006) but it was created and first chatted by the Saxon deejay Peterking in Nov. 1982.

with the fact that Rastafari and its advocacy of Garveyism[9] provided black youth in the UK with a template to make their alternative claims known. Thus the words 'Mi fling way di slackness, cause now a culture | the conscious lyrics yuh a go hear me utter' are a phenomenological statement as they speak to a subjective experience that has resulted in a conscious choice to do 'Jah works'. No longer is it acceptable for deejays just to chat anything that comes to mind (as will be explored below): their contributions must speak to the reality of life in the UK, exposing the crowdah-people[10] to forms of knowledge that are both informed and transcendental. Hence doing Jah works means speaking truth to power, while exemplifying Garvey's notion that 'The white man's propaganda has made him the master of the world, and all those who have come in contact with it and accepted it have become his slaves' (cited in Martin, 1976, p 89). Hence:

> Living in babylon as a black man,
> All me face is racialism,
> When mi weak dem seh dat me strong,
> When mi right dem seh dat me wrong,
> Tru mi no check fi politician,
> Noh care who win di election,[11]
> Pon di mike mi please everyone,
> Flashing down style and fashion.
>
> (Papa Levi, Ghetto-tone Sound System, Blues Dance (house party), London, March 1983)

Similarly, Papa Benji, a deejay from the West London sound system Diamonds The Girls Best Friend, suggests:

> Me born ah England, me know me black me nar seh me British,
> cau to some of de politician black man don't exist,
> me nuh care bout de liberal, tory or socialist,
> cau long time now blackman we ah fight prejudice,
> through some live good in them neighbourhood them lack awareness.
>
> (Papa Benji, Diamonds The Girls Best Friend Sound System, Club Willows, London, August 1984)

The above observations from these lyricists challenge the manner in which the influence of Rastafari and Garveyism were widely regarded as merely escapist, as advocated by social commentators who argued, 'Garvey was not interested in

---

9   A form of pan-African black nationalism inspired by the social, cultural, economic and political policies of the Jamaican Marcus Garvey, who founded the 'Universal Negro Improvement Association in Jamaica – African Communities League' (UNIA-ACL). In 1916 he moved to Harlem, New York and the organisation became a global entity with 'Africa for the Africans' and 'Race First' as central points of its ideology. By 1919 the UNIA-ACL had more than 30 branches with over two million members worldwide.
10 The amassed live audience which not only listens to the music but also partakes in antiphonic exchanges with the deejay performance.
11 The 1983 General Election in the UK, won by Margaret Thatcher's Conservative Party.

modifications of the present society but sought only one objective: the return of black peoples to Africa' (Cashmore, 1979, p. 19). This interpretation runs counter to Levi's and Benji's suggestion that until black people in the UK 'close ranks' and reappraise the reality of their oppressed social status, from their own racial and cultural perspective, they will continuously be politically neutered within the open (white) society. Hence:

> I am pro Black in my thinking, in my actions and I try my best to support my own people, you know. It is not that I am opposing any other nation, but I feel that I must stand for my own first and then if I am able to, I will stretch out my hand to help others, but self first. So first and foremost Papa Levi sees himself as an African descendant, not a European, even though I was born here in this part of the world. I see myself as an African stolen from abroad, you know (Papa Levi, cited in Eden, 2012 [n.p.]).

The onus is therefore firmly placed on black people to rediscover their African heritage, to counter the 'white lies' that rob them of a knowledge of self, because 'me nuh care bout de liberal, tory or socialist | cau long time now blackman we ah fight prejudice'. Thus the spaces and places where this counterargument could be heard were where the deejays knew that their role was 'pon di mike mi please everyone | flashing down style and fashion' within the black community. Obviously, then, the inspiration these black youths received from Rastafari, who preached self-empowerment as biblical and Garveyite philosophies, as well as the alternative politics of Minister Louis Farrakhan,[12] expressed among other things the need for black people to be more pragmatic in their dealings with white society. Indeed, Farrakhan had a profound influence on black youth in the UK during this moment, including on Papa Levi's lyricism, exemplified in the highly controversial song 'Ram Jam Capitalism' (1986), in which Papa Levi argued:

> **Spoken intro:** I dare any MC in this whole wide world to chat ah lyric, such as this.
> **Chorus:** Ram Jam Capitalism, Papa Levi with chi Ram Jam capitalism, we cufn man, Ram Jam Capitalism, Papa Levi with chi Ram Jam Capitalism, well hear me man.
> Deejaying:
> Certain Deejay love fi boost rob an gaan,
> I Papa Levi am not one,
> the little baldhead Caucasian who believe him ah don,
> practise everyday fi talk Jamaican,
> ah bade aafah artist an musician,
> seh in ah Jamaica an England,
> all the money weh him skank him buy house an land,
> ungle [only] conscious people understand,

---

12 Louis Farrakhan is the African American leader of the Nation of Islam (NOI) who are commonly regarded as a black nationalist group, founded by the former NOI leader Elijah Muhammad, 4 July 1930, in Detroit, Michigan.

> rob an gaan ah deal with exploitation …
> The bwoy ah put himself in ah the position,
> fi capitalise aafah the black nation,
> cau who support Reggae? Nuh we same one,
> it coming like we brainbox nah function …
> Seh wah we need now is organisation,
> an conscious man like Louis Farrakan,
> fi tek control of the situation,
> an run-out the leeches like rob an gaan,
> an all ah the puppet pon string musician.
>
> (Papa Levi, cited in Henry, 2006, pp. 227–8)[13]

I have dealt with this song and its impact on the reggae world in great depth (Henry, 2006), but what is telling is that Papa Levi begins the track with a challenge: 'I dare any MC in this whole wide world to chat ah lyric, such as this'. The challenge is recognition of the global reach of reggae music and how its potent voice draws on current as well as historical narratives in a pragmatic way to confront myriad forms of black exploitation. It is this notion of being more pragmatic that led to a reformulation of what it meant to be black in Britain, which was missed by many who failed to overstand the profundity of doing Jah works, works premised on the idea that 'we're not preaching to go out and kill anybody, we're just preaching about the injustices and trying to right certain wrongs that were done to Africans by racist Europeans' (Macka B, cited in Henry, 2006, p. 235).[14] For Macka B his mission as a deejay is simply:

> Me doing my little bit to help my people cau every time you hear a word
> it conjures up an image, therefore my mission is to fashion my words
> in a way that reflects the plight of the Afrikan and doesn't reinforce the
> negativity that is associated with the Motherland. If you look at the world
> and look for the poorest people, invariably they will be black, so my lyrics
> are like a stepping stone to help us get back to where we once were and
> Reggae music is the vehicle to carry the message (cited in Henry 2006, pp.
> 168–9).

By suggesting that 'Reggae music is the vehicle to carry the message', Macka B demonstrates the relationship between the performer and the audience and the types of reasoning that are disseminated within the culture. He clearly recognises that people tune in to his lyrics to be uplifted/enlightened because he speaks to the types of problems black people encounter in a racist society. His 'message' is therefore 'consciously' constructed in a manner that is both easily digested and informative, the provider of the 'stepping stone' black people require to 'get back to where we once were'. Yet what is of even more significance is his mentioning of the associative power of words and their ability to 'conjure up images', thereby demonstrating how crucial the notion of

---

13 Lyrics transcribed by the author, but otherwise unpublished.
14 Original source: recorded interview at Ariwa Studios, London, 8 April 1999.

overstanding original wordplay, 'my lyrics', is within the culture, a topic which is covered in the next section.

While nuff ah right and rahbit; we write and arrange

> Dancehall pirate ah dem deh mi fraid ah, tief San lyrics gwaan like originator, so when mi ah talk it them ah call mi imitator, when him talk it dem ah seh dat him greater (Papa San, cited in Henry, 2006, p. 184).

> Old pirates yes they rob I, yes they thief a-way my lyrics, run gaan ah studio, an put them pon plastic (Asher Senator, cited in Henry, 2006, p. 215).

The cultural sensibilities that allow the community to recognise a person who has created lyrics, as opposed to being a 'dancehall pirate' whom Papa San 'fraid ah', are similarly used to determine the merit of the deejay that is performing in the dancehall. Yet unlike in everyday interactions, when naturally occurring speech is utilised to ensure that effective communication is achieved and maintained, the deejay has to create a dialogue that makes sense in the present to a wider community of listeners, while being able to entertain through original wordplay. The point is that while deejaying, words, sounds and gestures, the 'illocutionary' act, ensure that a meaningful dialogic exchange takes place between audience and the performer, the latter providing, in the words of Macka B, 'a stepping stone to help us get back to where we once were'. Thus the language used, patwa, was more than just Jamaican language, it was the language of the black experience in Britain, containing myriad words and phrases drawn from this crucible of black cultural knowledge which has antiphony at its core, because there is no physical distance in African musical cultures between audience and performer (Gilroy, 1987; Back, 1987, 1996; Stolzoff, 2000; Bradley, 2001; Liverpool, 2001; Henry, 2006). This usage of call and response, led through the mouth of the modern-day *griot* or *jali*, enables the community vicariously to voice their opinions, representing a functionally expressive part of a greater artistic whole. To embellish this point, the British deejay Culture Mark (2016) states:

> I first picked up the microphone in 1979 at the age of 10 years old at my cousin Wingey's house. Her husband was proper into sound tapes and I was always listening to the likes of Johnny Ringo, Lone Ranger, General Echo, Welton Ire, Jah Thomas, Buru Banton and many more.

> One of the Lyrics I used to chat back then (1981), which was a call and response song, was called Free Africa:

> If it's the truth Culture ah talk shout out free Africa,
> from poverty come mek we free Africa,
> from brutality come mek we free Africa,
> Africa ah we country come mek we free Africa,
> all gang and posse come mek we free Africa,

> Eddie Grant sing ah song name Give me Hope Joanna,
> nuff respect to Eddie Grant cause that deh song ah seller,
> but one record is not enough we want something more stronger,
> like a massive army of ragamuffin solider,
> nuff aeroplane, nuff submarine, nuff ship in ah di water,
> meck we fill them up of ragamuffin solider,
> tek one trip down to south Africa,
> fi sort out the bwoy weh dem call Botha.[15]

Hence consideration should be given to the notion that mass communication is achieved with the audience recognising the 'glocal' nature of language usage that has tangible links to various African oral traditions. In this case antiphonic exchanges are fused with Europe's 'New World' polyglot cultures and utilised to deal with racial oppression in our endeavours to 'free Africa'. More importantly, Culture Mark further suggests that his love of reggae and deejaying, and the messages contained therein, were key factors in his continued social, cultural, political and Africentric development:

In 2007 my wife and I started our organisation called 'Black History Studies' and our mission statement is 'Educating the community to educate themselves'. We teach black history and black studies, so from back then until now I have been informing the masses about our condition as a people all around the globe and recently recorded this tune, which was released in 2017 for our tenth anniversary:

> Black History studies, knowledge is our wealth,
> educating the community to educate themselves
> we're doing what we can to rebuild our nation,
> www.blackhistorystudies.com.
> We come fi tell you about ya history,
> fi make sure it doesn't remain ah mystery,
> and anything they have hidden we will try to reveal,
> no more legacies will we allow them to steal.
>
> (Culture Mark, 2016)[16]

This is a crucial point for us to consider because Culture Mark's narrative speaks to the transcendental nature of reggae musical culture, that which enables its conscious participants to continue the works, in line with the ongoing struggles for African liberation, across the diaspora. This point is endorsed by Veal, who suggests: '[T]he hybridized redeployment of European musical traits in an Africanized musical agenda is encoded with the self-determination at the heart of the nationalist and postcolonial projects' (2007, p. 16).

The suggestion is that at the centre of this language usage is the promotion of a 'black aesthetic' to encourage an appreciation of the validity of a form of creativity and artistic expression which is in direct contrast to the 'European

---

15 Original source: Culture Mark, recorded interview, London, 17 Jan. 2016.
16 Available at https://www.youtube.com/watch?v=F9eIsZEq8pQ

aesthetic' which dictated social, racial, cultural and political worth. Thus the expression of group values, beliefs and consciousness, 'hybridised redeployment', through deejay lyricism is related to the position of the performer, whose ideas and beliefs are transmitted as a 'natural' counter to the dominant culture. That is why an 'Africanised musical agenda' must encode/promote a black aesthetic because 'beauty' is seldom in the 'eye of the beholder'. Rather, it is more often than not determined through the eye of the controller, in this sense as a by-product of the way black personalities are packaged, repackaged and sold to the British public, which is intrinsically linked to the problem of black 'acceptance' in the wider society. Consequently, postcolonial projects in this sense are complicated by the fact that the language of 'acceptable' communication is standard English, that which is rejected by the deejay who directly challenges the 'white' aesthetic that underpins it. In fact, according to reggae deejay Reds: 'I always made sure that my lyrics reflected London themes, so that anyone who lived in London would instantly appreciate what I was dropping was original, whether it was what I said or just the way I said it. Like in one lyric I talked about driving me jam-jar [car] fi goh check me spar, down the frog an toad [road] before the dance overload' (cited in Henry, 2006, p. 191).[17] However, locked within these types of cultural expression of London themes is a wariness towards those on the outside who want to crossover and come inside during moments of border crossing with the white world. The wariness is heightened because of the reality of white appropriation and misrepresentation of black cultural forms, so the racialised 'other' is found to operate out of a hermeneutic of suspicion when dealing with white 'acceptance'. For instance, according to Papa Benji:

> Bredrin, we were educated in a certain way to make us think a certain way, so it mek good sense to think that the white people who hate us are victims as well. In fact in 1982 I worked in the private sector as a draughtsman and this white boy, Barry Jones, said to me, 'all you niggers should go to the Falklands first. Yeh they should out you lot first as you shouldn't fucking be here.' I am not really into fighting but this rankled me as I thought if I was in the wrong place he would have done me something. The next thing I knew we ended up fighting on the floor. I got the sack for that and I honestly don't know what happened to him, but I know that when I started to deejay these were the things I would chat about, what it's like to be hated in your own, ha ha, country (cited in Henry, 2006, p. 134).[18]

Crucially, it is Benji who makes the observation as to how we are 'educated' in the wider society to view alterity as problematic, even though we are speaking of individuals and communities that are subject to the same acculturation processes in the wider public arena. The point is that if Benji was Jamaican with an accent you could in some ways understand Barry Jones's reaction, as

17 Original source: recorded interview, MCS recording studio, Kent, 18 March 1999.
18 Diamonds The Girls Best Friend Sound System, Club Willows, London, Aug. 1984.

the differences, while racialised, would also be linguistically evident. Yet this is not the case here, as for this racist the statement 'you shouldn't fucking be here' makes his position on this matter plain, while at the same time reminding Benji that shared language and culture are not enough to be 'accepted' in the country of your birth. Unsurprisingly, then, 'blacks and whites assume they are operating according to identical speech and cultural conventions and that these are the conventions the socially dominant white group has established as standard' (Kochman, 1981, p. 8). However, the said notions of identical speech and cultural conventions are ideologically based, which means these notions are subject to what we may believe is our own personal view or perspective, but our perceptions are influenced by our position within the ideology, which suggests the following response: 'The task of importance must be to construct a model or a framework that can deal with culture both as "becoming" and as "being": both as an evolution from a given cultural base, however much transformed, and as a creative response to and structural component of the social context' (Alleyne, 1988, p. 5).

The utilisation of other types of speech/language, especially the 'island talk' from the Caribbean, and British urban dialects like cockney or Brummie, is an ultimate marker of difference from white society and perhaps the greatest claim for originality within the social context. Therefore, no matter how much sharing there is in the realm of language usage with white society, acknowledging the strengths of the stark differences between a black and a white mind-set and mentality is crucial to overstanding why acceptance was sought amongst 'your own'. This is the reason why, especially as 'a creative response' in urban London, there was a proliferation of cockney phraseology in both the deejay's written accounts, as well as during those moments of spontaneity, as stated by Reds. Yet at their core was a critique of white racism, oftentimes in the 'common tongue' that now represented a morphing of various languages/vernaculars, creating novel ways of speaking that cannot be reduced to mere 'black talk' or 'London English'.[19] Furthermore, that this is the key stage in the deejay's development is given currency by the fact that within the wider black community people who have the 'gift of the gab', highly proficient orators, are said to have 'lyrics'. On Sound Systems such performers became known by the title of a 'lyric banton',[20] a title first associated with the Jamaican deejay Burro Banton and several others since that time who chatted original lyrics 'non-stop'. Such performers are the antithesis of Trevor Natch's[21] perspective as for him those who 'right an rahbit' are unable to 'write an arrange', which means they lack the natural skill or ability to be little more than 'extemporisers' (Henriques, 2011, p. 188). In

19   See Sebba (1993) for an interesting take on this theme.
20   See Henry (2006), chapter 5, for a more comprehensive take on what it means to be a lyrics banton.
21   Trevor Natch (deceased) was a deejay on West London's Diamonds The Girls Best Friend Sound System.

contrast, the iconographic importance of what it meant within the culture to be regarded as a lyric banton is captured in the following extract:

> Me ah the lyrics banton me no need no introduction,
> well ichi ni san is how them count in Japan,
> but hear me, fling weh the vocal make me ride the version,
> say people gather round me have the mic in ah me hand,
> say all pirate activate you walkman,
> and listen Lezlee Lyrix in origination,
> I gwine tell you why them call me the lyrics banton,
> cos me have the lyrics match any version,
> it could ah buck like bronco, wild like stallion,
> Lezlee, sit-down-in-the-saddle like a damn horse-man,
> but the difference with me and Willie Carson,
> well him ah use the whip me have the mic in ah me hand,
> me in ah, jockey fashion, me in ah jockey fashion, rihbitt,
> jockey fashion, me in ah jockey fashion,
> But how me ah go pass the gateman?
> Jah man, cause me say how me ah go pass the gateman?
> Well first thing I don't have no cash in ah me hand,
> cos I am Lezlee Lyrix true born lyric banton,
> him look me up and down say 'you no favour mic man,
> say where is the Chaplin, the buckers and the tam?'
> Me tell him 'me no wear them cause me born ah England,
> me dress fi suit me self, me no follow fashion.'
> Him say 'if you ah joke you better pull the other one.'
> Jah man, me give him one demonstration, hear weh me say.
> 'Say Lezlee no pirate, Lezlee no imitate, people appreciate, what I originate, some of them ah pirate, live pon dance tape, just like baby live pon Cow and Gate!' Ah murder hitch it up bow yah!
>
> (Lezlee Lyrix, cited in Henry, 2012, pp. 22–3)[22]

The fact that amplified voices such as this drew on aspects of Jamaican deejay culture that went beyond mere imitation speaks to how these voices traversed virtual spaces and places for decades, long before the popularity of the internet, making their own unique presence known on vinyl and cassettes in alternative public arenas. We therefore need to regard these patterns of behaviour within these spaces as the types of conscious thought and action that produce meaning by being constantly reflective, while at the same time future-oriented in an outernational way. To illustrate this point, consider for a moment that the gateman at a dance in Britain failed to recognise the British deejay presence due to the latter's not being suitably attired. This event is telling; and, according to the British deejay Reds, 'people were looking at it from the wrong angle'

---

22 Lezlee Lyrix, Diamonds The Girls Best Friend Sound System, Club Willows, London, Aug. 1984.

(Henry, 2006, p. 192)[23] because uppermost in the minds of these originators were the lyrical content and rhythmic delivery – unlike, perhaps, the external view of the gateman, who ended up receiving a demonstration of the seismic shift within the culture from a British perspective. Moreover, the 'Chaplin' mentioned in the lyrics above are baggy trousers, 'buckers' are Clarks shoes and the 'tam' is the type of headwear associated with Rastafari, which speaks to how many 'British born deejays … thought you had to act/speak/dress a certain way to be "accepted" as a dancehall performer' (Henry, 2012, pp. 2–3). Unsurprisingly, then, not only did this unique presence in the reggae world disrupt the sensibilities of many within the black communities, it also had a wider, and perhaps equally telling, role to play in countering white racism as: 'Black speech, and refiguring of English and "White" spaces transmits the power to trouble, re-formulate and re-define Eurocentric patriarchal constructions of a national past and present … it is through the music where Jamaican *patwa* has been best represented and disseminated throughout urban diasporic spaces outside of Jamaica' (Thomlinson, 2013, p. 63). Thomlinson makes known why the excavation of these voices is necessary to overstanding not just the global reach of patwa, Jamaican language, but crucially how the local (British/Canadian etc.) dialects take on its usage, and how this became central to black diasporic consciousness. The suggestion is that alterity becomes an organising principle whereby a unified countercultural voice is recognised, far beyond geo-political borders, by partakers in the cultural milieu with liberation at its core. Eurocentric ideas and philosophies are therefore resisted and the sites where that resistance takes place, which are the DNA of Africentric speech and social commentary. These constitute historical narratives that have an African provenance, especially when viewed as an authentic form of transcultural dialogue that manifests across Gilroy's 'Black Atlantic' (1994) as deejay lyricism. Authenticity in the case of the British deejay arguably occurred when performers decided to confront the social, cultural, racial and political issues head on during the early 1980s, while striving to be accepted for what they were: speakers of a patwa differing from that spoken by our Jamaican counterparts. Sullivan explains this aspect of the culture through an interview with Sir Coxsone's Blacker Dread, suggesting that 'while Coxone was more like a Jamaican yard sound, Saxon had a different English vibe' (2014, p. 116). Further, and of equal importance, the Saxon deejay Tippa Irie suggests: 'Saxon deejays began to write their lyrics down because they were becoming longer and longer. We used to pride ourselves on fulling up the riddim. While I was on Sounds like Tubby's before, we just made lyrics up … they were more repetitive in them days, not so much lyrical content, more on the hook' (ibid., p. 117):

> Now operator play the music,
> turn the vocal make me chat it,

23 Original source: personal communication, recorded interview, MCS recording studio, Kent, 18 March 1999.

let me give them lyrics I've originated,
nuff bwoy come in ah the dance run up them mouth pon Lezlee Lyrix,
and it's my lyrics they chat they've incorporated.
(Lezlee Lyrix, cited in Henry, 2012, p. 102)[24]

Tippa Irie explains why deejays had to step up their game and 'come original'; and this shift in emphasis is crucial to any overstanding of the significance of the written and spoken word, where 'extemporising' (Henriques, 2011) for many was no longer good enough. The crowdah-people had an expectation of being not only entertained but also educated/uplifted by lyrics that spoke to a lived reality of everyday life in the UK premised on a black experience. Added to this is the importance of being a composer, evidenced in 'let me give them lyrics I've originated', which unequivocally states that what the listener is about to experience is the product of the deejay's mind. Emphasising this distance between the originator and the pirate or 'incorporator' was expected and naturally enhanced the deejay's standing within the culture, the more so if what was chatted on the mic uplifted culturally, spiritually and politically, filling many significant gaps in their 'education'. Hence the deejay 'voice' is a manifestation of those traditional types of African resistance to European cultural hegemony that recognise why the battle for the African mind must also be fought on the terrain of knowledge-exchanges as forms of education. The suggestion is that British deejay lyricism is an exemplar of the practical nature of a black cultural production which focuses on where alternative world views can be exchanged as historical documents to educate the masses in the language used on the mic, because: 'I remember when I first started chatting an nuff people tell me seh me couldn't last because I was chatting so different, I was chatting about being a black youth in London. Later on me fine out seh nuff of who was saying that was just pirating the Yard-style and once everybody get the tape, yuh done know seh is them who couldn't last' (Champion, cited in Henry, 2006, p. 163).[25] Champion states that during this moment, when certain deejays were being rated for their lyrics, what they were actually doing was mimicking the Jamaican deejays, as is suggested above by Tippa Irie when he explains why the Saxon deejays began to compose their lyrics. For Champion, his detractors were uncritically accepting the pirated re-presentation of Jamaican lyricism as authentic, while largely ignoring the content of his rhymes, which related directly to the black experience in London. Champion's position leads us to consider how the process of writing and performing lyrics, in the British context, became accepted as sources of knowledge that allowed the listener to access original perspectives on a lived social reality. However, recognising originality is not always that straightforward when the form is

---

24 Lezlee Lyrix, Diamonds The Girls Best Friend Sound System, Club Willows, London, Aug. 1984.
25 Original source: personal communication, telephone interview, London, 21 March 1999.

largely associated with Jamaican performers, a perspective that fundamentally argues that reggae music can only be produced in Jamaica by Jamaicans, a point that is further endorsed in the following, where the realisation of the crucial role the original deejay played is evidenced:

> Me and Culture (Smiley) were in the dance and nuff deejays were just chatting Yard-style when we took the mic an started chatting our own ting. First is like them never know weh fi do, you wouldah thought that we came from another planet when all we was chatting was South (London) stuff. Anyway, after we 'juggled' and did a couple of combi's people came round the Set and started to beat down the place. It's funny but Jah know that was the first time I felt, yeh man you can do this ting (Asher Senator cited in Henry, 2006, p. 186).[26]

Asher makes known that the positive reaction of the crowd made him realise that he possessed the skill and ability to deliver original lyrics grounded in a black British experience. This led to Asher establishing himself as one of the conscious originators who were not expected to chat the yard-style, although the culture was dominated by Jamaican performers during this moment. Similarly, Champion gives further insight into this aspect of the culture of acceptance that represented a key moment in the evolution of the British deejay scene:

> When I first took the mic, summer 81, I was round my bredrin's yard and I knew I couldn't sing so me just do ah ting. I had some rhymes that I made up pon spot, you know more humorous dan anything else, but the man them did love it cause I was chatting about what happens out ah-road. To me it was more like when you ah reason an mek two joke, so to me it wasn't a big deal and through me never really hear the Yard-tape too tough them time deh my flavour was different. Little later in October 81 I had a clash with ah deejay on 'Dub Natty' [a local Sound System] an me dust him, cau by this time I had started to build proper lyrics even though me never have nuh name. After me rough him up, which was no big deal cau the bwoy did ah pirate; every-ting was Jamdown this an Jamdown that, so me seh me ah goh show you wah gwaan in ah London. The man them [the audience] did quiet at first an then them start galang[27] bad when me run him out [his opponent ran out of lyrics]. Then them start call me the Champion and you done know how the rest ah it goh, the name just stick (Champion, cited in Henry, 2006, p. 185).[28]

Of crucial importance is the mentioning of the 'silence' Champion encountered, which sums up the collective experience of many British deejays, who were initially greeted with this reaction. The main reasons for this being so was the obvious difference in the ways language was used, coupled with the themes being presented, which no longer mirrored a Jamaican world view but

26 Original source: personal communication, Code 7 studio, recorded interview, London, 20 Feb. 2006.
27 'Galang' or 'gwaan' means 'go along' or 'carry on'.
28 Original source: personal communication, telephone interview, London, 21 March 1999.

a uniquely British one. For many who came to dance halls to hear the yard style this was a shock to their system because what was being expressed differed from the pirated performances that dominated the early reggae dance-hall scene. Similarly, Champion's explanation of how the British deejays won over the crowd centres on recognising that we were living in the UK and not in Jamaica. Moreover, by stating that he created his lyrics spontaneously, 'head top',[29] he demonstrates how 'self-reflection is often one of the key characteristics of [...] extemporised performance' (Henriques, 2011, p. 188). However, Champion adds, 'I had some rhymes that I made up pon spot', thereby explaining that he also had compositions because 'I had started to build proper lyrics even though me never have nuh name'. Yet it was these 'proper lyrics' by the 'nameless' deejay that were used to 'dust out' the pirate, making known that the expectations within the culture had shifted and the emergent British deejay voice was coming to the fore, a vocal presence that was further established when many British deejays decided to recreate their own experiences in a more representative original voice, realising that 'yeh man you can do this ting'.

Conclusion

Black youth in Britain, by way of the deejay performance, created a living history that challenged their negative depiction across a range of contexts, a factor that was missed by many of the theorists who sought to explain their affiliations to reggae music and Sound System culture. As argued above, an explanation of this perspective is firmly rooted in a lack of knowledge and understanding of the alternative public spaces in which these claims were articulated. The point is that more consideration is needed when interpreting resistant cultures due to the manner in which past experiences are appropriated and passed on in a performance that outwardly masks an inner reality. Moreover, a space was created for alternative ideas of being black/African to be expressed in patwa, whereby the conscious, original deejay becomes the 'mouthpiece' for what are arguably outernational 'interpretive communities'. Of equal importance, by using the transcendental voice in this way the deejay continues a tradition of thinking oneself into being which is beyond the hegemonic scope of a dominant, racist society. That is why explanations that did not appreciate what it meant to be scorned and rejected in the land of your birth, constantly being told to 'fuck off back home', were inadequate and misleading. Similarly, a failure to consider why Standard English was rejected and patwa was embraced as the language of choice, within certain spaces and places, serves little more than to reinforce the well-documented idea that black youth were 'rebels without a cause'. Yet the profound nature of the rhyming skills and intellectualised rendering of various social, cultural and political events, such as those featured

---

29 See Henry (2006), chapter 6, for an insight into the role of the 'head top' (off the cuff/improvised) deejay within the culture.

above, demonstrate the necessity for the inclusion of the undocumented side to any viable discussion of the black-British experience as seen through the lens of deejay culture. Without the inclusion of the significant contributions presented above, a large part of the 'glocal' worth of reggae musical history and Sound System culture will stay hidden, and hence the picture will remain incomplete.

Bibliography

Alleyne, M. (1988) *Roots of Jamaican Culture* (London: Pluto Press).

Back, L. (1988) 'Coughing up fire: sound systems in southeast London', *New Formations*, 5: 141–52.

— (1996) *New Ethnicities and Urban Culture: Racisms and Multiculture in Young Lives* (London: UCL Press).

Bourne, J. (1980) '"Cheerleaders and ombudsmen": the sociology of race relations in Britain', *Race and Class*, 21: 331–52.

Bradley, L. (2001) *Bass Culture: When Reggae Was King* (London: Penguin).

Cashmore, E. (1979) *Rastaman: The Rastafarian Movement in England* (London: Unwin).

Cashmore, E. and B. Troyna, (1982) 'Black Youth in Crisis', in E. Cashmore and B. Troyna (eds.), *Black Youth in Crisis* (London: Allen and Unwin), pp. 15–34.

Dagnini, J.K. (2010) 'The importance of reggae music in the worldwide cultural universe', *Études caribéennes*, 16: 1–16.

Davis, G. (1989) *I Got the Word in Me and I Can Sing It, You Know: A Study of the Performed African-American Sermon* (Philadelphia, PA: University of Pennsylvania Press).

Eden, J. (2012) 'Uncarved', http://uncarved.org/dub/papalevi.html [accessed 6 Feb. 2019].

Gilroy, P. (1987) *There Ain't No Black in the Union Jack: The Cultural Politics of Race and Nation* (London: Hutchinson).

— (1994) *The Black Atlantic: Modernity and Double Consciousness* (London: Verso).

Gordon, A. (1998) *Ghostly Matters: Haunting and the Sociological Imagination* (Minneapolis, MN: University of Minnesota Press).

Hall, S., C. Critcher, T. Jefferson and B. Roberts (1978) *Policing the Crisis: Mugging, the State, and Law and Order* (London: Hutchinson).

Henriques, J. (2011) *Sonic Bodies: Reggae Sound Systems, Performance Techniques and Ways of Knowing* (London and New York: Continuum).

Henry, W. 'Lez' (2006) *What the Deejay Said: A Critique From The Street!* (London: Learning By Choice).

— (2007) *Whiteness Made Simple: Stepping into the GREY Zone* (London: Learning By Choice).

— (2012) *Carry-Beyond Reflections: An Audiography by Lezlee Lyrix* (London: Learning By Choice).

Kochman, T. (1981) *Black and White Styles in Conflict* (Chicago, IL: University of Chicago Press).

Liverpool, H. (2001) *Rituals of Power and Rebellion: The Carnival Tradition in Trinidad & Tobago 1763–1962* (Chicago, IL: Research Associates School Times Publications).

Martin, T. (1976) *Race First: The Ideological and Organisational Struggles of Marcus Garvey and the Universal Negro Improvement Association* (Dover, MA.: The Majority Press).

Rietveld, H. C. (2013) 'Journey to the light? Immersion, spectacle and meditation', in B. A. Attias, A. Gavanas and H. C. Rietveld (eds.), *DJ Culture in the Mix: Power, Technology, and Social Change in Electronic Dance Music* (New York and London: Bloomsbury).

Rigby, P. (1996) *African Images: Racism and the End of Anthropology* (Oxford: Berg).

Roach, J. (1996) *Cities of the Dead: Circum-Atlantic Performance* (New York: Columbia University Press).

Sebba, M. (1993) *London Jamaican: Language Systems in Interaction* (London: Longman).

Small, C. (1994) *Music of the Common Tongue: Survival and Celebration in Afro-American Music* (London: Calder).

Stolzoff, N.C. (2000) *Wake the Town & Tell The People: Dancehall Culture in Jamaica* (Durham, NC and London: Duke University Press).

Sullivan, P. (2014) *Remixology: Tracing the Dub Diaspora* (London: Reaktion).

Sutcliffe, D. and A. Wong (1986) *The Language of the Black Experience: Cultural Expression through Word and Sound in the Caribbean and Black Britain* (Oxford: Blackwell).

Thomlinson, L. (2013) 'Cultures of resistance: hip hop, music and black youth culture in Toronto', in D. P. Hope (ed.), *International Reggae: Current and Future Trends in Jamaican Popular Music* (Kingston, Jamaica: Pelican), pp. 63–92.

Veal, M. E. (2007) *Dub: Soundscapes & Shattered Songs in Jamaican Reggae* (Middletown, CT: Wesleyan University Press).

Webster-Prince, M. (2013) 'Putting up resistance: indigenous radio serial drama and reggae music', in D. P. Hope (ed.), *International Reggae: Current and Future Trends in Jamaican Popular Music* (Kingston, Jamaica: Pelican), pp. 225–58.

Wolff, J. (1993) *The Social Production of Art* (London: Palgrave).

5. Journeying through the 'motherland'

Peter Ramrayka

Your beliefs become your thoughts. Your thoughts become your words. Your words become your actions. Your actions become your habits. Your habits become your values. Your values become your destiny.

Mahatma Gandhi

Assimilation for an immigrant in any society presents enormous challenges with race, language and culture being regarded as the most significant. People from the Caribbean have had mixed experiences in overcoming these barriers. Some have been successful in jumping over the hurdles; others less so. Reflecting on my own experience I was fortunate in haing been involved for substantial periods in the two sectors in the UK that British people are proudest of: the National Health Service (NHS) (which ranks as number one in most surveys) and the Armed Forces (ranked number three). Gratitude, pride and support for current and ex-Armed Forces personnel in Britain, encapsulated in the Armed Forces Covenant (2000), subtitled 'An Enduring Covenant between the People of the United Kingdom, Her Majesty's Government and All those who serve or have served in the Armed Forces of the Crown and their Families', extend not only to those born in the UK but also to people from the Commonwealth.[1] Caribbean personnel who took part in both world wars, in particular those who joined the Royal Air Force (RAF) in World War Two, have a special place in the hearts of British people; and their legacy has benefited those of us who followed militarily, albeit in my case in 1961, 16 years after the end of the war. It was an honour and pleasure to play a part in the unveiling in 2017 of the African and Caribbean War Memorial in Brixton Square, London, organised by the Nubian Jak Community Trust and financially supported by the government. The ceremony was attended by, among others, African and Caribbean veterans, the Secretary of State for Defence, and the mayors of London and Lambeth.

1 See The Amed Forces Covenant, https://assets.publishing.service.gov.uk/government/uploads/system/uploads/attachment_data/file/49470/the_armed_forces_covenant_today_and_tomorrow.pdf [accessed 24 Feb. 2019].

P. Ramrayka, 'Journey through the "motherland"' , in J.D. Webb, R. Westmaas, M. del Pilar Kaladeen and W. Tantam (eds.), *Memory, migration and (de)colonisation in the Caribbean and beyond* (London: University of London Press, 2019), pp. 79–84. License: CC-BY-NC-ND 4.0.

As an NHS worker, regardless of your profession or status, you are perceived as someone who fundamentally cares for others; and your interaction within the community tends to be positive on the whole. Nurses of Caribbean extraction are particularly admired for their longevity of service, professionalism, dedication and empathy with patients and clients. Some postulate that coming from colonial British societies, with English as their first language, has given them added advantages over other immigrant groups, despite the huge bars of race and colour which need to be overcome. Until relatively recently few British Caribbean nurses obtained top general-management positions. I believe that when I entered the NHS in 1970 I benefited to some extent from the goodwill which the nurses who had come before me had engendered; and, coupled with the managerial and leadership skills I had acquired from nine years in the RAF, this enabled me to pursue an eventful and successful NHS career. Race was, and to a certain extent still is, a major hurdle but I feel the NHS has moved a considerable distance in promoting equality of opportunity, as is evidenced by the number of people of colour who are now in top leadership positions in the sector. Language for me, as with other Caribbean people, was never an issue. There is now a realisation among large sections of the indigenous community that as English is our first, and in many cases only, language, our distinctive accents, with their sometimes peculiar pronunciation, should be regarded as no different to regional language variations. Culture is, perhaps, one of the most challenging areas. It is very dependent on how early in one's life the immigrant journey starts and how linked to culture one's religion is. Most Caribbean people come from cultures which are predominantly Christian although the degree of practice can vary significantly. As I was closely exposed at an early age to three of the great world religions (Hinduism, Christianity and Islam), this helped me to adjust, relatively easily, to British culture in general and particularly to the multiracial environments of the RAF and the NHS.

My journey

The year is 1961. As a 17-year-old Indian-Guyanese boy I left the comfort of my tropical paradise, multiracial home, bound for the streets of London, which I thought were paved with gold. Imbued with a sense of excited anticipation and harbouring ambitions of becoming a lawyer, I soon found out they were not. Instead, I settled into bed-sit accommodation and embarked on a journey of discovery which would not only open my mind to social values and different cultural behaviour but would also take me around the world, including to the sub-continent of my ancestors, India.

Back in British Guiana (as it then was), my place of birth, I had been told that the 'Mother England' was inhabited by decent, fair-minded and friendly people who would welcome me and my colonial brothers with open arms. The British Empire would not have been the greatest in the world without us – would it? But over a period of more than half a century I would discover that issues of race, religion, creed and culture were as divisive as they were cohesive. In a twist of fate that led me to the top of my profession, I somehow managed to escape the clutches of such serious discrimination. This juxtaposition between what I was taught at home and what I found in the metropolis did, though, lead to profound confusion.

My first career stop was the RAF in July 1961, where I spent nine formative years rising up the ranks of the medical administration branch and, working and living closely with my fellow teenagers, acquiring British traits: fairness, moderation, punctiliousness, respect for heritage (albeit culturally slanted), self-confidence, a gift for innovation and a readiness to take up a challenge. I travelled the length and breadth of the UK and was based for lengthy periods in many parts of the country, experiencing regional differences in accents, outlooks and attitudes, especially towards persons of a different colour. An overseas posting to Cyprus between 1963 and 1964 exposed me to life during an active military campaign, where I was awarded the General Service and United Nations Medals.

Those born in Guyana make a powerful statement by joining the British Armed Services. For an immigrant it can be regarded as a leap into the dark, a belief that your colleagues will welcome you, despite many of them coming from envirnoments where reports of heightened racial tensions have been made publicly. That was my position in 1961. However, as an immigrant teenager several aspects of military life could be compared with those at a boarding school as the authorities control your entire life: you sleep, wake up, eat, study and socialise in very close proximity to your colleagues. If you bond well and your experiences are positive, your pride in your alma mater and your comradeship last a lifetime. I believe that life in the RAF gave me a deep appreciation and understanding of the British way of doing things, the inner concerns of my fellow citizens and the ability to recognise and respond positively to contradictions. I also took advantage of the extensive continuous educational programmes available, gained success in trade, professional and national qualifications and was deemed by my commanding officer to be eligible to be considered for a commission.

In 1970 I applied the skills, competencies and educational qualifications that I had acquired in the RAF to the NHS. Despite the passing of the Race Relations Act in 1965, most people of colour knew that there was still covert discrimination in most aspects of life, especially in employment. The NHS was an exception to this. It is the institution which makes British people proudest, the envy of the world. To many immigrants the NHS, as one of the largest employers of labour, was a natural home, particularly for nursing and ancillary workers – porters, domestic assistants, caterers. Indeed, the need for nurses was so great that there were recruitment campaigns in Caribbean countries in the 1960s. However, although the NHS wanted nurses and ancillary staff, it was not a natural home for people of colour who were interested in general management and leadership roles, as there was a perception in the 1960s and 1970s that, despite the Race

Relations Acts of 1965 and 1968, covert racial discrimination would form a barrier to managerial progression, the notion of people of colour supervising or managing indigenous British staff being anathema to large sections of society. Always open to a challenge and with the confidence which service in the RAF had given me, I thought I would enter the fray. Suggestions that my surname would also act as a barrier in gaining an interview were set aside.

My first application for a managerial position was indeed a success and I embarked on a stellar career. I started my NHS journey at the National Temperance Hospital in London as a staff officer. Essentially, my role was as number three in the administrative hierarchy of the hospital, responsible for coordinating general administrative activities, human resources and overseeing ancillary staff, mainly porters. From here, I worked my way up to a more senior appointment,[2] one step below board level for the north sector of Greenwich Health District. My rapid promotion not only reflected my hard work, but also the opportunities afforded by the NHS for career advancement. For instance, I secured this senior appointment from a shortlist of four local British colleagues. This was a particular achievement as there were no visible ethnic minorities at that level, nationally or locally, in that area of work at the time. Implementation of general management meant that the top tiers were constantly changing. Within the south-east region appointments to district general manager posts included several senior ex-military officers, plus an array of commercial and industrial people who felt, supported by the appointing authorities, that their experience of senior or top management in other fields was directly transferable to the NHS's managerial culture. The fact that most of them left after a relatively short space of time is evidence of the peculiar nature of leadership and management in the NHS, in which a combination of institutional knowledge, cultural fit, empathy and, some would say, vocational commitment and public-sector ethos predominates.

My substantive appointment as district administrator for Dartford and Gravesham Health Authority in 1985 was welcomed by many locally, and more widely, as I was the first person in the country from a visible ethnic minority to obtain this much-coveted position. As mentioned previously, although the NHS had recruited ethnic minorities as doctors and nurses, and to fulfil catering, domestic and portering duties, at the time administration and general management leadership roles either did not appeal to ethnic minorities or the prevailing national culture dissuaded those who were so inclined due to the belief that they were unlikely to succeed because of the perceived colour barrier. To a certain extent the barrier was slightly raised when, with the NHS's constantly changing structure, there was an influx of ethnic minorities (mainly doctors from the Indian sub-continent) into leadership roles as chairpersons of new primary care groups and the primary care trusts that succeeded them. These were

2 Namely north east sector administrator of Greenwich Health District, administratively responsible for three hospitals (St Nicholas Plumstead, Goldie Leigh, British Hospitals for Mothers and babies) and certain community services in the area.

non-executive appointments but hugely important in providing leadership in a changing environment.

By 1986 the new general management structure had been developed and it was time for title changes. Most members of the district management team acquired positions as board directors and I became director of administration, personnel and estate management, secretary to the authority and deputy district general manager: a mouthful, but my role embraced district-level responsibility for the district heads of services as well as running the health authority's administrative functions.

A serious event occurred when I was in this role: on the night of 15 October 1987 a severe storm – some referred to it as a mini-hurricane – hit the Greater London area and caused devastation to buildings, with trees falling on hospital roofs across the health district. Rare trees and shrubs at Joyce Green Hospital, which had been provided many years previously due to the connection between one of the head gardeners and the Royal Botanic Gardens at Kew, were unfortunately lost forever. Prompt remedial action by the estates department, one of my principal areas of responsibility, ensured that power was quickly restored, emergency repairs carried out, and the effect on patients was minimal. By responding to such problems, the local trust began to gain something of a reputation in the community.

Managers in the NHS often come in for wild and in many cases unfounded criticism from those who see them as people employed to put obstacles in the way of effective healthcare. But these critics fail to recognise that, in fact, managers are enablers: we provide the infrastructure and support to keep the organisation efficient and effective, as well as looking out for opportunities to promote innovation. Following the announcement of a joint venture between myself and Colin Rodden, the town clerk of Swanley, to provide a £400,000 state-of-the-art clinic, the *Kentish Times* ran the headline: 'Pioneer Clinic to be proud of …'. This initiative brought a range of community services to the people in the area. The working together of health and local authorities with a four-doctor partnership was early evidence of collaboration which continues to be a challenge in present-day healthcare.

After eight years in the district, five of which were spent at the top management table, what had I achieved? I was proud that I had led some major development projects: a college of healthcare studies in Dartford, Kent (1986–8); an intensive care unit at Joyce Green Hospital; and Archery House, a facility for the remaining learning-disability residents from Darenth Park Hospital (Kent; closed 1988) who needed continuing care in a domiciliary setting as they could not be returned to their original homes. In addition, I had satisfactorily managed multi-million-pound budgets; mentored and supported senior managers across the district who, in turn, were responsible for hundreds of staff; and had led or contributed to the development strategies of the Dartford and Gravesham health authority.

In 1990 I decided to leave the NHS, but to take its values and systems to developing countries, in particular working as a paid consultant in Botswana and Pakistan and as a volunteer in Tanzania.[3] The *Kentish Times* reported: 'Health chief leaves for job in Botswana', adding in the opening paragraph that 'the man who has helped shaped the district's health service set off last weekend to work in the third world … He has helped to influence many of the decisions of the health authority and believes there have been significant improvements in patient care'.[4] With these warm words and the customary send-off party thrown by friends and colleagues, I was ready for my new adventure. A tie emblazoned with the Gravesend borough council motto and a ghetto-blaster were among the parting gifts.

Reflections on service in the NHS

Reflecting on 28 years' service in the NHS, I feel that my time in the RAF medical branch had provided a solid ground on which to build. I also attribute some of my successes to the initial grounding I had in my country of birth, where growing up in a multiracial environment, especially in the capital city, Georgetown, where I attended St George's Anglican School, conditioned me to accept and celebrate diversity. A balance struck by me and other like-minded diaspora people is that we use our expertise and contacts in the adopted country to provide a voluntary service for our country of birth. I am pleased to have taken the lead in 1994 in bringing together a number of organisations to form Guyhealth (UK). Although changed from its original membership, it continues to provide assistance to the health sector in Guyana, recently in the area of mental health.

In 2018, the 70th anniversary of the NHS, it is recognised that there continue to be hurdles for visible ethnic minorities to overcome, but public acknowledgement and celebration of the contributions they have made is widespread, which highlights the impact of the Windrush (1948) generation. There is a certain point in an immigrant's life when, depending on their outlook and achievements, their adopted home becomes their chosen place of retirement, even though the pull from their country of birth remains constant. I believe if you become engrossed in all aspects of life in an adopted country, earnestly take in its values and ways of doing things, especially if these were acquired at an early age, you become a citizen of the world.

---

3   In Botswana I worked at the Princess Marina hospital, Gaborone; in Pakistan I worked for the Second Family Health Project/Pakistan-wide stratgic health project for Lahore, Karachi, Rawalpindi, Quetta, Azad Kashmir, Peshawar; in Tanzania I worked for the British Executive Service Overseas/ Voluntary Services Overseas as a management consultant/programme leader.

4   27 Sept. 1990.

6. De Zie Contre Menti Kaba – when two eyes meet the lie ends: a Caribbean meditation on decolonising academic methodologies

Nadine King Chambers

Ayiti as the starting point[1]

This chapter opens with the Haitian-Canadian poetry of Junie Désil to honour the overlooked space where black people in the Caribbean uphold more than just a singular lineage in the effort to keep our stolen selves uncolonised. The Haitian revolution (1791–1804) represents one of the greatest blows against all the wrack and ruin various European colonisers brought to Haiti. Its stories and legacies continue to be under siege from anti-black, anti-indigenous, pro-colonial forces; therefore I chose to begin to tell this complicated living tale of life, land and law by turning to literature and art, refusing white hetero-patriarchal systems of power and expanding space for our science and our fact to breathe freely in our fugitive stronghold labelled 'fiction'.

The best work begins at home and lives in the generative economy of poetry at the kitchen table:

> *At Grandma's knees*
> *The lines etched on my face my hands*
> *are the history of our people she says to me*
> *but I can't read it*
> *So*
> *Grandma traces herstory with my fingers*
> *"La-oui", she says*
> *here*

---

1   Ayiti is the original Taíno name of the island of Haiti. Following a visit in 2015 to an exhibition of work of one of her most famous artist sons (Jean-Michel Basquiat: *Now's the Time* at the Art Gallery of Ontario), I sent a postcard of the 1988-piece 'Exu' from Jamaica to a beloved Marxist friend on 19 May 2015, writing: 'Go against your thought that the Soviet/Russian [revolution] overrides everything including the centrality of the Haitian Revolution … relentlessly seeking freedom as it exists in our pulsing imaginary and this question of the flesh'.

N. King Chambers, 'De Zie Contre Menti Kaba – when two eyes meet the lie ends: a Caribbean meditation on decolonising academic methodologies', in J.D. Webb, R. Westmaas, M. del Pilar Kaladeen and W. Tantam (eds.), *Memory, migration and (de)colonisation in the Caribbean and beyond* (London: University of London Press, 2019), pp. 85–105. License: CC-BY-NC-ND 4.0.

dragging my index across the deepest brown line
in her palm starting farthest left
She says:
Before you
before your mother
before many women before me
there was Anacaona
everyone carries her name
in the bone
in the blood
in the soul
in the flesh
Pause
Then: 'ici-mem'
here she says
placing my finger now in the centre of her timeline
Anacaona she repeats again
Golden flower Queen of Haiti
She sighs
In a rush
words a staccato rhythm so fast maybe I never heard them
Leogane.
Anacaona
Canaobo
Christophe Colomb
Gold
Greed
Conquest
Treason
Deaths
Hung
1503
this more slowly enunciated
she was hung
Each word stabbed into her palm
three spaced intervals to the right of that deep brown line
Haiti was born when Christopher Columbus discovered her. He traded peacefully with the accomodating Taino/Arawaks of Ayiti. Such nice friendly people.
'Yo ravage peup-la. Yo ravage la te'
They ravaged the people. They ravaged the earth.
Tears
They look icy cold on her cinnamon brown face
they fall hot on my trapped hand
caught in her grip
at the venerable age of 500 plus years
the hurt is fresh in her eyes the memory too

in her mind
Still coursing down her face
Loosening her grip
my fingernail has left a crescent shaped indent
on her palm cutting
vertically across herstory's line
Now her eyes are dry
My finger is near the end of her line
'Ou we?'
you see right here she asks
this is where Anacaona was born
Leogane. And here?
This is where I was born
Jacmel.
And see over here? This is where your mother was born
Grand-Gosier.
This is you ce ou mem oui
Montreal.
And the women before us? (Désil, 2006)

This poem is the power of a Black Haitian elder transmitting herstories – unsettling authorised space and time – to make an indigenous and black map that tells the stories we need,[2] hard ones included. These are the guides bequeathed, not via the internet but within the web of our palms resisting being 'blanked' to continue the sacred work of decolonising what we remember *and* reinforcing our ability to revolt against the colonial present in which we find ourselves.

Jamaica: an instructive contrast

On the Jamaican coat of arms, Anacaona's people are portrayed resting comfortably with hands palm-down on either side of the British shield. The original inscription from 1906 reads 'INDUS UNTERQUE SERVIET VNI', meaning, 'The Indians twain shall serve one Lord'. The inscription was changed in 1962 to 'Out of Many, One People', yet post-independence there is no substantive reference to indigenous presence as shaping the present.[3] The now 113-year-old image keeps indigenous peoples of the region symbolically re-purposed by the coloniser's drive 'to make flat all that is high and rolling; to make invisible and wutliss [worthless] plenty things', as noted by the Rastaman in Kei Miller's *The Cartographer Tries to Map a Way to Zion* (2014, p. 17). In Junie's grandmother's 500-year memory-as-living-flesh piece Anacaona is

---

2 The oldest known maternal ancestor in my Jamaican family story is Catherine LaFebre, who sailed from Haiti to Jamaica with her father and stayed there rather than sailing with him to France.

3 See *The Gleaner*, http://jamaica-gleaner.com/gleaner/20120404/lead/lead93.html [accessed 15 Aug. 2018).

recognised as the original royalty; the poem is a living recognition of *this island's mine*.[4] How different this is from the amnesia riddling Jamaican memory, created when the British hid this inheritance in the 1906 coat of arms and covered over the jacket of the Spanish who arrived as traders to Xaymaca and left as *génocidaires*.[5] All colonisers made maps; and in those maps lie all their intentions about territories and systematic political imperatives. Kei Miller's Rastaman protagonist would salute Junie's grandmother as a force against the imperial cartographic drive 'to make thin and crushable | all that is big and as real as ourselves' (2014, p. 17).

I am the granddaughter of Jamaican campaigners for the federation dream and a daughter raised on the Mona campus of the University of the West Indies (UWI) on Jamaica at a time when all the rich and varied demotic speech of the Caribbean surrounded me as fact. For me, there is pride in wishing federation existed, coupled with the attempt to understand the shadows of things done by the British, with Caribbean countries' names listed on colonial contracts or agreements before federated or untethered independence was even a thought. My desire has run over more than ten years of slow research about the Aluminium Company of Canada (ALCAN) and how its corporate control, granted by colonial authority, altered hopes, rivers, dreams and rocks for smelters – connecting Jamaica to British Columbia. My work is about finding a way through the wide range of 'out of many [arrivals], one people' in order to shift the Jamaican sense of indigeneity, complicated by our histories as peoples 'trafficked', 'travelled' or 'having made their way' in a society built on enslavement post-genocide. The far-ranging consequence of the generally accepted reports of indigenous death may have created an inability to see indigeneity elsewhere. What was jest for Twain is no joke for existing Taínos and other indigenous peoples. Patricia Mohammed wrote: 'Undoubtedly, the scars of enslavement of African peoples are deepest. No other group apart from the Indigenous Amerindian population under colonization in the West Indies, suffered so much in terms of inhumanity, both physical as well as in the disruption and eradication of its cultural memory' (1998, p. 7). But is that true in all ways and all places? Not necessarily; and I am most moved by black Haitian women's memory of Anacaona, the female Taíno *cacique* [local chiefs] as proof that 'Dé zié contré menti kaba': when two eyes meet, the lie ends – or cannot start.[6]

4 W. Shakespeare, *The Tempest*, re-purposed by Chickasaw scholar J. Byrd. It is important to note that concepts of land and ownership are vastly different in indigenous cosmologies from capitalist concepts and practices.

5 A 'jacket' is a Jamaican term for a child being raised by a man who is unaware that he is not the biological father.

6 Personal exchange with Luz Guerra (Boriken/Puerto Rico) confirmed by a Désil elder: 'I am talking to you about a third person, who is absent, and I lie against him/her. You manage to bring the victim and me together and discuss the matter, at some point you will discover that I lied'.

This is what this chapter attempts: an invitation to attend to long relationships or lack thereof between racialised communities. It is an invitation to my own community to take up the new challenges because 'risk demands that we look at blackness across the diaspora and acknowledge not just black subordination but those historical and social moments in which blackness is articulated with and through settler and other forms of colonial power' (Jackson, 2014, p. 64). My work is primarily directed towards those of us in the diaspora located between the Caribbean and Canada, for whom the term 'decolonisation' includes acknowledgement of indigenous sovereignty and stolen land.[7] I am acutely aware that in Canada and other parts of the black diaspora of the Caribbean (such as the UK) the term 'decolonisation' is also used for various systems and structures in our fight for self-determination as part of our diaspora's complex, layered sense of 'at home and abroad'. My aim is to find a way for my community and its diaspora to take indigenous struggles for sovereignty over life and land seriously. I will do so by considering how the economies of settler colonialism in British Columbia were unified with slave colonialism in the Caribbean through multinational state and corporate engineering.

Journey in the Caribbean and Canada: 1803 to the present

In 1991, after two fantastic years in Trinidad and several years in Ontario, I arrived in Vancouver knowing nothing of the lies riddling the story about British Columbia's beginnings. Vancouver was not ceded by Musqueam, Tsleil-Waututh and Squamish peoples. In such places one has to grapple with the terms 'settler of colour' and 'uninvited guest'. As if that were not enough, it was a trial to answer folks from Jamaica asking, 'Weh yu deh?' Often my answer drew a response of, 'I couldn't live so far'. However, I did live 'so far' and it was there that my sense of indigenous 'Canada' was clearest and, unlike in Brampton, Ontario, I learned to see the presence of many indigenous nations and their traditional name-places. Oddly, the clarity was starkest when my citizenship test revealed the lie: not one question asked whether I knew anything about indigenous Canada. In 1997 I set out to remedy my swearing of allegiance to that discursive violence representing past and present horror by going off the 'grateful immigrant' path to seek some truths. I had not realised that some history of my own – things done by the British with Jamaica's name

7   These times require attention to deployment of the term 'indigenous'. I considered past, present and possible usage of the terminology in reference to black communities who arrived in eastern parts of Canada from the 1800s onwards and used it to identify themselves as separate from later waves of black migrants; as well as in reference to scholarship created in the Caribbean by arrivants as 'indigenous'. Within the body of this chapter I use it to designate communities of distinct peoples living in a *sui generis* relationship with land which has been under siege by European colonial expansion into north, south and central parts of the Americas.

on them – had arrived ahead of me in that region and directly to a nation that has never signed a treaty.

One afternoon in a Crossroads Restaurant, Kingston, on a trip to Jamaica in 2015, I ran into a friend who had just repaired a traditional African drum and was returning it to its owner. By chance, this exchange included mention of my research about ALCAN. This elder from Manchester (Jamaica) lit up and spoke about the impact of mining on land her family had struggled to acquire post-emancipation. 'We were flooded out', she said, adding, 'Even the graves went under water'. I was shocked, because I had only ever considered the process of displacement by man-made flooding to have existed on the British Columbia side of the story I had been tracking for more than a decade.

In the mid 1930s a sample of Jamaican soil, unfit for sustaining grass for animal husbandry, was sent off to be tested for other possible usage. Slowly Jamaica – a colony with barely a glimmer of self-governance by its majority – moved from a fading plantation system back into the global realm as part of a mining commodity chain. Across two seas in Britain and Canada, horizontal plan-cabinets were opening as hands searched for and pulled out early 20th-century water-power maps of British Columbia, eventually narrowing down to the Gitamaat and Henaksiala territories in north-central British Columbia on the Pacific north coast of Canada for the building of a smelter and power-generating facilities (Powell, 2011).

A timeline – one entwined from many to give context

- 1834: Abolition of British slavery, 272 years too long while indigenous communities of North America, like the Gitamaat and the Henaksiala stewarding their territory since 'time immemorial' meet Hudson Bay Company traders.
- 1865: Morant Bay War in Jamaica; and HMS Clio is part of the Royal Navy's gunboat policy directed at Kitamaat village (British Colombia).
- 1883: Missionaries arrive at Tsee-Motsa (Kitamaat village); and my beloved paternal great-grandmother is born in Airy Castle, St Thomas.
- 1947: Jamaica's Minerals (Vesting) Act and Mining Act.
- 1948–9: Gitamaat and Henaksiala communities merge and are referred to jointly as 'Haisla'.
- 1951: Building of the Kemano Generating Station in Haisla territory.[8]
- 1952: First shipment of ore leaves Jamaica (for the US).
- 1953: ALCAN town of Kitimat (northern coastal region of British Columbia) opens.[9]

8   This was preceded by the creation of the Kenney Dam in north-west British Columbia (opened in 1954) and the destruction of Cheslatta T'En communities, as described in B. Christensen (1995).
9   Kitimat is the town built by ALCAN. Kitamaat is the Haisla village/landmark.

- 1960s: Armed with a UK degree my father is an engineer with ALCAN in Jamaica. My first home is an ALCAN company house. Meanwhile in Kitimat the smelter is now a major wage-economy employer of the Haisla.

In the 1950s Gitimaat and Henaksiala (collectively identified as Haisla) spaces were violently restructured to build a smelter as part of the processing of Jamaican ore. Anglophone world powers' desire for bauxite for war as well as reconstruction after war required two things: the ore itself and the power to transform it. Yet this start has connections to Guyana and Barbados and so more than one of the nation states in the Caribbean Basin stand in the shadow of things done and imprinted as 'the West Indies' almost exactly one hundred years earlier in what is now known as British Columbia, Canada.

In 1803 James Douglas was born in Demerara, Guyana, to a Scottish man and a mixed-race mother from Barbados. By 1851 he was both chief factor of the powerful Hudson Bay Company and governor of Vancouver Island, the colonial starting place for what became British Columbia. The relationships between settler societies and indigenous peoples on Vancouver Island was discussed in 2017 as the focus of a powerful gathering, aptly titled *The First Nations, Land, and James Douglas: Indigenous and Treaty Rights in the Colonies of Vancouver Island and British Columbia, 1849–1864*.[10] By the 1920s the British had also tied Guyana (the southern root of the Caribbean with the largest indigenous populations) to Saguenay, Québec and Innu people in eastern Canada in a mining relationship that one might consider an administrative blueprint (echoed in the 'lakes' of Linden, Guyana) for the subsequent mining relationship forged between Kitimat and Jamaica.

What I am unearthing keeps revealing just how deep colonisation is, how vast, how complicated and how problematic if narrowly assessed from different locations, and without considering the possibility of connected histories. On the question of legal certainty, the erasure of Taínos from Jamaica works as de facto ownership by colonisers. Not so on the other side of this geographic equation in Canada: the definition of British Columbia is completely unlike most of Canada from Alberta to almost all parts to the east, and from the general discourse around treaty-making. In British Columbia the record shows only a handful of treaties, or in some cases agreements interpreted as treaties, made on Vancouver Island. The fact is that after 1854 the British crown simply refused to provide Douglas with more funds for the complete legal annexation of Vancouver Island and the mainland west of Alberta. At the time of confederation (1867), and to this day, the bulk of British Columbia, including Haisla space, is (in legal terminology) unceded to any crown entity, whether British or Canadian.

---

10   See https://hcmc.uvic.ca/songheesconference [accessed 25 Feb. 2019].

Before methodology, what kind of intention is needed to handle this complexity?

How should one discuss a colonial relationship between two geographical areas, time lines and peoples who on the surface appear not to have met? How should one centre unwritten ethical guidelines that traditional research checklists do not include? How should one research and write this, having lived in these two different worlds marked by settler-colonial horrors? Precisely because of these challenges I hold fast to a commitment to 'just see clearly'[11] and understand fully. I meditate often on the following quotation from Dorothy Allison, who explains her commitment to the high stakes of truth-telling: 'If we are not to sacrifice some part of ourselves or our community we will have to go through the grief, the fear of exposure, and struggle, with only a thin layer of trust that we will emerge whole and unbroken. I know of no other way to do this than to start by saying, I will give up nothing. I will give up no one' (1994, p. xx).

Inspiration comes in the work of Métis-Dene author Marie Clements through reading her play *Burning Vision* (2003) about uranium mining by Dene people and the destruction of Nagasaki which uses a fantastic theatrical writing device called chronotopic dramaturgy. Space and time are restructured to bring together more closely the lives and deaths of indigenous miners and Japanese civilians from multilinear chronologies. Clements starts in the late 1800s with the prophecy of a Dene seer and ends with the journey of Dene elders to Hiroshima in 1998. Her work inspires me with its structure of character, stories and ethical commitment to 'breaking space and time' to reveal relationships.

This indigenous play is one of my keystones, a guide to challenging the arch of colonial time through my personal search for reparative research justice within and outwith the frameworks set by academic arenas. Furthermore, to undo colonial structures by serving the community as encouraged by Shona Jackson – to do the work of 'making visible and intelligible research that does not fit into the balkanised categories of difference produced by predominantly white, academic departments, social worlds, and ways of knowing the colonial world' (2013, p. 63). In 2015, unaware of Jackson's journal piece, I decided to restart my own research on the topic, while being soberly attuned to the risk and potential rejection of work that refused the centring of white academics or the abundance of work done by racialised scholars *with* white scholars rather than with one another. In 2016 I wrote: '[S]ince inception this "Western academic life" has been a settler-colonial project purposed to structure time so whiteness must perpetually be ahead ... The work of centring our own bodies, experiences and thought was – and still is – a long and dangerous journey'.[12] My

11 Personal communication with M.A. Logan (Lele/Trinidad) over 24 years.
12 N. Chambers, unpublished letter to the editorial board of the now defunct, formerly independent e-journal *Decolonization: Indigeneity, Education and Society*, 25 April 2016.

personal academic journey starts by remembering I was born and first housed in a space shadowed by a Canadian mine. To understand the impact of mining in Jamaica, I *also* turn my attention to the other side of the shadow – to the lands and indigenous peoples who exist before and after ALCAN's smelter and power line. Turning the focus on to Kitimat and Kirkvine, I have committed to trying to find ways to remove the concrete of colonial timelines that have been told as separate 'marches of progress' bequeathed to the 'wilderness', 'savages' and 'sub-humans' as well as humans and/or identities categorised as 'extinct'.

First, the courage to start was guided by the familiarity of resource-extraction without value-added means of production and the sense of hinterland. What I learned about periphery and centres within the Caribbean, I could now apply to processes that seemed to be happening in British Colombia.[13] Somehow putting my findings together brought me to this rocky place of straddling two connected worlds as if I were both an optometrist and the client sitting in the dark squinting and attempting to focus my vision on some sort of 'flim' shown while fumbling with lenses marked 'colonial', 'post-colonial' and 'neo-colonial'.

Second, paying close attention to things that do not fit the meta-narratives of 'civilisation', for example: the red mud lake Jamaicans have lived with my entire life, and which I have flown over many times, gains a different significance if I think about how we do not really use the word 'lake' in our patois. We discuss river water, sea water or holes. Words that imply a natural or neutral phenomenon – 'red', 'mud', 'lake' – hide the violence that is an artificial holding pen created for tailings that seep into our aquifers and in drought times turns to carcinogenic dust drifting through the breathable air.

Lucky for me there are clear coincidences in broad daylight, one of my two favourites being talking to an older Jamaican neighbour whose childhood friend, he recalled, had gone to Kitimat. He mentioned his unique name. I wrote it down. A few days later, back at work in the university and standing in a queue talking, my accent was pronounced. A young blonde woman timidly asked me whether I was Jamaican. I said yes, and she said she was not, but her father was, to which I gave my standard response: 'If you were raised in a Jamaican household anywhere in the world, to me you are'. Welcomed, she gave me her name, which was of course the name my neighbour had given me, that person being her uncle. My other favourite coincidence was a conversation in Vancouver with an Italian-Canadian horse-trainer during a year away from academia in 'by-the-sweat-of-your-brow-you-will-be-known' *wuk* as a hotwalker (work as a stable worker). 'You Jamaican?', he asked. 'Yes', I answered; and he proceeded to tell me that in his long and varied employment record he had run a barber shop in Kitimat where he had drunk good rum

---

13 I am indebted to the late Dr Eric Grass, a Metis instructor on urban aboriginal issues at Langara College (Vancouver). In 2004 he answered my suspicion with a quick, gracious, firm affirmation based on his time as a postgraduate student in conversation with African students about mining in their respective countries.

with Jamaican workers at the smelter. Every time these coincidences happen, I know I am bound into them and required to be serious about how our eyes could possibly 'make four' with Haisla people to stare straight into the face of those who set the table for white supremacy's voracious capitalism in our lives.

The set-up for the take

Multinational arrangements are key drivers of this Kitimat-Jamaica connection, linkages between Canada, Britain (through its Caribbean colonies) and the US by means of the shifting of global power over the course of World War Two. Through war-acquisition rights to resources, these deals for extraction and production had already occurred in the name of 'national defence' long before the Caribbean independence celebrations of the 1960s. By drawing on a range of scholars from various disciplines and historical as well as geographical regions, it is possible to begin to understand the interlocking framework of power that allows the unchecked extraction of water and soil for ALCAN's endeavours in Canada and Jamaica.

In 1967 Jamaican economist Norman Girvan noted: 'Within each Caribbean territory, as a rule, there is zero internal mobility of bauxite – factors controlled by different companies and a *full international mobility within each company*' (1967, p. 19; emphasis by the author). ALCAN is one such company. Girvan's *Foreign Capital and Underdevelopment in Jamaica* (1971) notes the following:

> Between 1950 and 1965, two important developments relevant to our analysis took place within Aluminium Ltd. On the output side, the company's Canadian subsidiary more than doubled its smelter output from 360,000 to 788,000 tons; and the company also developed a world-wide network of affiliates which brought its wholly or partly owned output up to 1 million tons, 18 percent [sic] of non-communist world output. And on the input side, Jamaica replaced Guyana as the chief supplier of the company's raw material needs, in the form of alumina rather than raw bauxite.

> The decision to build an alumina plant in Jamaica in 1950 was part and parcel of an enormous integrated development scheme which represented the basis of Alcan's [sic] plans for post-war expansion. At the foundation lay the construction, at a cost of Can. $450 million, of a huge complex at Kitimat, British Columbia, embracing hydro-electricity, smelter, city, and port. Jamaica was the locus of bauxite-mining-alumina manufacture section of the project. The alumina plant, known as 'Kirkvine' works partly financed by a loan from Marshall Plan funds.

Attention to the impact of deeply localised pre-operation clearings first seems to appear in the academic realm in 1987. The late George Beckford's compilation of essays were published in that year in the journal of the Institute for Social and Economic Research (now the Sir Arthur Lewis Institute for Social and Economic Studies, University of the West Indies) (Beckford, 1987). Within that home-grown scholarly publication lives critical academic attention to the silent, subtle power or deliberate absence of the state as corporations removed farming communities for access to bauxite reserves – rarely cited. Certainly, there is scholarship on Jamaica as part of the global commodity chain. However, many of those texts replicate the same extractive method around academic knowledge that presents the global reach. For example, a close examination of one of the most recent pieces of scholarship, Mimi Sheller's *Aluminium Dreams* (2014), a documentation of the global network of mining companies which penetrated the Caribbean, reveals two key omissions. First, in Sheller's book, the word 'Jamaica' appears multiple times, yet Jamaican scholarship goes either unmentioned in the bibliography or appears as nothing more than minor endnotes in her work: Norman Girvan (1971) and Beckford's afore-mentioned compilation of essays by various scholars, all of which predate Sheller's text. Second, the British and Canadian settler-colonial histories are missing. These allowed a state-corporate partnership facilitating the dispossession of shoreline vital to Haisla subsistence for the creation of the port, smelter and power lines. In other words, attention is not paid to a key issue in the social and cultural impact of mining and manufacture on local peoples from distinct areas connected by the path carved out by a single company. That company controlled the transportation of ore extracted from one location and created a value-added product in another location.

My work – by contrast – strives to shine a light on locations; to encourage letting go of linear macro space-time frameworks which sometimes reduce our ability to see precisely how distinct communities are assaulted in networked isolation and appear to be mute in the retelling of globally scaled tales. From the shadow of the mine I am inspired by black feminist geographer Ruthie Gilmore, who states:

> What I wish to do is disarticulate common sense couplings of sites and struggles and disrupt assumptions such as the idea that politics happens in the milieu of the state or that value comes from wage-controlled work places ... My goal is to emulate the work of engaged scholars who try ... something other than perpetual recapitulation of ongoing place-based struggles that are displaced but never resolved (Gilmore, 2002, p. 15).

In line with that wish, it is possible to trip up what is conceived of as 'territory of the state' by returning to Kari Polanyi Levitt's work (2002), which is only a small part of a lifetime of solidarity with Caribbean economists and social scientists of the New World Group who were instrumental in founding the consortium of Institutes for Social and Economic Research (UWI) (cf. Girvan, 1967). This is my contribution: to support new ways of thinking through the impact of multinational entities within and through the Canadian state which connects these two far-apart locations. Gilmore inspires me to recognise the importance of attention to the devaluation and dispossession through settler-colonialism *that precedes the wage-controlled work places* controlled by ALCAN in Kitimat, tied to the ease with which dispossession of land occurred in the afterlife of slavery in Jamaica.[14]

British Columbia-based academic Matthew Evenden's explanation, using the pattern found in commodity chains, works well, as long as one is willing to keep the impact discussion in the realm of 'dynamics of warfare and environmental change over distance', and to speak of 'mobilized distant peoples, places, and environments' (2011, pp. 70–1) without paying close attention to how factors such as race, rural location and colonialism allow scholarship to remain distant. This distancing leads to crucial details about people becoming footnoted material.

On the other hand, in both concert and contrast with Evenden, Tina Loo's work extends Levitt's work in a sense, by tracing relationships of power in studies of forced relocations in Canada. This grants a Canadian scholarly entry point into a more direct link between northern British Columbia and Jamaica when she points out:

> [G]iven the international dominance of the nation's mining companies, historians might look at the emergence of Canada as an extractive, imperial 'metropolis,' tracing how its entrepreneurs and capital came to exploit the human and material resources of other 'hinterlands' with the same voracious appetite and devastating effects on local peoples and places as were visited upon it in earlier centuries (2014, pp. 621).

I also draw affirmation from Loo's earlier work on Africville, where she states: 'The process … reveals how contingent and subtle state power could be … In addition to giving us insights into its dynamics, these negotiations allow us to understand something of the amplitude, tone, and timbre of that power – of how it was experienced by those who exercised it and those over whom it was exercised' (2010, p. 627).

Evenden and Loo are just two possible examples of Canadian academic points of entry to unpack generally understood ideas of simple citizenship in reference to mining corporations: definitions of peoples without reference to the abysmal gap between indigenous peoples and white settlers or racialised migrants who may, on the surface, be listed together under 'local citizenry', although the latter are dealt discriminatory treatment. Finally, as another example, studies of the operation of mining always require an expanded definition of 'hinterlands', that is, located within and outside Canada concurrently – in the past and present.

---

14 I seek a new *Das Kapital* by black and indigenous authors working on systems and resistance to settler-colonial capitalism and its concomitant 'development' trajectory.

Beyond land acknowledgements that recapitulate but do not resolve injustice

How can one apply the term 'post-colonial' to racialised people who never agreed to colonisation and have not died? What does it mean to understand how minerals, such as bauxite ore, black and Asian people had been removed and shipped to cement displacement of indigenous folks in the 1500s Caribbean? How can one trace the linkages from that southern series of displacements to northern displacements in Canada in both countries through the profit-for-war and war-for-profit in the 1940s and 1950s? Why have we not seen more documentation about what triggered more long migratory journeys for many Jamaicans who had no other prospects once land struggled-for had been appropriated? What are the consequences of those processes before independence and as forms of neo-colonialism after it? How do we clarify the difference between European colonisation and modern-day Caribbean immigration: is it or can it be different in significant elements? I take heart when reading indigenous scholar Jodi Byrd (Chickasaw):

> What of Caribbean nations shaped both by settler plantation societies and the decolonial struggles waged by the descendants of African slaves? How could one begin to address the complexities of the historical collisions between colonisation of indigenous peoples within the Caribbean and the legacies of slavery [and freed Africans and Asian indentureship]? (2002, p. 7).

In hindsight, there are silences in indigenous studies as well as Caribbean studies which although not equal, are critical to approach with a sharp awareness. These studies are written by people (and here I can say 'us') refusing to remain subjects of colonial or historical studies. I speak of those silences (and there are many kinds) without blame, recognising the sheer survival, stamina and strategy required for ethical authorship, but also the corrosive effect of white supremacy on academic endeavours in multiple forms. I look at where areas of postcolonial studies have met (or not) and grappled with (or not) areas of indigenous studies in my quest to re-frame Kitimat and Kirkvine. The critical distinction is that I choose to focus on indigenous studies created by indigenous scholars who are not all dead or published posthumously. Key to this focus is an understanding that the crime called colonisation is not over. Therefore, I must ask different questions of postcolonial readings by valuing the indigenous academics who have spent time critically examining the literary output of the postcolonial Caribbean. The late Banaban/I-Kiribati (Pacific) scholar Teresia Teaiwa said: 'I tried to … draw closer comparisons between the Pacific and the Caribbean in the area of cultural politics, as some glaring discrepancies emerged, most notably when it came to accounting for the enduring power of discourses of indigeneity in the Pacific – something superseded in the Caribbean by discourses of race and class' (Teaiwa, 2006, p. 76).

Modern-day Canada began as a process of confederation in 1868, without the consent of indigenous peoples, while corporate entities continued to build as a result of British Columbia's shift in 1871 from British colony to Dominion of Canada – illegally. The 1950s are the start of multivalent exploitative linkages between Kitimat and Kirkvine, which become two contemporaneous places with markers of indigenous relationship to land and markers of black relationship to labour. Perhaps this connection could be a starting point for revealing deeper truths about celebrated states and corporations?

I started wrestling with this issue in 2001 after a series of mind-opening classes by an indigenous lawyer and instructor who took students, case-by-case, through 113 years of indigenous people's legal battles with settler Canada's policies and courts.[15] Taking those classes in Indigenous studies at the Institute for Indigenous Government and Langara College was life-changing. It explained things that my citizenship test of two hundred questions had failed to cover in terms of the knowledge a 'Canadian' should have. It explained what a 'multicultural' act graph did not make visible since indigeneity was shown as separate from racialised peoples categorised as migrants from 'founding' or 'settler' nation-states. Furthermore, postcolonial studies in academia and anti-racism work in the 1990s and early 2000s in Canada generally lacked consistent and connected attention to indigenous struggles.

In 2011 Byrd named a key problem:

> Often, scholars who try to sustain a conversation between post-colonial studies and indigenous studies end with the assessment that geographic localities that fall within the purview of subaltern and indigenous theories are too disparate, that the histories are, too ... and that postcolonial scholars are too imbricated within settler agendas when they speak from academic centres in the United States, Canada ... or the Caribbean (2011, p. xxiii).

Today, fortified by Clements' *Burning Vision*, I frame my personal demon in academic terms: how does one begin to address collisions outside the indigenous Caribbean in settler-industrial societies such as Canada and the position of the Caribbean racialised arrivant-cum-immigrant who unwittingly, by presence of numbers, forms part of the ongoing colonisation of indigenous nations in Canada? Furthermore, plantation wealth was migrated out of the Caribbean into other parts of the Commonwealth, such as Canada, by settler-colonialism and its attendant racial capitalism. This exploitation developed into the corporate, militarised and civic assault for which reparations are also due to indigenous peoples in those territories. I have coined the term 'settler-industrial' to name the ways in which the industrial age was financed by

---

15 I am indebted to Barbara Buckman for 17 years and counting of unflagging mentorship.

plantation profits and the public funds used to reimburse the white and near-white plantocracy for the loss of slavery.

I find it important to think carefully about that Caribbean pre-independence history as someone who inherits it, not from a position of ruling power or whiteness, although the markers of a white, Western education are inscribed on me like an old skin and difficult to free myself from what often feels like a solitary quest for transformation.[16] The focus of much of our post-independence Caribbean history is quite rightly the struggle to recover from slavery. Beloved academic and performance ancestor R.M. Nettleford's book title *Inward Stretch, Outward Reach* (1993) inspires me as an instruction to understand racialised peoples who also have been unjustly othered – in the case of the Caribbean – and the indigenous inhabitants impacted by the arrival of gold and spice-driven colonialism before their capture was entrenched by the arrival of black people and Asians. Poet and librarian ancestor Audre Lorde makes it plain: 'I am not free while any woman is unfree, even when her shackles are very different from my own. And I am not free as long as one person of Color remains chained. Nor is any one of you'.[17]

I strive, both through reading outside of my identities and being anchored by deeply personal reasons, to revolt against the anti-indigenous Canadian settler-colonial agenda in which I am imbedded. Ground, the heart of Jamaican agriculture, was transformed by extraction after the discovery of bauxite. I closely followed the red dirt of my memory torn out of 'that island's mine',[18] washed in acid, shipped and electrocuted to form aluminium in unceded Haisla territory. However, the machinations that facilitated these changes are not part of everyday black people's discussion of the struggles within societies riddled by the legacies of invasion and slavery. These complex decolonisation discussions – beyond silence or quick platitudes – need to intensify now.

Resisting terra nullification when black diasporas celebrate Black History Month

In the academic arena, I can see a productive encounter between Caribbean studies and indigenous studies, mindful of Tiffany King's interrogation of the academic structure of settler-colonial studies that spread from antipode to 'centre'. White settler-colonial studies, she states, 'focus on terra nullius

---

16 Critical to this quest are the works of and conversations with Luz Guerra, Claude Brown, Karina Vernon, Tyler Bellis, Cease Wyss, Esther, Marcus Briggs Cloud, Barbara Binns, Larissa Lai, Rain Prud'homme-Cranford, Ivan Drury, Chimwemwe Undi as well as the people I have cited here. All errors and omissions on this unfolding journey remain mine.

17 A. Lorde, 'The uses of anger: women responding to racism', keynote presentation at the National Women's Studies Association Conference, Storrs, Connecticut, June 1981, https://academicworks.cuny.edu/cgi/viewcontent.cgi?article=1654&context=wsq [accessed 26 Feb. 2019].

18 Shakespeare, *The Tempest*; Byrd (2011), p. 30.

and land disappears the settler's relationship to violence and the intricate and violent processes' (2016, p. 4). I work to upset the logic that comes with only thinking of a settler-*terra nullius* construction, as we understand the clearing done by invasion and by the creation of reserves on the west coast of British Columbia. In the 1800s the Canadian corporation-settler-state coming into formation was in various kinds of fraught relationship with indigenous peoples. Therefore, academic texts which centre the commodity chain and the relationship of colonisers in the process of commodification make actual racialised people living in forms of relationship with the land disappear by retelling the story of corporate-state-arranged business conducted to steal land and labour without mentioning what happened or to whom it happened, then and now.

I need to be clear that it is not ethical for me to conflate land loss by indigenous people living in their traditional territory and – remembering the drummer I met – the land loss of formerly enslaved people in spaces from which indigenous people were cleared away by genocide (although not entirely). That said, these losses are displacements and for me they do collide with each other, although administratively and geographically separated. I would need various maps to be remade to enable these losses to be recognised meaningfully and, as Noxolo et al. state, 'recognition that not only are some spaces, times, places, peoples and relationships apart from this postcolonial interaction … but beyond this, that they might also want to actively refuse some forms of responsible relationships that northern [read: white Western-trained] academics want to imagine' (2011, p. 8).

On the community side, I remember Black History Month in 2014, when I spoke on three occasions in Vancouver, a city which probably has the highest number of international mining-corporation headquarters per square foot in and around the intersection of Burrard Street and Hastings Street in the city centre. I spoke first to an audience of black students, many from Caribbean and African continental bauxite-mining areas of the global South, to speak of the solidarity of decolonial action by the 1974 bauxite levy. Second, I spoke to elders, some of whom came from communities in Jamaica that had been pushed out by land expropriation in the 1950s. Finally, I was an invited speaker at an indigenous-led event filled with people currently dealing with mining and tailings-pond proposals in the lands and natural lakes they call their ancestral home. I kept the unsettling question the same: what could the celebration of Black History Month mean in unceded indigenous territory?[19]

19 Black History Month 2017 opened with the Vancouver chapter of representatives from an international black organisation with the city's mayor and chief of police celebrating the production of the Canada Post stamp image of Mathieu Da Costa (d. after 1619). Mathieu was an African robbed of his name and birth location who survived or sidestepped being acquired, stolen, kidnapped or sold by competing settler-colonial forces in the days of black enslavement in the New World by trading his language skills for work that was integral to European colonisers in what became Canada. The event at city hall occurred two weeks before

In 2017 the illegal celebration of the 150th anniversary of Canada required – no, demanded – that immigrants ignore the structure of colonial incursion that dishonours treaties and the reasons for treaty. As an immigrant scholar I must pay close attention to the realm of academia, a location of knowledge production that actively and consistently works to control time and definitions without challenging settler colonialism. I draw inspiration from the impetus that drives black British academic and community activist Robbie Shilliam in his book *The Black Pacific*. This academic text is anchored in the presence of ancestral/spirit/root work in engagement with, and respect for, the power of the arts and history. Shilliam brings to light South-South anti-colonial connections, calling for '[p]olitical commitment among critical intellectuals (especially those occupying the Western academy) to displace current academic endorsements of privileged narcissism and, instead, to help make more intelligible the deep, global infrastructure of anti-colonial connectivity. To this provocation … colonial science is a science you can use or discard; decolonial science is another science' (2015).

Reading *Burning Vision* has allowed me to pay attention to the framing of the story; and Clements' deployment of chronotopic dramaturgy girds how I imagine my decolonial responsibility to resist the path of 'terra nullification' before inscribing anything on a blank page with the aluminium of the pen or the laptop frame I am using. I work against the ease with which the grain of academia runs, which positions the writer as a surveyor who 'replicates not just the "environment" in some abstract sense but equally the territorial imperatives of a particular political system' (Gilbert and Tompkins, 1996, p. 279). Let the blank page be a warning, to remind me of the risk of an uncritical postcolonial-coloniality in unceded territory; my responsibility to silences in these two places; and, finally, when I ask 'whether the question itself is worth asking or is necessary to answer, whether the question itself is not the first in a series of violations' (Sangari, 2011, p. 8).

I have seen those violations, where the academic questions steeped in settler-colonialism today make an equivalence between discussing the damage as a matter of fact (as if that were enough), and doing something about it. Too many times I have seen 'groundbreaking' intellectual work as a sort of absolution or abdication due to the objective status accorded the academic, whereby the responsibility is simply passed on to the listener. Instead of a race to do something groundbreaking, what I aim to do is to look at the breaking of rocks that were of ritual significance to the Haisla in order to situate the smelter, to process in turn the broken grounds of Jamaica that were ripped out of that island's mine.

---

the multi-decade annual memorial March for Murdered and Missing Aboriginal women, which is an embodied survival song against settler-colonial violence enabled by city and federal police actions of neglect and brutality in unceded and treaty territory.

Slowly coming, coming home

The good news is that this change has already started in the Caribbean, notably in the Antilles with Melanie Newton of Barbados and her article '"The race leapt at Sauteurs"' (2014), as well as Shona Jackson from Guyana and her book *Creole Indigeneity* (2013). We need more conversation in the vein of Jacqui Alexander pondering on the scholarship and activism 'when a regional feminist movement in the Caribbean ... by the 1980s had begun to chart the failures of anticolonial nationalism, implicating capitalism and colonialism in the unequal organization of gender' (2005, p. 9). Respectfully, I ask whether the same can be done for regarding the exclusion of indigenous peoples from our discussions related to race at home (and within Canada)?

In 2017 the Institute for Gender and Development Studies in Trinidad at UWI (St Augustine) received the support, in the form of an organisational grant from the AntipodeFoundation [sic], earnestly to start what I believe will work to supersede the scholarship by non-Caribbean people that still dominates the authorship of early histories of the Caribbean. In this new effort, perhaps we can spend more time listening to past and present stories of indigeneity as it manifested, survived and survives in smaller and equally important places such as Grenada, Saint Vincent, Dominica and most predominantly in the big southern root of the Caribbean – Guyana.

The distance of 5,902 km between Kirkvine and Kitimat is simplest when I am just travelling from A to B, harder when I hunt colonisation in archives and hardest when I commit to revealing the linkages between geographical spaces of sea and mountains. How exactly might communities in Jamaica and British Columbia be linked by the paths of colonial industry? I commit to looking at places that appear as blanked, stripped of texture, stories and peoples in the official records, then beyond to listen for libations for the rocks, people and trees in the living land and human resisters and the utterance of the resilient in the present: still alive, still standing, still holding.

A Jamaican teacher in the audience of the presentation on the 'Slave Ownership Project'[20] organised by the History and Archaeology Department of the UWI (Mona) commented in distress, saying, 'We got the writing of it wrong'. Without hesitation I said, 'No, it was the best we could do at the time'. Perhaps now is the moment to return to the records in the archives and beyond to speak again to the *macomeres*,[21] the village lawyers, the corner preachers, the market women and the reasoners to do the work Professor Augier urges us to do to keep the nation together. I believe it is the work of every one of us who understands something about the wake of these ships of history to decolonise

---

20 'The structure and significance of British Caribbean slave-ownership 1763–1833', Department of History workshop, University of West Indies (Mona), 2 June 2015.
21 A Caribbean term used to reference one's closest female friends, godmothers to children, bridesmaids, and so on.

the relationship between the indigenous Caribbean and those of us trafficked and travelled and migrated (Sharpe, 2016). My chapter is an invitation to join a decolonisation quest to re-navigate history and make room to undo the lie that leaves unexplained our Caribbean relationship to place names and food that began in what my Boriken sistren Luz Guerra calls the 'mothers' story' echoed in the opening poem.[22] This journey is not complete and occasions constantly arise to drive these very questions into the present in which I stand, whether in Jamaica or in British Columbia.[23] I close with Lorna Goodison's encouragement that we:

> .... *take up divining again*
> *and go inna interpretation*
> *and believe the flat truth*
> *left to dry on our tongues*[24]
> *Truth say*
> *Heartease distance*
> *cannot hold in a measure*
> *it say*
> *travel light*
> *you are the treasure*
> *It say even if you born*
> *a Jubilee*
> *and grow with your granny*
> *and eat crackers for your tea*
> *It say*
> *you can get licence*
> *to navigate.*[25]

The first time I stood as an uninvited guest at the edge of Tsee-Motsa (Kitamaat Village), facing the smelter that forms the other side of the shadow of the mine under which I was born, my head was held high, but my eyes were cast low … listening. I will continue my slow research work to do something beyond the structure of academia to obey protocols of higher laws than a tri-council policy-statement certificate on research ethics.[26] May I first – and, I hope, always – return to that memory before uttering even one question.

Dé zié contré menti kaba.

---

22 This was relayed to me in a personal exchange.
23 E.g., when Hurucán (the god of storms) strikes *and* Guyana issues an invitation that the country's vast land mass can serve as 'a gift' to all people from several affected Caribbean nations with no mention of indigenous title or rights to said same lands (http://newsday.co.tt/2017/09/21/guyana-offers-land-for-hurricane-victims [accessed 15 Aug. 2018]).
24 I always hear 'hand-miggle' in conversation with 'History lesson at grandma's knees'.
25 Goodison (1988).
26 See http://www.pre.ethics.gc.ca/eng/index [last accessed 15 Aug. 2018].

Bibliography

Alexander, M. J. (2005) *Pedagogies of Crossing: Meditations on Feminism, Sexual Politics, Memory, and the Sacred* (Durham, NC: Duke University Press).

Allison, D. (1994) *Skin: Talking about Sex, Class and Literature* (Ithaca, NY: Firebrand Books).

Byrd, J.A. (2002) 'Colonialism's cacophony: natives and arrivants at the limits of postcolonial theory' (unpublished doctoral thesis, University of Iowa).

— (2011) *The Transit of Empire: Indigenous Critiques of Colonialism* (Minneapolis, MN: University of Minnesota Press).

Christensen, B. (1995) *Too Good To Be True: Alcan's Kemano Completion Project* (Vancouver: Talonbooks).

Clements, M. (2003) *Burning Vision* (Vancouver: Talonbooks).

Désil, J. (2006) 'History lessons (at grandma's knees) room of one's own', *The Mother and the Virgin*, 29: 75–7.

Evenden, M. (2011) 'Aluminium, commodity chains, and the environmental history of the Second World War', *Environmental History*, 16: 69–93.

Gilbert, H. and J. Tompkins (1996) *Post-Colonial Drama: Theory, Practice, Politics* (London and New York: Routledge).

Gilmore, R. W. (2002) 'Fatal couplings of power and difference: notes on racism and geography', *The Professional Geographer*, 54: 15–24.

Girvan, N. (1967) 'The Caribbean bauxite industry', *Institute of Social and Economic Research, University of the West Indies, Jamaica*, 2 (4).

— (1971) *Foreign Capital and Underdevelopment in Jamaica* (Kingston, Jamaica: Institute of Social and Economic Research).

Goodison, L. (1988) 'Heartease I', in *Collected Poems* (New Beacon Books).

Jackson, S. N. (2013) *Creole Indigeneity: Between Myth and Nation in the Caribbean* (Minneapolis: University of Minnesota Press).

King, T. L. (2016) 'New world grammars: the "unthought" black discourses of conquest', *Theory and Event*, 19.

Levitt, K. (2002) *Silent Surrender: The Multinational Corporation in Canada* (Kingston and Montreal: McGill-Queen's University Press).

Loo, T. (2010) 'Africville and the dynamics of state power in postwar Canada', *Acadiensis*, 39: 23–47.

— (2014) 'Missed connections: Why Canadian environmental history could use more of the world, and vice versa', *Canadian Historical Review*, 95: 621–7.

Lorde, A. (1981) 'The uses of anger: women responding to racism', https://academicworks.cuny.edu/cgi/viewcontent.cgi?article=1654&context=wsq [accessed 26 Feb. 2019].

Miller, K. (2014) *The Cartographer Tries to Map a Way to Zion* (Manchester: Carcanet).

Mohammed, P. (1998) 'Towards indigenous feminist theorizing in the Caribbean', *Feminist Review*, 59: 6–33.

Nettleford, R. M. (1993) *Inward Stretch, Outward Reach: A Voice from the Caribbean* (London: Macmillan Caribbean).

Newton, M. J. (2014) '"The race leapt at Sauteurs": genocide, narrative, and indigenous exile from the Caribbean Archipelago', *Caribbean Quarterly*, 60: 5–28.

Noxolo, P., P. Raghuram and C. Madge (2011) 'Unsettling responsibility: postcolonial interventions', *Transactions of the Institute of British Geographers*, n.s., 37: 418–29.

Powell, J. (2011) *Stewards of the Land: Haisla Ownership and Use of their Traditional Territory, and their Concerns regarding the Northern Gateway Project and Proposed Tanker Traffic in the Douglas Channel and Kitimat Arm*, https://www.canada.ca/en/environmental-assessment-agency.html

Sheller, Mimi. (2014) *Aluminum Dreams: The Making of Light Modernity* (Cambridge, MA: MIT Press).

Sharpe, C. (2016) *In the Wake: On Blackness and Being* (Durham, NC: Duke University Press).

Shilliam, R. (2015) *The Black Pacific: Anti-Colonial Struggles and Oceanic Connections* (London: Bloomsbury).

Teaiwa, T. K. (2006) 'On analogies: rethinking the Pacific in a global context', *The Contemporary Pacific*, 18: 71–87.

7. Organising for the Caribbean

Anne Braithwaite

Recent years have seen several former British colonies that attained independence in Britain's post-war winds of change mark golden jubilees. Those 50th anniversary tailwinds swirled from India and Pakistan, Sri Lanka and Jordan, Israel and Myanmar in the 1990s to Libya and Sudan, Ghana and Malaysia, Cyprus and Nigeria in the early 2000s. The current decade sees several more African and Caribbean countries marking golden jubilees, including Sierra Leone, Kenya, Tanzania, Jamaica, Trinidad and Tobago, Guyana, Barbados and Botswana, to name just a few. I had thus been on the lookout for accessible reviews of the 50-year post-imperial period that explored the complex and unresolved development-deficit questions.

Unfortunately, there is a dearth of public access to the vibrant intellectual discourse about and rigorous analyses of decolonisation, political economy and development studies. Such access is necessary for encouraging research and informing policy thinking. The conference from which this volume has emerged – which bore the same name as this book – was therefore a most welcome opportunity. The focus on the Caribbean is especially salient as the question of decolonisation in the Caribbean demands a much more serious consideration by scholars. Indeed, it is imperative that further discussion takes place between academics and the broader Caribbean population who lived, and continue to live, with the effects of colonisation and decolonisation. This chapter outlines the memories of one post-Windrush migrant who sought to organise for positive change in Guyana, and in the process gained valuable insights into [de]colonisation, Caribbean history and our place in Britain. Here I reflect on how those experiences have shaped my political thinking and the organising lessons learnt along the way.

Seeking to understand

If colonisation is the process by which a central system of power establishes control over indigenous peoples of an area, then dominates and plunders those peoples and the surrounding resources, I was glad that Guyana had gained independence. And of course I would be returning there, in about five years,

---

A. Braithwaite, 'Organising for the Caribbean', in J.D. Webb, R. Westmaas, M. del Pilar Kaladeen and W. Tantam (eds.), *Memory, migration and (de)colonisation in the Caribbean and beyond* (London: University of London Press, 2019), pp. 107–15. License: CC-BY-NC-ND 4.0.

having completed my education and established myself. But this was merely a vague notion on my arrival in the UK in 1972. My curiosity about the politics of decolonisation was aroused through attempts at understanding, from a distance, the intrigues of a newly independent Guyana (1966), the home I had just left, aged 20, full of anticipation for life in London. For the first time I needed to talk about Guyana, not only to family and friends, but to others who knew mostly nothing about it. And what I knew was not that easy to articulate. But what *did* I really know? The major shocks of events in Guyana induced a steep learning curve.

Discussions with UK-resident family and friends, mainly students, eased the rapid adjustment necessary to face the cultural booby traps of London life and the disappointment of my first London winter. It was a real struggle trying to reconcile 'mother-country' myths with the lived realities of striving to carve out a productive adult life. At the heart of my quest was a desire to understand Guyana's position in the world, but mainly my place in it here – and there. My delight in the vibrant Caribbean social scene and the spectacular rise to dominance of the West Indies cricket team was tempered by the subtle assertions of everyday racism and the disturbing developments in Guyana.

Newly independent Guyana was now home to the seat of the Caribbean Community secretariat (CARICOM), formed in 1973. I had worked a wonderful stint with the inaugural Caribbean Festival of Arts (CARIFESTA), which Guyana had successfully hosted in 1972. In the wake of the US 1960s civil rights and Black Power era, I shared the abundant optimism of most African-Guyanese, led by Forbes Burnham's ruling People's National Congress (the PNC), which embraced the current Black Power slogans. Most Indian-Guyanese, under Cheddi Jagan's ousted People's Progressive Party (PPP), had been sidelined along with Burnham's 1964 coalition partner, the United Force. They had lost the battle for power, thoroughly vanquished in the ethnic violence and notorious electoral violations which I had experienced as a child in 1960s Guyana.

The Burnham-led administration had now ostensibly embarked on concerted efforts aimed at the decolonisation and restructuring of Guyana's economy, while taking steps to attract Guyanese and people of African descent to (re)settle in Guyana. The administration saw this repopulation effort as having dual benefits: stemming Guyana's crippling emigration tide while also fostering new potential votes, thereby challenging what was perceived as the ethnic disadvantage of African-Guyanese. These matters were usually thoroughly discussed at the almost exclusively African-Guyanese social gatherings that I frequented.

And I generally supported these views. I grew up in Victoria, Guyana's iconic first post-emancipation African village – named after Queen Victoria. Here, African-Guyanese had lived harmoniously with Indian-Guyanese villagers until the Indians were driven out by the US- and UK-sponsored regime-change race terror that fuelled the early civil violence in the early 1960s. I saw myself and Guyana's other 'races' as I had been taught to – through colonial eyes, with all the manipulative racism and self-hatred that entails. Although a product of Guyana's elite Bishops' High School for girls, and having mostly accepted the race, class and colour status quo, fortunately I was not such a good student. My lived experience of my formative years in Victoria had sewn little seeds of dissent from this order.

When in London in 1973 I heard that Guyana's High Commission was recruiting for part-time evening office work and jumped at the chance to meet other Bishops' and Queen's College high school alumni. This would allow great opportunities to catch up on news and gossip without the intrusion of loud party music – and to be paid. And there was a lot of partying – mostly at house parties and the Earls Court West Indian Students' Centre, which were responsible for many romantic encounters, including my first in London.

In fact, our part-time office work at Guyana's High Commission was rigging Guyana's 1973 election – although I was amazingly slow to realise this at the time. Many questions bothered me. How did these black-power projects reconcile with the meaning of Guyana's motto: 'One People, One Nation, One Destiny'? In what context were the widely documented, covert 1960s US and UK interventions in Guyana to be seen?[1] And why was Guyana's notorious election-rigging continuing and, indeed, becoming worse (1980, 1985 and the 1978 referendum)? What difference did Guyana becoming a 'co-operative republic' in 1970 make? For that matter, what difference did it make when Forbes Burnham's ruling party declared itself a socialist party and paramount to the state?

Guyana's hosting of the 1972 Foreign Ministers Non-Aligned Conference, the first of its kind to be held in Guyana, gave Burnham the opportunity to address the evils of imperialism and actively to support African liberation struggles – which I supported. These, however, served to reinforce the Burnham regime's progressive mask abroad, while it was ruling as a brutal dictatorship at home. If neo-colonialism uses capitalism, globalisation and cultural imperialism to influence a developing country, then the Burnham regime's collusion with capital epitomised neo-colonialism. This was manifest in London when, in a depressed 1970s' sugar market, sugar giant Booker – nationalised by the Burnham regime – was able to herald increased shareholder dividends as a result of Guyana's compensation and marketing payments.

Guyana was becoming subject to increasingly acute economic hardship. Burnham's PNC government, as part of an IMF bailout deal, was forced to implement severe cuts in government expenditure and the removal of subsidies on food items. There were severe shortages of essential food items such as flour, cooking oil and split-peas. Many Guyanese living abroad began sending

---

1   These interventions had been going on since 1945.

essential foodstuff items, to help relieve the suffering of their relatives in Guyana. Working people were the hardest hit, with those least able to cope bearing the brunt of its floundering economy and politically repressive woes and blows. Then came the Jonestown horror in 1978. Jonestown was a US-based religious-type cult which had relocated to a large, remote area of land in Guyana. Led by Jim Jones – a white self-styled reincarnation of figures such as Christ and Buddha – this 'peoples temple' settlement was secretly gifted by Guyana's PNC government in exchange for political support, for example, by participating in government marches. Jonestown – like Guyana's more urban and thuggish House of Israel sect, which also supported the government – operated outside the scope of most of Guyana's laws. When US congressman Leo Ryan arrived with a delegation to investigate US citizens' complaints, they were attacked as they boarded an aircraft to leave Jonestown. Ryan and five others were killed. This precipitated the mass murder/suicide, in which nearly a thousand people died – mostly African-Americans – instantly thrusting Guyana to international notoriety. The Guyana government at the time dismissed it as an 'American problem'.

This event was pivotal in focusing and propelling my fledgling activism. With each new state-sponsored outrage against the Guyanese populace, I became anxious. The Working People's Alliance (WPA) formed in 1974, exposed Guyana's neo-colonial absurdities, manipulations and class contradictions. And when renowned Guyanese historian, Walter Rodney, joined and co-led the WPA on his return in 1974, he used his exceptional ability to analyse and synthesise centuries of history to illuminate Guyana's issues of the day. The WPA's organising and education created a serious threat to Guyana's dictatorship. Their teaching explained the submerged links between imperialism, slavery, indenture and neo-colonialism, and thereby uncovered the nature of Guyana's tragic Indian/African conflicts. I had found a political home. Following a spell with the Committee Against Repression in Guyana, I became a founding member of the WPA Support Group (WPASG) UK after the WPA became a political party in 1979. I was also a founding member of the Justice for Walter Rodney campaign following Rodney's assassination in 1980; and of the Campaign Against Waste Dumping in Guyana. Exposure to Rodney's and the WPA's progressive ideas and the organising work were transformative in my political development.

Education, reparation, self-emancipation

Although organising principles for the Caribbean, as elsewhere, are universal, I see the fundamentals of organising for positive change in the Caribbean as rooted in education, reparations and self-emancipation, wherever those involved might reside. The value of education – particularly about one's own history – for understanding why, and how, there has been such widespread ignorance about empire, colonisation, resistance and decolonisation cannot be overstated. The critical need to change the narratives that we have been taught is predicated on being able to understand and articulate – particularly for non-academics – why powerful neo-colonial interests remain deeply invested in perpetuating existing, incomplete and distorted historic narratives. In tandem with this, new forms of extraction and plunder of human and economic resources are evolved. Working with the WPASG (UK), I began to understand the power dynamics at play among the individuals, groups, governments and institutions in Guyana, here in the UK and within the geo-political and economic webs that drive those relationships. Reading late 20th-century Foreign and Commonwealth Office records at the National Archives in Kew, I also began to recognise the importance of effective, methodical and reliable information systems in colonial and neo-colonial control. But whose truth do they tell?

My political and cultural encounters for the first time with other UK-based workers and students from all over the world – not to mention the many artists, politicians, non-governmental organisation (NGO) workers, activists and scholars – was invaluable in helping to fill the huge gaps in my knowledge of other peoples. These interactions, particularly with British-born children of the Windrush generation, brought home to me the importance of looking at the global picture, of taking the long view. Finally, I began to understand the deep significance of knowledge about pre-15th-century Africa and the pivotal nature of Haiti in the machinations of imperialism, decolonisation and reparations.

A 21st-century, pan-African perspective is imperative for revealing those hidden histories, particularly of Africans, that pervade the grossly distorted narratives expounded for centuries to serve imperialism. Knowing our history enables better contextualisation of current issues such as the Windrush scandal, Brexit, the immigration crises and the CARICOM position on reparations, while devising better solutions. We must recognise, protect and build on what has been done before. To remain effective, organisations must change: adapt processes, but retain values and be strategic to achieve their goals. Today's generation could learn from earlier generations about conflict resolution, care for the environment, and creating new ways to meet the challenges of developing their full potential. Organising needs ancestral wisdom to be vigilant and alert to attempts to thwart, frustrate or destroy activities that challenge or disrupt the established order. Meeting CIA whistle-blower Philip Agee was an eye-opener to the destruction of the gains secured by workers' struggles to improve their lives. Agee was a CIA operative (case officer) between 1957 and 1968. His 1975 book *Inside the Company: CIA Diary* exposed the involvement of the CIA in undermining and overthrowing legitimate progressive governments around the world, while at the same time supporting murderous dictatorships. This is particularly relevant to Guyana because the CIA also intervened in order to undermine and split the progressive anti-colonial movement of the early 1950s. One of the main techniques used was the promotion of racial division and violence. Guyana has never recovered from this intervention, and now more than 50 years later, racial animosity is still strong. And neither of the two major parties which dominate is securing Guyana's long-term future.

Self-emancipation means that workers, constituents and social movements must push power holders, power brokers and politicians to deliver on their promises. As Frederick Douglass observed in 1857:

> Power concedes nothing without a demand. It never did and it never will. Find out just what any people will submit to, and you have found out the exact amount of injustice and wrong which will be imposed upon them; and these will continue until they are resisted with either words or blows, or with both. The limits of tyrants are prescribed by the endurance of those whom they oppress.[2]

Douglass makes it clear: organising works best by doing. And a good place to start is with the burning issues that are of concern here and now. What can I do to make my world better? This was our ethos when we established the Campaign Against Waste Dumping in Guyana. This successful campaign helped to abort the Guyana government's decision to import and store toxic waste from the US in 1988.

We must work with others to channel our anger into positive outcomes. Struggles that appear to be ineffective, unsuccessful or even failures still help to change existing conditions, whatever official spin is applied and irrespective of whether or not power concedes the impact of those struggles. Remember that whatever is 'given' can be taken away; no struggle, no progress – and struggle involves sacrifice. Whether as an artist, administrator or athlete, child, cleric or carer, educator or engineer, layabout, lawyer or linguist, scholar or scientist, parent, police or politician, artisan or activist, bartender or boss: we *all* play a role in shaping our world and all can be included in organising. We all – actively or passively – contribute as part of the problem, part of the solution or sometimes both by our own ignorance, contradictions or naivety. Although Guyana's state/PNC violence of the 1970s and 1980s assassinated young Walter Rodney and crushed the WPA as a mass party, the WPA's work remains transformative in abating Guyana's ethnic traumas. If only working people knew their power. We are limited only by our imagination.

The effects of rising income inequality and the polarisation of societies pose risks beyond national economies to global migration and environmental consequences. Economists' cult of growth, consumer fetishism and large-scale privatisation, monetisation, industrialisation of goods and services all have their considerable and seductive attractions, particularly to those whose primary interest is money-making. Such calculations, however, seldom attempt to value

---

2   Extract from a speech entitled 'West India Emancipation' given at Canandaigua, New York, on 3 Aug. 1857 to mark the 23rd anniversary of the event.

the many social and environmental costs and benefits. These are excluded from their financial calculations – or only included in very selective and superficial ways. By the time the long-term consequences become apparent, those responsible for the decisions and the major beneficiaries are long gone – or have morphed into new projects and entities. Britain's utilities, prison, health and social care, education, criminal-justice services and financial markets attest to this. Gold rush 'investors' have left Guyana polluted. In 1995 at Omai mines, owned by a Canadian and an American company, there was a horrific accident in which about three million cubic metres of cyanide-tainted waste, that was being stored in a reservoir, burst its banks and flowed into the Essiquibo river. The danger was immediate to the local indigenous people and others who use the river for fishing and drinking-water.

Mercury pollution is also a problem, as it is barely monitored, and there is little regulation of the thousands of small-scale gold-miners who use and carelessly dispose of mercury in the local rivers. Such inadequate protection, management and redress systems do not bode well for Guyana's much vaunted impending oil boom.

Great people – even those we love – make wrong calls and do bad things (and bad people and people we dislike make correct calls and do good things). Do not go with something that matters just because of who says or does it if it does not make sense to you. If someone cannot explain something in clear, plain language that a bright young person can understand, it is because they themselves do not quite understand it. Idolise no one. The personal is the political, hence we also need to challenge colleagues' wrongdoing and bad behaviour and hold each other to account, privately with colleagues first, then within groups, in a kind and constructive way and in a spirit of love. It is a very important part of political work that to some extent we (community groups, colleagues and family) see ourselves as accountable to and responsible for each other. To remain silent about blatant wrongdoing by holders of public office, or those who live and work among us in our cultural, political, professional, social and even familial domains, tacitly endorses that behaviour. Once people become habituated to all sorts of unacceptable practices they go to sleep while terrible things are done. The repugnant is normalised and becomes the status quo.

To survive and thrive, carrying generations of trauma, we need to repair ourselves. That is why reparations must start with the self. Most of us – British and Caribbean people – have been brainwashed by imperial doctrines and, unwittingly or otherwise, become co-opted into the neo-colonial ethos. Britain's reparations must address the historic terror and damage of human trafficking and exploitation; the British government must issue an apology and seek to make restitution. Whatever the challenges, there is always something that can be done; we must keep going. Many Caribbean people now live the life our ancestors dreamt of; they would see in us their dream come true. We know that there is still much further to go, but we must recognise how far we have come. Imagine what could be achieved if only working people knew their power. We must address the global, sustained and macro-economic forces that impact business, economy, society, cultures and personal lives – to reinvent today. The use of 'nudge science' – relatively subtle, inexpensive techniques used to change people's behaviours – could be a useful tool, for example. Major socioeconomic, demographic and technological shifts occurring across the globe will have a sustained, transformative impact on the world and humanity in the decades ahead. In the face of rapid urbanisation, changing demographics and accelerated innovation a better world is possible. We must remain hopeful.

Those with discernible migrant heritage are so often told that empire and enslavement were a long time ago and that they should move on. Yet any probe beyond the surface divulges the extent to which we *all* continue to live the legacy of empire, enslavement and colonisation.[3] Forms of colonisation have evolved; however, robust structures that maintain and reinforce exploitation of the many by the few remain. The continuing role played by white supremacy and racism also remains manifest in 21st-century hyper-globalisation. The rich elite ('the one per cent') manage networks of control which include major mass-media conglomerates. Many states have been captured and governments so influenced by them that the financing of elections subordinates the civil voice and democracy is deformed. Both Caribbean and British communities continue to be prey to these vagaries.

Some folks yearn for the past: bring back empire, bring back the British, bring back the good old days. The legacy of empire remains palpable in all our lives, quite flagrant in Guyana's abysmal oil-boom negotiations: corporations make a killing and the local elite live large at poor taxpayers' expense. The plight of Guyana's working people is that the remnants of an elite manoeuvred into power in the 1960s to 1980s by the UK and USA continue to serve the interests of mostly western capital. In 2015 the Guyana government gave themselves salary increases of 50 per cent on their election, on top of the generous allowances and benefits (including medical treatment abroad) at the taxpayers' expense. It is as if they had simply swapped places with the former colonial settlers. Even Guyana's immigration practices of the 1970s and 1980s are repeated with Haitians, Cubans and Venezuelans today. Indian-African conflict to this day hinders Guyana's development. Thirty-five years of campaigning finally won, under Guyana's PPP government, an independent commission of inquiry into Walter Rodney's death. The commission, comprising three respected Caribbean Jurists: Sir Richard Cheltenham, KA, QC (chairman); Mr. Seenath Jairam, SC; and Mrs. Jacqueline Samuels-Browne, QC, started taking evidence in April 2014. The current APNU-AFC government, however, immediately and abruptly halted the commission's work after its election in 2015. At the

---

3 See, for instance, the research project 'Legacies of British Slave-Ownership', based at University College London.

time the commissioners requested a further two weeks to complete the inquiry, but the government refused to grant it.

Some British media, NGOs and individuals spoke out against Guyana's colonial and neo-colonial plight: Granada Television's 'World in Action' programmes of 1968 ('The trail of the vanishing voter', broadcast 11 December 1968 and 'The making of a prime minister', broadcast 6 January 1969) clearly illustrated the vote-rigging that took place with overseas voters. Individuals, such as the late Lord Avebury, played a leading role in exposing the fraudulent elections that the PNC used to keep itself in power. He led an international team of observers to the 1980 elections. Their final report stated that 'we were obliged to conclude, on the basis of abundant and clear evidence, that the election was rigged massively and flagrantly'.[4] But British economic gain prevailed. Britain colluded in or acquiesced to overt and covert US actions to ensure that the right people won power in Guyana and elsewhere. Educational institutions in both British and Guyanese establishments are yet to decolonise their curricula. The Brexit strategy in trade, aid and culture now re-ignites neo-colonialism to court the Commonwealth. Nearly half a century later I am still here in London, living the 21st-century colonial legacy and working towards decolonisation. I have a reason and a right to be here – and there is work to be done.

---

4   UK Constitutional Law available at: https://ukconstitutionallaw.org/2014/07/29/derek-obrien-comment-on-the-caribbean-commonwealth-caribbean-elections/

8. The consular Caribbean: consuls as agents of colonialism and decolonisation in the revolutionary Caribbean (1795–1848)

Simeon Simeonov

In the last decades of the 18th and first decades of the 19th century an official who had previously remained all but unknown in the Caribbean made a forceful and lasting appearance in the region (de Goey, 2014; Ulbert and Prijac, 2010; Dickie, 2008; Kennedy, 1990; Simpson and Weiner, 1989; Fernández, 1971). The consul, a public official residing in a foreign country and representing the interests of his nation's mercantile community, had become a main feature of European socioeconomic life since at least the 12th century, yet he had remained conspicuously absent from the Americas (de Goey, 2014, pp. 1–32).[1] In the age of mercantilism, when trade between the European colonies in the Americas bore the stigma of illegality, foreign consuls seemed unnecessary for American colonial development. Moreover, because consuls were often foreign nationals, European states expelled them from their colonies to increase colonial security.[2] Therefore, at the dawn of the so-called age of revolutions (1776–1848), British, French, Dutch and Spanish consuls crowded the important sea ports in Europe and the Mediterranean, but they were nowhere to be seen in the Americas (de Goey, 2014, pp. 1–17; Hobsbawm, 1996, pp. 1–7).

The emergence of Caribbean consulates during ths period would play a significant role in the transformations that shattered the old colonial order in the age of revolutions. Only recently have scholars begun to suggest that examining the history of Atlantic revolutions through the lens of Caribbean consular establishments can provide a unique opportunity for exploring the transnational and extra-territorial origins of Atlantic revolutionary thought and action (de Goey, 2014, ch. 4; Rugemer, 2008, pp. 180–221; Horne, 2012). Because Caribbean consulates were so crucial to the development

---

1 The masculine gender is used when describing early 19th-century consular officials to emphasise that this group comprised exclusively (mostly upper-class, white) men.
2 On the effects of mercantilism in the Americas, see Fisher, 1997, esp. pp. 134–216.

S. Simeonov, 'The consular Caribbean: consuls as agents of colonialism and decolonisation in the revolutionary Caribbean (1795–1848)', in J.D. Webb, R. Westmaas, M. del Pilar Kaladeen and W. Tantam (eds.), *Memory, migration and (de)colonisation in the Caribbean and beyond* (London: University of London Press, 2019), pp. 117–32. License: CC-BY-NC-ND 4.0.

and sustainment of imperial, trans-imperial, and transnational networks of information and commerce, their study can inform a more integrated approach to the age of revolutions that mitigates the nationalist biases entailed by an exclusive emphasis on particular colonial empires. As information brokers interlinking colonial spaces, consuls shed invaluable light on the interplay between such important processes as colonisation and decolonisation, nation-building and empire-making – processes that stood at the very heart of what Atlantic revolution was about. As state agents promoting national commercial interests and disseminating scarce – often invaluable and secret – information about foreign places, peoples and empires, studying consuls provides an opportunity for examining how colonial practices of control and surveillance intersected with revolutionary ideas about citizenship and national sovereignty.

Consulship made its first forceful impact on American politics following the US-French Treaty of Amity and Commerce (1778), which provided for the establishment of bilateral, reciprocal consular relations between the contracting parties. With the revolutionary war still raging, US state officials realised that consulates could be highly advantageous both diplomatically, in securing US independence, and economically, for the development of national commerce. Politicians such as John Adams, John Jay and Thomas Jefferson familiarised themselves with European consular systems and informed Congress about the importance of consular institutions in Europe, paving the way for the creation of the US consular service.[3] Over the following decade, leading US officials emphasised the importance of consuls as a major institution of the federal government and enshrined it in the US constitution.[4] As a result of these revolutionary developments, the United States became the first country in the western hemisphere to establish consular relations. In the 1780s and 1790s the first European consulates in the western hemisphere appeared in such important maritime hubs as Philadelphia, New York, Boston, Norfolk, Charleston and Baltimore. Simultaneously, US consuls opened their establishments on both sides of the Atlantic, gradually gaining importance as key players in transatlantic affairs. For example, consuls featured prominently in the first treaties between the United States and European nations, including the US–French Consular Convention (1788), the Jay Treaty (1794) and the Treaty of San Lorenzo (1795) (Kennedy, 1990, ch. 1–3). In all these agreements,

---

3   E.g., Thomas Jefferson, 'Proclamation Concerning Consuls', *Virginia Gazette*, 8 Jan. 1780; C. W. F. Dumas to John Adams, 25 Feb. 1785, in: Massachusetts Historical Society, Adams Papers <http://www.masshist.org/publications/adams-papers/index.php/view/ADMS-06-16-02-0313> [accessed 2 April 2019].

4   The constitution of the United States, article II, section 2: '[The President] . . . shall appoint Ambassadors, other public Ministers and Consuls, Judges of the supreme Court, and all other Officers of the United States'; article III, section 2: 'The judicial Power shall extend . . . to all cases affecting Ambassadors, other public Ministers and Consuls . . . in all cases affecting Ambassadors, other public Ministers and Consuls, and those in which a State shall be Party, the supreme Court shall have original Jurisdiction.'

consulates became an important attribute of US national sovereignty, yet the prolonged and highly divisive debates around them also testify to the fact that US leaders remained apprehensive about the potential of consulates to confer non-reciprocal commercial advantages, or even to act as secret agencies of foreign colonisation.[5]

Indeed, the greatest clashes over the conduct of consular affairs in the late 18th century revolved around the application of the principle of reciprocity to the practice of establishing consulates in two particular regions: the North American Gulf Coast and the Caribbean Basin. In 1795 the Treaty of San Lorenzo, remembered for settling boundary disputes between the US and Spain in North America and opening the Mississippi to free trade between the Spanish colonies and the American republic, enshrined the principle of reciprocal consular relations and paved the way for a new age in Atlantic political history.[6] One of the treaty's most significant consequences was that US consular appointees and officials began to use the principle of reciprocity and push for the recognition of US consulates in the Spanish Caribbean, which Spanish officials held to be exempt from the treaty provisions.

These debates over the limits and meaning of an emergent 'consular Caribbean', a political geography of contested, unauthorised, elusive and entangled (by virtue of treaty-reciprocity) consulates, left an important, indelible imprint on the birth of the modern Caribbean and its complex history of colonialism and decolonisation. This chapter argues that the emergence of Caribbean consulates in the period between 1795 and 1848 transformed the history of the western hemisphere and the Atlantic world in four important ways: (1) consulates placed the Caribbean at the centre of Atlantic debates about the meaning of colonial rule; (2) they fostered greater opportunities for inter-colonial trade and conflict; (3) as quintessentially European institutions, the consular establishments that proliferated throughout the Caribbean region sparked new questions about the meaning of colonial governance; and (4) finally, they fostered an ambiguous transition between colonial rule and decolonisation. When taken together, these four propositions suggest the crucial, complex and historically contingent role that consular establishments played in the age of revolutions.

First, between 1795 and 1815 consulates placed the Caribbean at the centre of international debates about the limits of colonial rule and the meaning of national sovereignty.[7] As state officials claiming jurisdiction over foreign

---

5 On the divergent issues and debates surrounding consulship, see 'Instructions to Benjamin Franklin in re Consuls, [2 January] 1783'; and Madison (1969 [1783]), pp. 5 and 15–7.

6 Treaty between the United States and His Catholic Majesty, 27 Nov. 1795, Article XIX.

7 In the years immediately following the Treaty of San Lorenzo, Presidents George Washington and John Adams took advantage of the treaty's reciprocity clause by making the first US consular appointments to the Spanish American colonies, to the towns of Havana, New Orleans and Caracas. What is interesting about these consular appointments is that they all

citizens or subjects, consuls challenged the common assumption entertained by colonial officials across the Caribbean that foreign representatives had no place in their jurisdictions. For the first time in the history of the region, colonial and consular jurisdictions were in open competition, which created new challenges for both colonial and metropolitan authorities. At the root of these contestations of the old colonial regime stood the new republics of France, the United States and, later, Haiti, which expressed a much greater interest in setting up Caribbean consulates than the imperial regimes of Spain and Great Britain. In the late 1790s and early 1800s consuls from these new republican governments proliferated in the Caribbean port cities, pressuring reactionary colonial elites into reactive measures that sought to curtail the reach of consular power (Michelena, 2010).

The aggressive policies of US, French and Saint-Dominguan/Haitian consuls in the Spanish empire, for example, confronted traditional views of the absoluteness of colonial jurisdictions. In the late 1790s a Saint-Dominguan consul by the name of Agustin Paris sought the recognition of local authorities in San Juan (Puerto Rico), sparking intensive exchanges about the threat such consular agents posed to the future of sovereign rule in the Spanish colonies.[8] In nearby Havana, a US consular appointee called Henry Hill championed new models of colonial rule that sought to accommodate the rising power of republican merchants in the revolutionary Caribbean. Like Paris, Hill encountered the complete refusal of local officials to recognise his consular character.[9] Hill's counterpart in Batavian Curaçao, the French consul Tierce Cadet, developed a wide-ranging network of correspondence with French republicans throughout the Caribbean, whose very existence unsettled Spanish colonial governors eager to block the bane of republican consulship and protect national sovereignty.[10] Even though Hill and Tierce Cadet pursued different objectives in different colonial jurisdictions, the fact that both of them claimed jurisdiction over their national citizens made them main targets of Spanish and Batavian colonial policies directed at asserting national sovereignty and

---

featured Caribbean ports. Already at the turn of the 19th century, the Spanish Caribbean was arguably one of the most important, if not the most important, theatres of US foreign policy in the Americas. The appointment of consuls to Havana, New Orleans and Caracas both confirmed and augmented the importance of Spanish Caribbean markets to early US foreign affairs. See Count de Someruelos to Pickering, Havana, 18 Sept. 1799 (Archivo General de Indias [henceforth AGI], Cuba 1660); Someruelos to Mariano Luis de Urquijo, 17 Sept. 1799 (AGI, Estado 2); Manuel de Guevara Vasconcelos to Secretary of State, Caracas, 31 July 1800 (AGI, Estado 67). On the US mercantile ties with the Spanish Caribbean, see Chambers (2015) and Salvucci (2003).

8   Melchor Josef de Foncerrada to Principe de la Paz, 16 July 1797 (AGI, Estado 13).

9   Manuel Gayoso de Lemos to Count de Someruelos, New Orleans, 21 Jan. 1806 (AGI, Cuba 134B).

10   Andrés Boggiero to José Antonio Caballero, Coro, 10 Nov. 1799 (AGI, Estado, 71, 4).

marginalising foreign migrants, particularly those from a republican or, in the case of Cadet, an abolitionist regime.

In the 1790s and 1800s, Spanish officials in Havana, New Orleans and Caracas came to regard US and French consular appointments as a dangerous precedent in colonial history. Spanish authorities were unsure of how to treat these republican officials, pondering whether they were private merchants representing discreet capitalist interests or whether they were public agents championing foreign policies. Were these foreign consuls beneficial to the commercial development of the islands, or were they actually undermining Spanish sovereignty by claiming jurisdiction over foreign subjects? In their voluminous correspondence, Spanish American officials came to regard US and French consuls as spies whose secret mission was to spark widespread discontent among a colonial underclass of slaves and people of colour with the goal of overthrowing colonial government and claiming these islands for a foreign power (Jordaan, 2011).

The harshest response to the consular appointments in the early 1800s came from Havana, where a new captain-general, the supreme civil and military officer on the island, came to power in 1799. Captain-General Salvador de Muro y Salazar, Marquis de Someruelos, immediately instructed the new US consular appointees that the Laws of the Indies – Spain's colonial body of law – did not permit the admission of consuls, agents or any foreign national representatives in the Spanish Indies. Strikingly, US consuls Henry Hill and Vincent Gray continued to exercise their consular jurisdiction despite Someruelos's explicit orders. Someruelos wrote an infuriating letter to consul Hill, arguing that US consuls were violating both US and international law.[11] The Cuban authorities then went on to detain Vincent Gray, creating a precedent of contesting the legal immunity of consular appointees. Disputes between US consuls and Cuban officials continued throughout the first half of the 19th century. In the wake of the Spanish American revolutions European consuls likewise faced an increased risk of criminal prosecution, which put a greater strain on the relations between the Spanish American republics and Europe.

The political transformations wrought by republican consuls in the Caribbean at the turn of the 19th century gradually began to recede in the face of a powerful reactionary backlash. In the 1800s Napoleon's ascendancy to the imperial throne in France and Thomas Jefferson's presidential terms in the United States contained the radical revolutionary impulses unleashed by the initial wave of Caribbean consular establishments. The shifting historical conjuncture was most evident in the US and French moratoria on Haitian consulship, which sought to foreclose the possibility of a radical redrawing of the hemispheric and global political map (Gaffield, 2015, pp. 1–15; Willentz, 2005, pp. 218–53; Matthewson, 2003; Logan, 1941). A similarly

11 Count de Someruelos, 'Introduccion o exordio', not signed or dated, but most probably late Aug. 1805 (AGI, Cuba 1660).

conservative approach to consulship animated the regulation of diplomatic ranks during the Congress of Vienna (1815), which sought to standardise consular establishments and sever their link to the diplomatic world. However, as subsequent contestations by various consular appointees demonstrated, the revolutionary 'opening' of diplomatic consulship left a lasting imprint that transcended the impact of the Congress of Vienna in the everyday practices of Caribbean consulates.[12]

Related, second, to the political and diplomatic aspects of the consular Caribbean is its importance within the history of European colonialism. The emergence of consuls in the Caribbean meant that states and empires now had a new tool at their disposal for conducting foreign policy. In their previous institutional history consuls had accrued myriad responsibilities, from certifying ship papers, providing passports and monitoring commerce to maintaining public relations and spying on foreign officials (de Goey, 2014, introduction). All these functions now became part of the history of the Caribbean and of Caribbean colonialism in particular.

Obviously, the political and diplomatic conflicts over consular affairs had profound implications for the system of Caribbean colonialism. In order to appreciate the impact of these new consulates on the trajectory of colonial rule, we have to comprehend the specific colonial context in which Caribbean consulship emerged. In the late 18th century, Spain introduced a new series of laws, within the framework of the so-called Bourbon reforms, in order to stimulate its colonial trade in the Americas and the wider Atlantic world. Historian John Fisher has described this age as a transitional period for Spanish Caribbean colonialism. Even though the Bourbon reforms opened up Spanish Caribbean ports to free trade, Spain's renewed wars against Britain and France undermined the beneficial operation of these legislative acts in the region. For almost two decades, from 1795 to 1815, constant warfare between these powers jeopardised the intercolonial links within the Caribbean and the transatlantic links between the Caribbean and Spain. The 'free trade' envisioned by the Bourbon reforms came under attack due to constant Caribbean warfare and privateering, giving way to a period of 'neutral trade' carried on ships from non-belligerent nations such as the United States, Sweden, Denmark or the Hanseatic League for the purpose of covering colonial shortages (Fisher, 1997, pp. 160–206). Even though neutral trade risked undermining colonial regulations and the development of colonial agriculture, Spanish-American officials quickly realised that it was absolutely necessary for the sustainment of monocultural, export-based colonial plantations. As Carlos Martinez de Irujo, the Spanish ambassador to the US, revealed in 1797, '[t]he declaration of

---

12 One of the best examples for such contestations is provided by a US consular letter from imperial Brazil. See Condy Raguet to Henry Clay (15 Sept. 15, 1825), in *Despatches from United States Ministers to Brazil*, vol. 4, File Microcopies of Records in the National Archives, no. 121.

war [against Britain] will no doubt expose [our] navigation to many risks and contingencies ... [so] I will take the opportunity to issue, from time to time, a license to an American merchant so that he can bring here a small quantity of provisions on his account'. Irujo's main reason for securing these contracts with US commercial agents was to 'prevent exposing the colony [of Cuba] to scarcity'.[13]

The fact that the Spanish ambassador in Philadelphia envisioned Spanish consuls and US commercial agents as vital to his plan of sustaining the 'pearl' of the Spanish Caribbean speaks to the centrality of consulates in sustaining an agricultural plantation economy in the age of revolution and neutral trade. Irujo's remarks also illustrate the vast scope of the consular Caribbean. In his letters the Spanish ambassador paints a picture in which the highest-ranking Spanish diplomat in the Americas was, in fact, a peripheral agent of the Cuban authorities.[14] As the Spanish-American revolutions intensified in the 1810s, the pre-eminence of Cuba within a Spanish-Caribbean system of governance, stretching from the Spanish consulates in Baltimore and Charleston to the South American littoral, only increased (Murray, 1980). Understanding the 'consular Caribbean' as the intelligence-gathering and policy-making centre of a new transnational economy, specialising in matching the supply and demand for news, foodstuffs, armaments, manufactured and agricultural goods, migrant labourers and African slaves, is crucial to reconsidering and reframing current narratives of colonialism and decolonisation.

It is in regard to Caribbean politics and colonialism that a third feature of the consular Caribbean merits closer discussion: the political geography of consulship. Until the 1820s the consular Caribbean remained a somewhat homogenous geography, largely shaped by US consular establishments, but over the next decades many new actors entered this region as revolutions in Spanish America were steering countries toward national independence. Studying this later stage of the consular Caribbean is important inasmuch as it enables us to understand the role of consulates in shaping, and being shaped by, revolutionary processes taking place at the intersection of Caribbean, Central and South American politics. By adopting a transnational institutional approach that integrates accounts of French, Spanish and British Atlantic revolutions into a single analytical framework, we can understand how the personal or structural changes in consular networks informed the trajectories of insurgency and counter-insurgency in a wider political geography. Such an approach, whose contours can only be suggested here, emphasises trans-imperial movement, miscommunication, the importance of timing and the significance of 'missed opportunities' as crucial factors in Caribbean – as well as

13 Carlos Martínez de Irujo to Baron de Carondelet, Philadelphia, 13 Jan. 1797 (AGI, Cuba, 104).
14 See also Carlos Martínez de Irujo to Baron de Carondelet, New York, 12 Dec. 1796; Philadelphia, 26 Jan. 1797; 29 April 1797 (AGI, Cuba, 104).

Atlantic – political history. In addition, this method provides a new perspective on the problem of Haitian exceptionalism by historicising one of its most lasting and central components: Haiti's exclusion from the consular Caribbean until 1825.

If the Napoleonic wars marked the emergence of the consular Caribbean, their end almost seamlessly merged into another series of world-historical events known as the Spanish American revolutions, which would in turn also play an important role in the changing meanings of consulship. Most historians date the beginning of these revolutions back to the year 1808, when the overthrow of the Spanish king Fernando VII by the Napoleonic armies created a crisis of legitimacy and sovereignty throughout the Spanish empire (Langley, 1996, pp. 166–9). Not surprisingly, Spanish officials came to suspect foreign consuls, particularly from the United States, of plotting to undermine Spanish sovereignty in the Americas. In 1808 the Spanish ambassador to the US exclaimed:

> With what right are [the United States] sending a Consul, if it has been repeated numerous times to them, that they cannot send one to any of our Colonies? If [the US] are treating this Island [of Cuba] as independent, they are committing an offense to the fealty of these Islanders. If they recognize, as they have to, Fernando VII as the King of that Island, it is an insult to not listen to his Representative in these States, who would answer them that their pretension [to send consuls to the Spanish colonies] is inadmissible.[15]

What promoted the US's interest in sending consuls to Cuba was the island's growing importance as a global exporter of sugar (Fraginals, 1978). In the years of the Napoleonic wars, US consuls in Cuba pursued two main objectives: stimulating commerce with this geographically proximate colony and stopping French privateering off Cuba's numerous privateering bays (Ferrer, 2014, pp. 157–204). Secretary of State James Madison came to regard consuls as the most effective means of putting an end to the notorious French assaults on US shipping, and pushed for the expansion of US consulates on the island.[16] In the eyes of Madison and other US officials, consuls could reshape the colonial regimes in the Spanish Caribbean into a sphere of increased US influence by fostering closer economic ties with the United States, establishing transnational networks of maritime regulation and adjudication, and contesting the imperial sovereignty of European metropoles.

The history of the consular Caribbean in the 1810s and 1820s thus took place against the backdrop of Cuba's 'sugar revolution', which had only been possible because two other revolutions – the French and the Haitian – ended the dominance of the world's greatest sugar-producing colony in the 18th century,

---

15 Valentin de Foronda to Captain-General Count de Someruelos, Philadelphia, 3 Nov. 1808 (AGI, Cuba 1710).

16 James Madison to Count de Someruelos, Philadelphia, 19 April 1805 (AGI, Cuba 1660).

Saint-Domingue (Ferrer, 2014). However, just as the Haitian revolutionaries had realised the importance of the United States as the hemisphere's largest weapons-manufacturer and market for colonial produce, so, too, did Cuban officials increasingly fix their eyes on the northern republic as a proximate and large supplier of foodstuffs able to cover the growing agricultural needs of an expansive, slave-importing, plantation economy.

Given these commercial relationships between Cuba, Saint-Domingue and the United States, it is not at all surprising that the first US consuls to Cuba and Saint-Domingue arrived at their destinations almost simultaneously. In 1799, in the middle of the quasi-war between the United States and France – a conflict which itself revolved around the issue of consular diplomacy – the newly appointed US consuls in Havana and Le Cap demonstrated a more assertive foreign policy as they ostensibly desired to legalise the illicit commercial links connecting these Caribbean islands with the northern republic. These US consuls would fulfil the dual purposes of fostering the already significant commercial ties of the early republic to the Caribbean and of undermining the imperial sovereignty of European metropoles (Salvucci, 2003). Nevertheless, while the US consular presence in Cuba continued and expanded throughout the first half of the 19th century, the US consulate in Saint-Domingue remained primarily a temporary policy to pressure France into a rapid conclusion of the quasi-war (Logan, 1941; Childs, 2006).[17]

The brief opening of the US consulate in Saint-Domingue seemed to suggest a radically new trajectory for the consular Caribbean, yet the ascendancy of Thomas Jefferson and Napoleon Bonaparte cut short this momentous window of opportunity. Thus, notwithstanding the short episode of US consulship, Haiti, the largest colonial economy at the end of the 18th century, remained strikingly peripheral to the political geography of Caribbean consulship in the first decades of the 19th century. Although Julia Gaffield has recently argued that Haiti's isolation from the world of Caribbean foreign relations remained more of a wishful thought than a reality, it is important to note that the lack of official consular representatives on the island nevertheless created a serious impediment to Haitian independence (Gaffield, 2015, p. 152). In an 1826 senate debate on the failed US prospect of joining the Pan American Congress, Senator Thomas Hart Benton, from the slaveholding state of Missouri, aptly summarised US foreign policy towards the black republic: 'Our policy towards Hayti ... has been fixed ... for three and thirty years ... [W]e interchange no consuls or ministers. We receive no mulatto consuls, or black ambassadors from her. And why? Because the peace of eleven states will not permit the fruits of a

---

17 M. Childs (2006, pp. 38–45) has described the 1790s and 1800s as a period of isolation in the island's political history, but the chronicle of unauthorised consulship illustrates that this political isolation was more a political desideratum of Havana's captain-general than a historical reality.

successful negro insurrection to be exhibited among them'.[18] Senator Benton skilfully turned the principle of consular reciprocity on its head. This principle had been incorporated in hemispheric relations as enabling the intercourse between equal partners, but Benton turned it into a grotesque rationale for the racist discrimination against the young Caribbean republic (Matthewson, 2003, pp. 1–4).

Benton's words are a cautious reminder to a new school of diplomatic historians who aim to illuminate the past and present conduct of foreign affairs through adopting a broader definition of diplomacy that questions and historicises the implicit assumptions behind the social construction of diplomatic affairs. Indeed, this 'new diplomatic' history has yielded important insights about the record of foreign affairs at the intersection of diplomatic, social, political, transnational and cultural history. However, the contestation of older and more exclusive definitions of diplomacy has at times engendered presentist assumptions about the historical trajectory of diplomatic affairs. The shortcomings of new diplomatic history are particularly evident in the problem of Haitian consulship in the age of revolution. On the one hand, while new diplomatic historians regard sailors, ship captains and foreign travellers as ambassadors of their country, such a view is at odds with 19th-century concepts of diplomacy (Rouleau, 2014, introduction). Indeed, as the history of Caribbean consuls attests, whether one received an accreditation as consul, and whether consuls had diplomatic character, were far from purely definitional or trivial matters (Logan, 1941, pp. 84–117). These questions were indeed among the most hotly contested issues in the age of revolution. It is only by appreciating the importance of consular recognition – rather than dismissing the construct of consulship as the mere paraphernalia of diplomatic affairs – that historians can appreciate the disavowed modernity of the Haitian revolutionary project and its wider repercussions throughout the Atlantic world.[19]

On the other hand, new diplomatic historians have also tended to obscure the crucial distinctions *within* the consular ranks. If one assumes that ambassadors, consuls, commercial agents and foreign merchants – not to mention mariners or travellers – were all diplomatic agents, then asking who

18 T.H. Benton, *Speech by Mr. Benton, of Missouri, Delivered in the Senate of the United States*, 13 March 1826 (Washington, DC: Columbian Star Office, 1826), pp. 84–5.

19 On the concept of disavowal, S. Fischer writes: 'The modernity that took shape in the Western Hemisphere (in theoretical discourse as well as in cultural and social institutions) in the course of the nineteenth century contains, as a crucial element, the suppression of a struggle whose aim was to give racial equality and racial liberation the same weight as those political goals that came to dominate nineteenth-century politics and thought – most particularly, those relating to the nation and national sovereignty. Unless we submit the concept of modernity to a radical critique, our emancipatory goals and strategies will continue to reproduce the biases that came to shape modern thought in the Age of Revolution' (2004, p. 274). Consulship was a crucial aspect of the struggle for emancipation, sovereignty and the nation-state and as such formed an important part of the contest for modernity that Fischer so aptly analyses.

received a diplomatic appointment, and what that diplomatic appointment entailed, seems irrelevant. In a similar interpretive approach, Julia Gaffield has de-emphasised the question of consular recognition and claimed that the opening of the US commercial agency in Haiti in 1813 presented a welcome economic opportunity for the fostering of international commerce (2015, p. 152). However, such an interpretation is at odds with the claims of historical actors, such as Senator Benton, as well as a host of contemporaneous observers who understood the gravity of the difference between consular and commercial agents. Indeed, the distinction between commercial and consular agents would arise many times during the age of revolution and plague international relations just as much as – if not more than – the ostensible similarity of these institutions would foster international understanding.[20]

Haiti's exceptional status in the consular Caribbean – its blurring of the practical line between a consul and a commercial agent – undoubtedly provided greater space for transnational commerce, yet it would be erroneous to assume that this was an indisputable blessing for the fledgling republic (González, 2015). Instead, such a policy clearly served the interests of the United States, which promulgated a rather porous distinction between consuls and commercial agents in order to pry open restrictive Caribbean colonial regimes to US manufacture. The presence of US commercial agents in Haiti suited the needs of US mercantile elites, who wished to tap into the island's considerable commerce without pledging the northern republic to any contractual reciprocity, to protect its seamen and – most importantly – without incensing the powerful southern elites who regarded Haiti as an existential threat to their economies. It is only by recognising the complexity of Haiti's exceptionalism in the consular Caribbean, by stressing the strong lobby of southern plantocrats in the federal capital and by historicising the boundaries of the 'diplomatic sphere' that we can attempt a contemporary re-evaluation of what it meant to be (or not to be) a consular representative in the age of Atlantic revolutions.

Finally, the investigation of all three previous points – politics, colonialism and revolution – touches on the question of decolonisation, the fourth key feature of the consular Caribbean. It is a little-known fact that consuls played a crucial role in the decolonisation of Haiti and the Spanish American republics encircling the Caribbean (Gaffield, 2015, pp. 1–15). Indeed, Haitian consulship – first in the late 1790s and early 1800s and then in the 1820s – played a crucial role in the first comprehensive debates about consulship, Eurocentrism and colonialism in international law (ibid., pp. 93–152). The presence of foreign consuls in Haiti, debates about consular reciprocity with the new republic, and a revolutionary discourse of 'black consulship' all helped

20 See, e.g., Count de Someruelos to Henry Hill, 22 Aug. 1805 (AGI, Cuba 1660); John Morton to James Madison, Newport (CT), 9 Aug. 1802, in *Despatches from U.S. Consuls in Havana, 1783–1906*, National Archives and Records Service, General Services Administration, Washington, D.C., microform T 20, reel 1.

to push the boundaries of the political imaginary in the early 19th century (James, 1963, pp. 241–68). They also created an important political precedent of linking the presence of consuls to anti-colonial revolution and political independence, providing a script for the Spanish American Creoles who would later apply the Haitian consular experience in establishing new republican governments.

With the establishment of the first independent Spanish American republics – a process in which Haiti played a crucial role – the consular Caribbean entered a new period of expansion and growing conflict over the meaning of freedom, the contours of citizenship and the future of slavery (Murray, 1980; Salvucci, 2005). It was not until the late 1820s and 1830s, in the wake of the Spanish American revolutions, that British consuls first came to contest US primacy in Caribbean consular affairs, both in terms of their expansive presence and in terms of their liberal, at times fervently abolitionist, ideology (Murray, 1980; Sonesson, 1999). Tellingly, in that same year that US slaveholders dominated the Senate debate on the exclusion of Haiti from the consular Caribbean, the English foreign secretary George Canning transformed the British approach to Caribbean consulship. Canning dispatched the first British consuls to Cartagena and Port-au-Prince in order to foster stronger links to both the newly emergent South American republics and the republic of Haiti, which had significantly contributed to their independence.[21] Although the US had had a head start in the consular Caribbean since the beginning of the Napoleonic Wars, it was British abolitionist consuls that came to transform the political discourse on Caribbean colonialism, slavery and anti-colonial rebellion in the late 1820s, 1830s and 1840s.

The British moment in the consular Caribbean came as a counterpoint to US dominance throughout the first quarter of the 19th century (Murray, 1980). Thus, just months after Senator Benton from Missouri discarded the possibility of admitting and sending consuls to Haiti, due to the increased risk of slave insurgency, Charles Mackenzie became the first man of colour to act as consul in the Haitian capital, Port-au-Prince (Horne, 2012, p. 88). Mackenzie neatly encapsulates the new dynamism of British consulship in the Caribbean under the Canning administration. Gathering experience during his first consular appointment at the Mexican Caribbean port of Veracruz, Mackenzie acquainted himself with the first emancipated Spanish American nation in order to transfer this experience to Haiti in a career move that was not uncommon in the consular Caribbean.

Mackenzie arrived in Haiti less than a year after France had recognised its independence. He studied the island's history with a particular emphasis on the revolutionary and post-revolutionary period. As a proponent of free trade,

21 George Canning to consuls in Columbia, Foreign Office, 10 Oct. 1823 (The National Archives, Kew [TNA], Foreign Office (FO) 18.1); George Canning to Joseph Planta, Foreign Office, 25 Dec. (TNA, FO 35.1).

Mackenzie used his consular authority to stimulate the liberalisation of Haitian regulations towards Great Britain, the island's second-biggest commercial partner after the US. His position as consul immediately suggested to his Haitian peers – the president and secretary-general of Haiti – the opportunity of signing a Treaty of Amity and Commerce and thus breaking Haiti's diplomatic non-recognition.[22] However, Canning cautioned Mackenzie that his authority did not cover the signing of transnational treaties, a prerogative reserved for British ambassadors.[23] In his later assessment of Haitian independence, Mackenzie did not emphasise Haiti's marginalisation in the consular Caribbean, instead arguing that the 'failure' of Haitian post-revolutionary recovery was the direct consequence of revolutionary anarchy and economic mismanagement.[24]

In Cuba, too, British consuls became proponents of economic liberalisation, a policy that had a different meaning for US, Cuban and British officials. Although Cuban authorities had initially resisted the admission of foreign consuls throughout the Napoleonic wars, they eventually realised that they could use this institution to their own advantage. In the 1830s and 1840s, Cuba's sugar complex would be intimately connected to the fate of the US and British consulates. United States' consuls could secure Cuba advantageous deals with the US and strengthen the ties of Cuban sugar planters to US slave traders. Conversely, British consuls threatened to undermine the Spanish colonial regime, as British public opinion and diplomacy in the 1830s and 1840s cast the continuation of the Cuban slave trade as an 'odious commerce' that had to be abolished immediately (Murray, 1980).

To be sure, the initial steps of British consuls against Cuban slave-trading were rather cautious and ambivalent, much like the early history of the mixed commission courts in Havana (Paquette, 1988; Murray, 1980). Characteristically, it is not until Great Britain abolished slavery in its own colonies that British consuls began to play a greater role in the abolition of the Cuban slave trade. Nevertheless, in the 1840s – a period marked by a British crusade to suppress the slave trade in the Atlantic – the diverging trajectory of US and British consulship in the Spanish Caribbean could not be more evident. Just as the US slaveholder Nicholas Trist had become the lifeline of Cuban sugar barons, his British counterpart and famous abolitionist David Turnbull turned into their worst nightmare.[25] In the subsequent decades the

22   Charles Mackenzie to George Canning, Port-au-Prince, 28 May 1826 (TNA, FO 35.3).
23   George Canning to Charles Mackenzie, Foreign Office, 26 Jan. 1826 (TNA, FO 35.2).
24   C. Mackenzie, *Notes on Haiti, Made during a Residence in that Republic* (London, 1830), pp. 24–53.
25   MacMaster observes that in his position as consul of the United States and Portugal in 1837 and 1838, Trist provided official papers for nearly every vessel in the Cuban slave trade (1968, p. 56). Charles P. Trant, US vice-consul at Matanzas, followed in Trist's footsteps, clearing out 'American' vessels which consisted entirely of Spanish slave-trading crews (cf. 'Enclosure 46. Abstract of the Papers of the Schooner "Traveller", Andrew Johnson, Master', in *Parliamentary Papers. Slave Trade, Class A. 1841*, p. 63).

tensions between US and British consuls in the Spanish Caribbean intensified, putting greater stress on the Cuban sugar planters and traders who dominated colonial governance. Just as the commercial activities of US consuls raised the prospects of Cuban annexation to the United States, the abolitionist agenda of Great Britain introduced uncertainty about Spain's ability to protect the local Creole elite. In the end these two opposite dynamics challenged the viability of Cuba's colonial subordination to Spain.

In conclusion, although consuls were a quintessentially colonial institution, in the age of revolution they also became – somewhat paradoxically – agents of decolonisation (de Goey, 2014). Characteristically, the leaders of the first free nation in the Caribbean – Haiti – realised that admitting and appointing consuls was a necessary part of attaining international recognition and national sovereignty.[26] Indeed, the first country to send a consul to revolutionary Saint-Domingue was the United States, a republic that had fought and won its own anti-colonial war (Johnson 2014; Girard, 2009; Rossignol, 2004).[27] The precedent of establishing consular relations as a precondition to securing international recognition, first established in the wake of the American and Haitian revolutions, had far-reaching consequences throughout the early half of the 19th century, challenging some of the basic assumptions and practices in the law of nations.

A focus on consular relations demonstrates that the institutions of colonialism and decolonisation are not inherently antithetical but, in fact, ambivalently interrelated. As the emergence of the consular Caribbean shows, the institution of consulship embodied practices of both colonial domination and anti-colonial emancipation. This chapter suggests that consulship provides a unique lens through which to explore the inherent ambiguities, inconsistencies and contradictions of colonialism and decolonisation, as well as the problematic relationship of these concepts to each other. By virtue of its extra-territorial and transnational emphasis, the concept of a consular Caribbean can help historians to rethink some of the basic assumptions that govern our analysis of the complex political and transnational history of the modern Caribbean.

Bibliography

Chambers, S. (2015) *No God But Gain: The Untold History of Cuban Slavery, the Monroe Doctrine, and the Making of the United States* (New York: Verso).

Childs, M. D. (2006) *The 1812 Aponte Rebellion in Cuba and the Struggle Against Atlantic Slavery* (Chapel Hill, NC: University of North Carolina Press).

26 Cf. C. Mackenzie to G. Canning, Port-au-Prince, 28 May 1826 (TNA, FO 35.3).
27 See also 'Letters of Toussaint Louverture and of Edward Stevens, 1798–1800', *American Historical Review*, 16 (1910): 64–101.

de Goey, F. (2014) *Consuls and the Institutions of Global Capitalism, 1783–1914* (London: Pickering and Chatto).

Dickie, J. (2008) *The British Consul: Heir to a Great Tradition* (New York: Columbia University Press).

Fernández, E.G. (1971) *Historia de la jurisdicción mercantil en España* (Seville: Publicaciones de la Universidad de Sevilla).

Ferrer, A. (2014) *Freedom's Mirror: Cuba and Haiti in the Age of Revolution* (Cambridge: Cambridge University Press).

Fischer, S. (2004) *Modernity Disavowed: Haiti and the Cultures of Slavery in the Age of Revolution* (Durham, NC: Duke University Press).

Fisher, J. (1997) *The Economic Aspects of Spanish Imperialism in America 1492–1810* (Liverpool: Liverpool University Press).

Fraginals, M. M. (1978 [1965]) *El ingenio: complejo económico social cubano del azúcar*, vol. 1 (Havana, Cuba: Editorial de Ciencias Sociales).

Gaffield, J. (2015) *Haitian Connections in the Atlantic World: Recognition After Revolution* (Chapel Hill, NC: University of North Carolina Press).

Girard, P. R. (2009) 'Black Talleyrand: Toussaint Louverture's diplomacy, 1798–1802', *William and Mary Quarterly*, 66: 87–124.

González, J. (2015) 'Defiant Haiti: free-soil runaways, ship seizures, and the politics of diplomatic non-recognition in the early nineteenth century', *Slavery and Abolition*, 36: 124–35.

Hobsbawm, E. (1996) *The Age of Revolution, 1789–1848* (New York: Vintage).

Horne, G. (2012) *Negro Comrades of the Crown: African Americans and the British Empire Fight the U.S. before Emancipation* (New York: New York University Press).

Hutchinson, W.T. and W.M.E. Rachal (1969) *The Papers of James Madison* (Chicago, IL: University of Chicago Press).

James, C.L.R. (1963) *The Black Jacobins; Toussaint L'Ouverture and the San Domingo Revolution* (New York: Vintage).

Johnson, R.A. (2014) *Diplomacy in Black and White: John Adams, Toussaint Louverture, and Their Atlantic World Alliance* (Athens, GA: University of Georgia Press).

Jordaan, H. (2011) 'Patriots, privateers and international politics: the myth of the conspiracy of Jean Baptiste Tierce Cadet', in W. Klooster (ed.), *Curaçao in the Age of Revolutions, 1795–1800* (Leiden: Brill), pp. 141–69.

Kennedy, C.S. (1990) *The American Consul: A History of the United States Consular Service, 1776–1924* (Westport, CT: Greenwood Press).

Langley, L. (1996) *The Americas in the Age of Revolution, 1750–1850* (New Haven, CT: Yale University Press).

Logan, R.W. (1941) *The Diplomatic Relations of the United States with Haiti* (Chapel Hill, NC: University of North Carolina Press).

MacMaster, R.K. (1968) 'The United States, Great Britain and the suppression of the Cuban slave trade, 1835–1860', unpublished doctoral thesis, Georgetown University.

Madison, J. (1969) 'Notes on Debates, 6 January 1783', in *The Papers of James Madison*, vol. 6, *1 January 1783–30 April 1783* (Chicago, IL: University of Chicago Press).

Matthewson, T. (2003) *A Proslavery Foreign Policy: Haitian-American Relations during the Early Republic* (Westport, CT: Praeger).

Michelena, C.L. (2010) *Luces revolucionarias. De la rebelión de Madrid (1795) a la rebelión de La Guaira (1797)* (Caracas: CELARG).

Murray, D. (1980) *Odious Commerce: Britain, Spain and the Abolition of the Cuban Slave Trade* (Cambridge: Cambridge University Press).

Paquette, R.L. (1988) *Sugar Is Made with Blood. The Conspiracy of La Escalera and the Conflict between Empires over Slavery in Cuba* (Middletown, CT: Wesleyan University Press).

Rossignol, M.-J. (2004) *The Nationalist Ferment: The Origins of U.S. Foreign Policy, 1789–1812*, trans. by L. A. Parrott (Columbus, OH: Ohio State University Press).

Rouleau, B. (2014) *With Sails Whitening Every Sea: Mariners and the Making of an American Maritime Empire* (Ithaca, NY and London: Cornell University Press).

Rugemer, E. (2008) *The Problem of Emancipation: The Caribbean Roots of the American Civil War* (Baton Rouge, LA: Louisiana State University Press).

Salvucci, L. (2003) 'Merchants and diplomats: Philadelphia's early trade with Cuba', *Pennsylvania Legacies*, 3: 6–10.

Sonesson, B. (1999) *Puerto Rico's Commerce: From Regional to Worldwide Market Relations* (Los Angeles, CA: UCLA Publications).

Ulbert, J. and L. Prijac (eds.) (2010) *Consulship in the 19th Century* (Hamburg: Dokumentation und Buch).

Wilentz, S. (2005) *The Rise of American Democracy: Jefferson to Lincoln* (New York: Norton).

9. To 'stay where you are' as a decolonial gesture: Glissant's philosophy of Antillean space in the context of Césaire and Fanon

Miguel Gualdrón Ramírez

What does the intensity of living in a 'paradise' do to its inhabitants? Jamaica Kincaid offers an answer in the closing pages of her book *A Small Place*: 'Antigua is beautiful. Antigua is too beautiful. Sometimes the beauty of it seems unreal. Sometimes the beauty of it seems as if it were stage sets for a play, for no real sunset could look like that; no real seawater could strike that many shades of blue at once' (1988, p. 77). The list of things too beautiful to be real in Antigua extends for two pages; it includes a detailed description of the perfection of every shade of colour in nature in Antigua, the unflawed simplicity of its small houses, the misery of those who inhabit its perfection: 'All of this is so beautiful, all of this is not real like any other real thing that there is. It is as if, then, the beauty … were a prison, and as if everything and everybody inside it were locked in and everything and everybody that is not inside were locked out' (ibid., p. 79).

A place like this becomes a small place, where small events are cultivated and where there are no other marks or events to compare the life one has in such an environment. The people who live in a paradise (one that has been created as such, too beautiful to be real) cannot give a complete account of their land, nor their history, nor themselves; the prison determines not only the homogeneity of their territory, the dullness of life in a tourist paradise, but also the uniformity of time, the lack of marks in history ('No Industrial Revolution, no revolution of any kind, no age of anything' (ibid., p. 79)) to distinguish what was from what is from what will be. And thus Antiguans do not know who they are: incapable of making a decision, Kincaid wonders whether she comes from children, artists or lunatics, 'or an exquisite combination of all three' (ibid., p. 57).

Is it possible to escape from a prison like this? If the colonised person's own land does not belong to him, and everything inside is trapped in a paradise constructed for others, how can this space be inhabited? Moreover, is it

M. Gualdrón Ramírez, 'To 'stay where you are' as a decolonial gesture: Glissant's philosophy of Antillean space in the context of Césaire and Fanon', in J.D. Webb, R. Westmaas, M. del Pilar Kaladeen and W. Tantam (eds.), *Memory, migration and (de)colonisation in the Caribbean and beyond* (London: University of London Press, 2019), pp. 133–51. License: CC-BY-NC-ND 4.0.

possible to resist the colonial construction of space that we grasp in Caribbean paradises? What does a decolonial, spatial strategy look like? The aim in this chapter is to consider the approach to the question of territorial contestation in the Caribbean as it has been discussed by an author from another small place, Martinique: Édouard Glissant.[1] In his 1981 book *Le discours Antillais* (*Caribbean Discourse*, hereafter *DA*), Glissant states that the combination of different decolonial strategies of resistance in the Antilles requires a return to what he calls '*le point d'intrication*' [the point of entanglement],[2] which has to occur in space as well as in time: it amounts to a seizure of the 'here' and 'now' and not of the past or an elsewhere, as is the case in other Caribbean thinkers. This focus on the present is a similar gesture to the one Glissant sees in Aimé Césaire and Frantz Fanon: in both of them the locus of the inquiry is also related to a 'now'. However, they see the necessity of the 'here' differently: their accounts of the Caribbean (colonial) spatiality, according to Glissant, would be limited in scope and incapable of creating a proper link between nature and culture, the main reason for not inhabiting their own land.

The place of Glissant's philosophy of decolonisation in relation to Fanon and Césaire has been theorised by some authors (Yountae, 2017, pp. 88–101). But the emphasis has not been placed on the fact that Glissant refers to both his predecessors as examples of the absence of a link between the two tactics of resistance – *un détour* [a tactical diversion] and *un retour* [a return]. For Glissant, both Césaire and Fanon are still diverters and not properly producers of a new reality, of a real Caribbean territory and history. Thus, following previous analyses by commentators, but departing from them (or adding a new layer, the layer of spatiality that should be combined with a traditional analysis of temporality), this chapter defends the idea that Glissant locates his decolonial thought between Césaire and Fanon: it neither advocates a reconstruction that points to a past located elsewhere (Africa), nor recommends the rejection and replacement of the here/now with a different, unknown spatiality and temporality. For Glissant, the locus of resistance is located in the present and in the possibilities of decolonisation already contained in the Caribbean, although concealed and understated. This chapter begins by showing what is, according to Glissant, the necessary conjunction between the different tactics of resistance, then focuses on some of Césaire's and Fanon's texts in order to show why they do not offer this necessary link. The final section comes back to

1   As shown in my article 'Transversality as disruption and connection' (2019), the question of the coloniality of space in the Caribbean cannot be separated from a colonial temporality and this is also true of the decolonial form of resistance to this rule. The present chapter will focus mainly on some of the spatial aspects of this resistance, which nevertheless presuppose what will be called, following J. Drabinski's use of the term, an 'abyssal beginning' of the Caribbean, a beginning that challenges a linear, continuous form of temporality (Drabinski, 2015, p. 141). This is what Glissant calls 'the abyss' (see Glissant's 'The open boat', in *Poetics of relation*, 1997, p. 5–9).
2   Glissant, 1997, p. 56.

Glissant to analyse the notion of *l'antillanité* as the possibility of truly focusing on a here/now as a multilayered strategy of resistance.

Going back to the point of entanglement (space/time)

The relocation of African slaves brought to the Americas, as part of the slave trade organised by European powers through the Middle Passage, is described by Glissant as a *transbord* [transference] or a re-invention (1981, pp. 41–55).[3] The slaves could not rely on their knowledge, heritage or tradition to deal with the horrifying situation into which they were forced because they were not transplanted as a community, but transferred to a new territory as already uprooted and disconnected, a situation their descendants inherited and just carried with them. There were no preceding collectivities on board ship, no previous common experience or expertise, usually not even a common language that would have provided a basis to cooperatively resist the new circumstances they were forced into. A collective resistance had to be created anew from this point forward.

In one of the first sections of *Le discours Antillais*, 'Le retour et le détour' [Reversion and diversion], Glissant focuses on two main historical strategies of resistance to this radical dispossession. The first is an almost automatic impulse towards reversion, to go back to the origins, a literal or metaphorical attempt to return to Africa on the part of the transported populations in the Americas. Without mentioning them directly, Glissant seems to be referring to some of the most important movements of decolonisation in the 19th and 20th centuries, at least for the African diaspora, such as the several metamorphoses of pan-Africanism and the négritude movement. In general, the impulse towards reversion describes the compulsion to retain and defend, in order to reconstruct, all the cultural elements of the previous life that are still alive in the communities. However, this propulsion of reversion ultimately constitutes for Glissant an unsatisfactory attempt to go back to a beginning, Africa, for example, that is no longer the origin of these populations: the Middle Passage (understood as a *gouffre* [abyss] in *Poétique de la Relation* [Poetics of Relation] effectively breaks any sustainable connection between both shores of the ocean.

If they wanted to survive and resist the tortures of slavery (and later the despair of their lives when 'freed'), the Caribbean populations had the option of mimicking a new culture that was imposed on them and assimilating to it, to the extent that something like this was possible. In a colonial condition, however, the 'enemy' is usually not completely known, or at least not enough to bypass and go back to the 'real' origins of the communities in peril. Since colonial history is erased in the very act of being imposed, in order to be

---

3 In the use of the primary texts throughout this chapter, the first reference will be to the original in French and then the English translation (when available). When the published translation has been modified, this will be indicated.

replaced by a narrative that portrays the colonial situation as necessary, the source of oppression is not immediately clear to the consciousness of these peoples. Thus, Glissant states that reversion is not enough: a *détour* is also necessary in order to find the source of an oppression that cannot always be seen from the current position. The concealed character of the enemy after hundreds of years of colonial domination requires a different approach, one that Glissant calls *parallactic*: since the source of oppression is not directly visible, the community needs to move and change its position in order to see an objective that was previously covered by an obstacle.

The condition for the success of this parallactic strategy, as a means to survive, depends on the possibility of finding concrete obstacles that the *détour* can elude by shifting positions. Examples of these obstacles in Glissant's works are the infantilised French language used by the masters when they spoke to the slaves; the interdiction for the slaves of planting their own food; the crusade against Creole in a 'post-colonial' Martinique, and so on. Against all these obstacles, the enslaved communities started to oppose creolised forms of culture.

Just as with *retour* strategies, however, the forms of resistance that constitute a *détour* are also insufficient if they are the only resource used by these communities. What they need is a *retour/détour* set of strategies, a constant shift in location that does not lose sight of the fact that the ultimate goal is always to (re)construct a liberated condition, and not just to avoid a particular colonial imposition. This is a major point that commentators usually forget, who tend to focus only on diversion as strategy, without realising that Glissant studies in detail examples that are exclusively forms of *détour* and shows them as having failed.[4] In the case of strategies of diversion that are not coupled with reversions, Glissant analyses the limitation of a series of intellectual and practical attempts to trick the enemy in order to find a different point of view from which the source of oppression can be seen; in all these cases, according to Glissant, the strategy is not linked with a *retour* strategy and thus ends up being a failed attempt.

How is it possible to link properly these two sets of strategies that Glissant has been analysing separately? How is it possible to try *retour/détour* strategies that overcome the failures of separating them? This chapter suggests the best method is to adopt the words and acts of Antillean writers and poets (Marcus Garvey, Aimé Césaire, George Padmore, Frantz Fanon) as 'diverters' and not as 'returners' (which they are usually considered to be) in order to find a way at last of attempting a real return. This is where the legacy of Martinican authors such as Césaire and Fanon is located, even in their radically different conceptions:

> The poetic word of Césaire, the political act of Fanon, led up *somewhere*, authorizing by diversion the return to the only point where our problems

4 Good examples of this approach in secondary literature are Britton (1999, ch. 1) and Yountae (2017, ch. 4)

lay in wait for us … They illustrate and establish the landscape of a shared Elsewhere [*d'un Ailleurs partagé*]. We must return to the place [*lieu*]. Diversion [*détour*] is not a useful ploy unless it is nourished by reversion [*retour*]: not a return to the longing for origins, to some immutable state of Being, but a return to the point of entanglement, from which we were forcefully turned away (Glissant, 1981, pp. 56–7; translation modified).

In my view, Glissant's main contribution lies in the possibility of theorising and poetising this connection, not only in relation to the studies of Césaire, Fanon and others but also to decolonial theory in the Caribbean. Both Césaire and Fanon attempted forms of diversion (masked sometimes as forms of return) that ultimately put *us* in the position of tackling the very issue that has been concealed: *le lieu* [that place] which constitutes the *point d'intrication* out of which Caribbean peoples have been removed. For Glissant there has never been a real possession of the land for these communities; they have always been renting their own space, *de passage* [in transit or passing through] (p. 149; not included in the English edition)). Thus, just as with the Antigua of Kincaid, the inhabitants are incapable of an account of themselves: only when Martinicans can spatially return to their land (not Africa, that is forever lost, but the Archipelago, the islands, the sea and its shores, its circularity, its submarine rootedness) can the tactic of diversion finally accomplish its purpose and the *détour* turn to a form of self-expression (Glissant, 1981, p. 57). This point of entanglement is not an idealised, mythical point of origin. It is a spatial point (here) and a temporal one (now): the Antilles.

Spatial variations on the present: Fanon and Césaire

'In this inert town'*: Aimé Césaire and the possibilities of the Caribbean*

As mentioned previously, one of the things the thought of these Martinican authors has in common is the fact that the philosophical enquiry, related to finding the possibilities of changing a social and political reality, points to the present, even when it looks for the origins of said reality. This is clear in Césaire, despite the usual claim that his intellectual activity is located in the African past of the Caribbean communities. As Drabinski (2015, pp. 148–51) shows, locating thought in the present does not mean accepting the present as it is; as we shall see, Césaire's evaluation of the colonised present leads to an almost visceral rejection of that same present, of the conditions under which the communities live in that situation, of the erasure of ancient forms of culture, in sum, of the incessant work of colonisation in replacing one civilisation with another. However, this rejection carries with it in Césaire not only a temporal meaning, but also a spatial one and this is what is emphasised here.

The connection between the 'present' and the 'here' is perhaps most evident in *Cahier d'un Retour au Pays Natal* [Notebook of a Return to the Native Land, hereafter *Cahier*], where place and moment become almost indistinguishable.[5] From the very first strophes Césaire identifies the present of his narration (the incessant repetition of a 'when': 'At the end of first light') with a dreadful description of the place, the Antilles, where this now takes place. Thus, from the very first page this 'now' is again and again interlaced with 'in this inert town', that is, a still space, perhaps even unmovable at this particular time. And there is nothing equivocal about the impression this narrator makes upon arrival: the present time and the present space are described from the beginning of the poem as rotten, ill and dirty: 'And aged poverty rotting under the sun, silently; an aged silence bursting with tepid pustules' (2013, p. 1).

The reasons for this account are, of course, related to the conditions of misery, poverty, illiteracy, famine and so on of the region. The population's economic conditions and the particular harshness of the form of production they are engaged in in the Antilles are emphasised in the text, making it extremely difficult to envisage the 'beauty' that tourists and colonisers alike usually associate with the colonial space. And just as described sarcastically by Kincaid in *A Small Place*, any escape from this unreal situation seems impossible (ibid., p. 6) because the people are not even capable of understanding and challenging their conditions; they cannot express themselves. The inert town and the mute multitude represent the real condition that renders impossible any form of redemption; denied their true cry, which is one of hunger, misery, revolt and so on (see Césaire, 2013, pp. 2–3) the people are disconnected not only from their own situation, which means that they cannot understand it and thus are unable to change it, but also from the space they inhabit. They are estranged from themselves and from their surroundings.

But what is the reason for these conditions? We know: a history of colonisation, dispossession, extraction of labour and resources and racism. However, this negative assessment of the here/now also has to do with the spatial, colonial construction of the Antilles themselves and not only with disconnection caused by the economic and social conditions imposed by the colonisers.[6] This chapter next focuses on three instances of Césaire's contempt for the Caribbean landscape: the beach (and the sea), the island and the archipelago. In all three the poet suggests the complicity of space in the people's muteness and inert character and thus the landscape itself becomes an ally of the oppressor and not a tool for liberation and resistance.

5   For the purposes of this analysis the focus is on the first version (1939) of the *Cahier* as edited by A. J. Arnold and C. Eshleman. For a detailed analysis of the differences between the multiple editions of the *Cahier* between 1939 and 1947, see Laforge, 2012.

6   This chapter does not suggest that the space of the Archipelago is independent of its economic conditions, or that for Césaire there is an essential rottenness of the landscape. Perhaps one is caused by the other.

With regard to the first, Césaire describes the character of the beach, the incessant movement of the waves breaking, as *lécher* [licking or sucking] the life out of the land. The beach seems to be merely the remnants of the earth that will be devoured by the sea, or the material itself being chewed, licked, decomposed: 'or rather the sea is a huge dog licking and biting the shins of the beach, biting them so fiercely that it will end up devouring it, the beach and Straw Street along with it' (ibid., p. 16).

In the Antilles, a place circumscribed by beaches hysterically licked by the sea (ibid., p. 10), the landscape thus becomes an eternal reminder of the death to come, of the gradual decomposition of the region, of the inescapability of misery. A similar thing happens with the island (Martinique) and the Archipelago which are described in strophe 32, for example, as 'this little ellipsoidal nothing trembling four fingers above the line [of the equator]'. The colonial landscape is nothing but the will to self-negation, destruction and death that offers no possibilities of redemption and liberation. The reason for this, as suggested in strophe 34, is the *non-clôture* [non-closure] of the landscape in question: the openness of the sea, the ellipsoidal shape of Martinique, the arch of the Antilles as if running away from itself. All these conditions mark for Césaire a negative non-closure incapable of keeping life within, incapable of delimiting and giving a steady identity.

What is, then, Césaire's response to this pale diagnosis of the Antillean here/now? He has at least two different answers (which sometimes seem contradictory) in some of his most important essays on the question. The first is an attempt to organise around a collective past represented in African civilisation and a certain survival of that past. That which survives, according to 'Culture et colonisation' (1956) [Culture and colonisation], is less the content, the knowledge, the culture of an African civilisation, but mostly what he calls its 'unity', one that enables a form of *solidarity in time* among African descendants from all over the world:

> There is a double solidarity among all those who are gathered here: first, *a horizontal solidarity*, a solidarity created by the colonial or semicolonial or paracolonial situation that has been imposed on us from without. And on the other hand, another solidarity that is vertical, *a solidarity in time*, which comes from the fact that out of an initial unity, the unity of African civilisation, there has been differentiated a whole series of cultures that all owe something to that civilisation (1955: 129–30).

The possibility of guaranteeing this 'vertical solidarity' among cultures, this form of common origin, is thus at the source of the possibility of resisting the work of colonisation, and thus perhaps the present that Césaire had described two decades before. And this verticality is *in time*: it follows time downwards and upwards, to and from a common past of greatness that has been lost *in the present*. But, how can people organise around this common harmonious past? Although, as we shall see, Césaire explicitly denies the possibilities of a return in texts such as *Discours sur le colonialisme* [Discourse on Colonialism; hereafter *Discours*], he sometimes explicitly uses the term when referring to the decolonial work that all those who share a 'horizontal solidarity' must carry out: '[T]his Congress is a return to origins [*un retour aux sources*] that all communities undertake at their moment of crisis, and at the same time it is an assembly bringing together men who have to grasp the same harsh reality, and hence of men fighting the same fight and sustained by the same hope' (2001, p. 130).

Despite the formulation, Césaire himself is not ambiguous regarding the possibility of continuing the process of an African civilisation at the moment of its disruption by Europe. The development of African civilisation cannot simply be continued: 'Let us say simply that it was struck at its base. At its base, and thus irrevocably' (ibid., p. 132). What Césaire suggests is thus not the taking up of a collective past, a return in the sense of continuing, but the acknowledgment of a unity in the origin, an origin irrecoverable as it was, but fashionable, shapeable, 'a return to the sources', and by creating these, a new African civilisation (ibid., pp. 51–2). It is thus not a matter of returning, going back, but of *dépassement* [going beyond] by acknowledging both a horizontal and a vertical solidarity. Césaire speaks of 'the African culture yet to be born, or in the para-African culture yet to be born' (1955: 141), perhaps as a form of future perfect.[7]

Challenging the immobility of the colonised by bringing about a new history: decolonisation in Les damnés de la terre *(Frantz Fanon)*

Frantz Fanon represents for Glissant a different side of a similar decolonial attitude, another form of *détour* to the one sketched in the previous section which follows Césaire's diagnosis of the present and the here. This chapter now offers an interpretation of Fanon's understanding of a decolonial strategy in a spatial sense and not just a temporal one. By emphasising two of the essays included in *Les damnés de la terre* [The Wretched of the Earth; hereafter *Damnés*], it shows how for Fanon the colonial space emerges as a political space of intervention, shaped by the colonial powers, and how the decolonial gesture is to retake these spaces which are not yet one's own. This understanding of spatiality, although from a very different perspective to that described in Césaire, would represent a similar attitude toward decolonisation: the search for an elsewhere, driving the impulse away from ourselves, in order to find liberation.

Even though Fanon does not refer explicitly to this distinction, it is possible to interpret his stance towards the temporality of decolonisation using Césaire's characterisation of two forms of solidarity among oppressed peoples in the contemporary world: a vertical one (between peoples that share a common

---

7   Drabinski, 2015, p. 150.

origin) and a horizontal one (between communities that share a similar form of (colonial) oppression). This is apparent in a veiled critique aimed by Fanon at Césaire, or rather at the notion of 'négritude' that the latter has defended as a form of vertical solidarity. As we see in 'Sur la culture nationale' [On national culture], an essay included in *Damnés*, 'négritude' constitutes the first answer to the question of how to resist the colonist claim that the black is a savage and lacks any form of culture (Fanon, 2010, p. 212, pp. 195–236). To this broad, unqualified judgment by European colonisers, 'l'intellectuel colonisé' [the colonised intellectual who defends 'négritude'] would oppose a similarly broad defence of a national culture in terms of a continent (ibid., pp. 211–2).

'Sur la culture nationale' constitutes a demolishing critique of this approach to the possibility of 'continental' national culture. Such critique is based on questioning the possibility of what Césaire calls a vertical solidarity. Fanon states, first, that almost no common issues unite communities made up of African descendants *as African descendants*: the only thing they have in common is being defined primarily in opposition to whites: as black, that is, they only share what Césaire calls a horizontal solidarity (ibid., pp. 215–6). But this horizontality constitutes an empty category for Fanon: it is never based on an actual denigration of particular peoples, traditions, languages and so on, but on a meaningless generalisation to which only an equally empty stereotype can be opposed in 'continental' terms.

Regarding the verticality that points back to a common past, as previously mentioned it would be a mistake to understand Césaire's decolonial gesture as a call for a return to Africa. Fanon also rejects the possibility of commonality in chronological terms; the verticality points more to the idea of constructing a 'myth of the black', criticised both in *Damnés* and in *Peau noir, masques blancs* [Black Skin, White Masks] (1952). In *Peau noir, masques blancs*, both in the introduction and chapter 5, embracing the idea of blackness, refining this idea in contraposition to what the white man is seen to be, amounts to nothing more than the embracing of an idea *created* by Europeans.[8]

Fanon replaces (or, perhaps, dialectically supersedes) black identity with a decolonial nation which actually shares that horizontal solidarity but now doesn't just include African descendants; we can extend this solidarity to all the wretched of the earth. In this regard, 'Sur la culture nationale' offers two insights relevant to this analysis of Glissant and Césaire: first, the decolonial

---

[8] G. Ciccariello-Maher, in his recent book *Decolonizing Dialectics* (2017), has a different interpretation of the role of self-assertion, of black identity, in the struggle for liberation and decolonisation in Fanon. (A similar understanding can be seen in G. Coulthart's *Red Skins, White Masks* (2014), ch. 5.) For Ciccariello-Maher, the affirmation of a black identity is the first step in the dialectic, one that has the power to jump-start a movement that is otherwise foreclosed, because of the ontological difference between black and white (2017, p. 50). Although I agree with the need to see the dialectical role of *négritude* in Fanon, it is important also to show the striking criticism to it, in particular of the fact that it is an intellectual, educated endeavour, a criticism that Ciccariello-Maher leaves aside in his book.

gesture in Fanon, in a different sense from that in Césaire, points to the present: one needs to be sceptical of the intellectuals and artists who turn their gaze towards the past when trying to attack the sources of oppression (2010, p. 225), because the past runs the risk of becoming only the traces of what has been lost, of what exists no more, the corpse of history.

Second, and at a deeper level, Fanon is determined to show in this essay that we can only talk about a national culture, perhaps a national identity, after actual liberation occurs; before that, under the colonial situation, struggle itself was the only form of culture and thus only reactive, forced, oppositional. A national consciousness, even nationalistic in its nature (fervent, blind, undifferentiated) becomes the only form of national culture, a form nevertheless empty in its formulation. As such, it becomes not just national, but international, given the shared conditions of colonised peoples all over the world. And if struggle is the only culture of the colonised, the old culture ought to be replaced as well: 'After the conflict there is not only the disappearance of colonialism but also the disappearance of the colonized man' (ibid., pp. 245–6).

This last idea can also be grasped in what Fanon developed in a different essay included in *Damnés*, 'De la violence' [On violence] (ibid., pp. 37–104). From the outset of this chapter decolonisation has been described as the basic replacement of the upper part of the colonial system by the lower part: the coloniser, settler, imperial power ought to be replaced by those who have historically been enslaved, colonised or left aside. To put it in Fanon's terms, 'decolonisation is quite simply the replacing of a certain "species" of men by another "species" of men' (ibid., p. 35). This replacement, this turning of the structure upside-down does not, however, simply put the colonised in charge and erase the colonial scar: that which would be put back in place is also a creation of the coloniser. It has been materially shaped into a colonised being, a thing, and thus also has to be undone by the process of liberation.

The premise of this argument is the idea that colonialism imposes a Manichean world, a clear distinction between two 'species' of humans that are opposed to each other, two species in separate spaces or zones. This distinction has at least two levels in Fanon's works: first, we can grasp the clear opposition between the spaces these two 'species' inhabit in the well-known statement that there is a zone of non-being in which 'the black man' has been enclosed (2001, pp. 6/xii). What we have on this first level is an almost ontological plane of discussion because the separation between species, although materially graspable, is nevertheless extended to the whole being of the black subject, who cannot change from one zone to the other. The idea of a replacement of species defended in *Damnés*, however, carries another level of interpretation. It is possible to think of this new separation in terms of compartments: the colonial world is *compartimenté* (Fanon, 2010, pp. 37–8). This constitutes a more geographical, architectural level of analysis, one that Fanon sees represented in the material distinctions of buildings for settlers and natives, institutions, lines in the cities separating neighbourhoods from slums or ghettos and so on: these are no longer ontological zones, but geographical ones.

I focus here on this second sense, the more material, geographical conception of the endeavour of decolonisation. As outlined above, Fanon's level of discussion in *Damnés* corresponds to this second one; and it is in this sense that he states that, since the colonial world is cut in two, the work of decolonisation is simply the abolition of one of these spaces (ibid., p. 41). But as a result of the Manichean, colonial world Fanon describes in the text, the abolition of one of these compartments necessarily carries with it the abolition of the other, because the compartmentalisation does not precede the colonial rule. Thus, the aforementioned replacement of one species by the other (ibid., p. 35) cannot be understood here as driving out the colonist to replace him by the native. This is why Fanon reaches a similar point of view here to that described in 'Sur la culture national': only in and through liberation is it possible to talk about a new human being who does not carry with him the burden of a past, not even a pre-colonial past (ibid., p. 36).

It is only in this regard, in this spatial, geographical conception of decolonisation, that Fanon understands the role of history in the struggle. Colonisation and decolonisation are finally recognised in terms of doing or undoing history in the sense of shaping the landscape of the country, their geographical zones, in a particular way. The settler has created a peaceful, beautiful land and this particular shape becomes its history:

> In this becalmed zone the sea has a smooth surface, the palm tree stirs gently in the breeze, the waves lap against the pebbles, and raw materials are ceaselessly transported, justifying the presence of the settler: and all the while the native, bent double, more dead than alive, exists interminably in an unchanging dream. The settler makes history; his life is an epoch, an Odyssey. He is the absolute beginning (Fanon, 2010, pp. 51, 52–3).

This space, which is not the space where the natives live, becomes the truth of the land and its only destiny: the almost unreal beauty of Antigua, as described by Kincaid. But by destroying this history and replacing it with a new one, the decolonial struggle does not go back to an ancient history of the land; it does not seek the *real*, pre-colonial truth of the country. Moving out of this colonised compartment can only be achieved by crafting a new history, by creating new sections (ibid., p. 51).

The consequences of this understanding of history are now clearly graspable, especially when confronted by Césaire's understanding of tradition and an African soul. The decolonial history, the only history of the nation, becomes a process of demystification in a double sense: first, as liberation from the image of the native created by the colonial forces; but, second, this also means that all the cultural practices of the native, all the dances, sensitivities, myths, magic, religion, faith, and so on, are seen as practices the native carries out in order to survive during this colonial rule, as ways to 'exorcize itself, to liberate itself, to say itself' (ibid., p. 57; translation modified). In this way, decolonisation, the creation of a new history, also requires a detachment from these practices, a demystification of the Manichaeism of a history externally imposed that engenders, only negatively, an equally colonised history of ancient practices (ibid., p. 58).

Thus, in contradistinction to Césaire – for whom the Caribbean space is rotten and cannot be redeemed and thus it is necessary to look elsewhere, in another space but at the same time – for Fanon, the spatiality itself of the colonised territory requires a total transformation, a creative task coming out of a detoxing force. Decolonisation is, according to this perspective, a possibility arising from the destruction of one's identity and space, in totally reorganising the current identity and in constructing that of the future following the aforesaid disconnection. Only out of this displacement can the real history of the country emerge, an absolute beginning for the liberated country.

L'antillanité as poetics of Caribbean spatiality

The temporal/spatial understanding undertaken here makes it possible to re-interpret Glissant's suggestion to take Césaire's and Fanon's work as an example of *détour* and not the joint strategy of *détour/retour*. In the case of Césaire, his poetic work amounts to a form of *détour* because it is unable to come back to the lived reality of the colonised peoples. Ironically, the '*retour au pays natal*' never takes place because the poet always remains on the surface of the reality he perceives; the narrator goes back to a land that is not *theirs*, but the land of the consequences of dispossession as imposed externally on the communities that inhabit it. Thus, the only path forward seems to be to reject it completely and to look elsewhere for the source of liberation, the construction of Africanness in the present. Fanon traces a similar movement, one which looks for an *elsewhere* in order to find the source of liberation. It is an *elsewhere* perceived almost only in negative terms: Fanon looks for the source of the oppression in a different place to the one the colonised subject inhabits, and the origin of liberation comes out of the attempt of taking over such a place and replacing those who live there. Neither a free past nor the culture created out of enslavement and colonisation constitute the source of decolonisation, because they are completely lost in the work of colonisation or are tainted with its production of subalternity. Once achieved, freedom rejects the culture of the Antillean, that is, Creolisation.

For Glissant, the Caribbean space as a form of resistance begins with a multilayered territory that is inhabited by all actors and where tactics of decolonial resistance also depend on the historical presence of colonisers. Reducing the colonial world to a Manichean one would artificially reduce the actual and diverse process of Creolisation. Culture comes before liberation: culture is actually the only thing that can liberate. For Glissant, the spaces are and are not one's own, but whatever the case, they are inhabited all the time. There is no absolute duality, as in Fanon, or absolute dispossession, as in Césaire, but space needs to be understood in all its complexity, as being home to simultaneous forms of oppression and resistance, limitations and openness, interdictions and freedom. In order to do that, Caribbean communities need to go back to this point, to this territory out of which they have been diverted. This is made possible by Glissant's notion of *l'antillanité* [Antillanity].

'The advance of America': conditions of Antillean, spatial poetics

Glissant wrote: 'Our landscape is its own monument. Its meaning can only be traced on the underside. It is all history' (1981, p. 11). This statement, part of one of the introductions to *Discours*, is the initial mention of a motif Glassant repeatedly revisits in the book. Antillean history is spatial, not just because history does not occur outside this region's spatial conditions (perhaps true of every region), but also because those conditions configure a particular form of history as Antillean, that is, as archipelagic, insular, abyssal, etc.

This connection between landscape and history, however, does not span only the island of Martinique, or the archipelago of the Antilles; there is a form of continuity between the archipelago and the continent itself, as becomes clear in Glissant's analysis in section 42, 'Chili'. But a consideration of this continuity does not imply an absolute connection, neither a linear route (in spatial terms) nor a causal relation (in temporal terms). Rather, because of the geography of the Antilles, continuity represents a disconnection from the mainland that nevertheless does not cut its ties to it, but also the continent's expectation of regaining, following after, or simply striving for movement, for expansion:

> What does this other America mean to us? What do we mean to it? Before its dense and multiple presence, we seem to fade into insignificance. Would we simply be several drops left by this immense river after it had broken up and slowed down? Could we in fact be the other source, I mean the necessary stop in the journey out of which the journey itself is constituted? In one way or another, the Caribbean is the advance of America [*l'avancée de l'Amérique*]. The part that escapes from the mass of continent and therefore participates of its weight. (ibid., p. 117; translation modified)

'L'avancée de l'Amérique', a spatial image that no longer looks at the archipelago as dead, sterile terrain (Césaire), or as a severed or occupied piece of land that must be replaced (Fanon), but as a source of movement and expansion, as openness.[9] There is, indeed, a sense of risk involved in this understanding of an

---

9   The focus on this optimistic image does not intend to suggest it is the only approach to the possibilities of the Caribbean. In many ways, this region was in the vanguard of the continent as a testing site of colonialism and definitively as a first contact space out of which the whole

'advance': the Caribbean is not just a part that expands itself outside the main body; it also constitutes an element, a group of elements, that momentarily escape the limits of the volume they normally inhabit to explore and investigate what comes ahead (in time, in space) and might not come back in one piece, or even alive.

To investigate this openness, to talk about history, identity, politics, culture and so on, the poetics coming from the Antilles must be able to open up for the openness itself; listening but also voicing, what Glissant calls *l'éclat* [explosion, spark, radiance] throughout *Discours*. This means not only witnessing it, but also being able to create the reality of this expansion, this openness, this explosion (ibid., p. 109). As will be shown, such openness of the archipelago no longer means, as it did in Césaire, a negative aspect, a harmful non-closure, an incompleteness.

What are, then, the particular geographical, territorial and spatial conditions of an Antillean discourse, following its landscape? Glissant occupies himself with this question in section 36, 'Techniques', where he addresses the possibilities of true national literature, that is, one that is at last actually concerned with the conditions of the existence of such a nation and one that attempts self-expression. Trying to express the reality of a community requires, then, a meditation on a suitable way and this is patently obvious in the shortcomings of realism as a poetic 'technique' when applied to the Antillean experience. These shortcomings are perceivable in at least three functions of Caribbean spatiality:

1. The function of landscape: whereas in realistic poetics landscape always constitutes a context, a background to the action, in the Antilles landscape it can only be a character in itself. This is even more crucial given the fact that, as already shown, colonialism is defined as that which causes an alienation of communities from their territories, the separation between culture and nature (ibid., pp. 104–5);
2. The absence of seasons and seasonal rhythms: an Antillean poetics has to be one of duration, of saturation. The environmental conditions of the Antilles demand this form of poetics, in opposition to a seasonal region in which the lived experience expects resolution, moments of ecstasy, twists in the narrative. What the absence of seasons implies for the Antilles is a monotony of narration, a 'plain-chant', inscribed in the lack of harmony of life without a determined cycle to explain it or to make it predictable and linear (ibid., pp. 106–5);
3. Chaos and anxiety: because of the chaos of memory in the Antilles, the region also expresses a complexity of levels which are not clearly graspable and should not be presented that way in the poetic work. No clarity is capable of addressing this chaos because the chaos should not be

---

imperial enterprise emerged. During World War Two it was a space which blocked economic possibilities for the continent, as the history of Martinique tragically exemplifies.

dissolved, but expressed. Spatiality in the Caribbean exhibits the anxiety of multilinear relationships, the absence of a single way of explaining that should not be reduced to a linear narrative. Therefore, expressing such chaos of memory and space implies a function that goes beyond mere description and embraces a work of production (ibid., p. 107). This new polyphony can be seen, for example, in Glissant's demand for new genres, given that novel and poem remain disconnected from an active communitarian production of this history and also privilege a written poetics.

L'antillanité: insularity as openness

> In this context, insularity takes on another meaning. Ordinarily, insularity is treated as a form of isolation, a neurotic reaction to place. However, in the Caribbean each island embodies openness. The dialectic between inside and outside is reflected in the relationship of land and sea. It is only those who are tied to the European continent who see insularity as confining. An Antillean imagination liberates us from being smothered (ibid., p. 139; translation modified).

In the context of the Antilles, to go back to the point of entanglement means to connect with an openness and expansion that allow a complicated set of hidden links demanding expression, but not complete clarification. It requires taking seriously the experience of landscape, the absence of seasons and the chaos of territory, but also the complicated relationship of the archipelago itself with the continent. The image of the Antilles as 'l'avancée de l'Amérique' suggests that the archipelago runs ahead of the continent, expanding it (calling it to move), but also risking losing touch with the mainland to the point that it has to be called back sometimes. As an imaginary, the Antilles mean freedom; and insularity has to become for the region's inhabitants an attitude toward liberation instead of a place of constraint and imprisonment.

Glissant refuses to define *l'antillanité* in the glossary to *Discours*, claiming that a term so extensively used has already acquired a reality. Faithful to this idea, Glissant uses it constantly as if it were already understood, as if what it communicates has already been established, or lived, or simply expressed by some communities, but on a different level. Whatever it is, it seems to be both a construction ('more than a theory, a vision', as he says in the glossary to *Discours* (p. 261)) and an already-lived attitude: 'Antillanity, an intellectual dream, lived at the same time in a subterranean way by our peoples' (ibid., p. 139; translation modified).

This gesture of refusal defines the most important word in the book. As a vision, as an intellectual dream, *l'antillanité* constitutes a form of theoretical construction on the part of the one who reflects upon the presence of an already-existing connection of the archipelago. However, *l'antillanité* already exists in a different dimension from this reflection: it is lived by Antillean peoples as the subterranean connection of the archipelago and of the island itself (Martinique). We can construct a theory, a vision, a plan for it, but it would only be tentative, because these connections cannot be exhaustively described or prefigured. Due to its opaqueness, it can never be just descriptive (it will never 'capture' its 'subject-matter' completely), but also not entirely prescriptive (it will never become a plan to be followed, or a set of criteria to be contrasted).

For the present purpose, this chapter will focus on the second sense of *l'antillanité*: the lived experience of the people. This is the subject of a brief section, number 82, 'Le vœu, le réel' [The hope, the real; translation modified]. In the title itself this notion is put at the site of an intersection between a reality and an aspiration, 'un vœu' [wish or hope]:

> The notion of *antillanité* emerges from a reality that we will have to question, but also corresponds to a hope that we must clarify and whose legitimacy must be demonstrated.
>
> A fragile reality (the experience of *l'antillanité*, woven together from one side of the Caribbean to the other) negatively twisted together in its urgency (*l'antillanité* as a hope, forever denied, often deferred, yet a strange, stubborn presence in our responses).
>
> This reality is virtual: dense (inscribed in fact) but threatened (not inscribed in consciousness).
>
> This hope is vital, but not obvious (ibid., p. 221; translation modified).

There is thus a play between two extremes, a fragile positivity and an imperious negativity. The first of these faces is undeniable, according to Glissant: although not everyone has heard about the Caribbean, its existence is indisputable for anyone who knows about the specificities of this remarkable region of the Earth.[10] But this indisputable reality, he says, is *virtual*: it has not been secured except in the common experience of these specificities and not in their conscious expression. This is why the positivity of this reality is fragile. The interesting point he adds here is that such a missing step towards expression corresponds to the necessity of transcending the élitaire aspect of manifestation, that is, the theoretical aspect *l'antillanité* (the 'intellectual dream') there has not been space for here.

The threat that the elitist, intellectual approach poses to self-expression is basically the same threat posed by the political, economic and, in general, historic conditions imposed on the Caribbean: severing the connections of transversality by imposing a deep isolation on every island. Whenever it is seen as separated, isolated from this common-lived experience of the people, *l'antillanité* runs the risk of becoming yet another external, disconnected form

---

10 This does not mean a simple affirmation of the ontic existence of the place: Glissant refers here to the particular character of a region whose geography, landscape, culture, historical conditions, etc. make it not only real, but noteworthy, perhaps even exceptional (pp. 221–2).

of expression, no matter how celebrated it is in international circles. In order to prevent this, it has to remain open to the insular/archipelagic character, which is in its turn an openness of the people towards its land, its experience in such a land and the connection to the rest of its inhabitants:

> The distant, uncertain openness [*ouverture*] of the Caribbean is nonetheless capable of carrying forward our people to self-renewal and of providing them with renewed ambition, by making them possess their world and their lived experience (wherein *l'antillanité* is present) and by making them fall into step with those who also share the same space (this too is implied in *l'antillanité*) (ibid., pp. 223–4; translation modified).

This is the closest we come to Glissant describing *l'antillanité*, this '*ouverture*' suggested in a Caribbean take on insularity, an openness towards openness. It cannot constitute a complete manifestation (and that is why he would refuse to define it), but a form of expression as an attunement to the spatial/temporal conditions of the Antilles and the lived-experience of its inhabitants, of the people.[11] A poetics of *l'antillanité* has to remain caught in this insoluble tension between a vision and a lived experience, between an aspiration and a reality.

To remain in tension, however, does not mean that *l'antillanité* cannot attain true expression, or that it always remains on the verge of arriving. Self-expression is possible in the Caribbean and it is possible to attune oneself to the conditions of the landscape and temporality, conditions that demand a commonality within the islands and in relation to the archipelago. This is, then, a direct answer to the question posed by Kincaid at the beginning of this chapter: it is indeed possible for these communities to give an account of themselves, to embrace an Antillean relationality (Kincaid, 1988, p. 165), but only as an attitude while searching for multirelationality. It is precisely because the Antilles (given their geographical configuration) are revealed as a 'une multi-relation' [multiple series of relationships] (ibid.) and not as a place: it does not describe the geographical demarcation of a location in America, but a mode of relation, of connection, of transversality.

This means as well that poetics of *l'antillanité* does not exist yet and that all these analyses prefigure, or predate, at least those forms of self-expression that would allow a liberation of the territories. But the possibility of attunement prefigures this as a poetics of anti-origins, presentist, disruptive, durable, intense. And the first gesture of configuring such a reaction is, according to Glissant, to 'remain where you are': 'The first reaction against this generalizing universality is the will of 'rester au lieu' [remaining where you are]. But for us this place is not only the land where our people were transplanted, it is also the

---

11 Attunement understood as putting oneself in the same key by sounding and listening the same (e.g., by uttering words, by writing) as something else (a landscape, a piece of music, a painting?). In that way one starts to sound like the other person or object without actually doing so (just like two instruments can be attuned to each other without playing the same sounds).

history they shared (experiencing it as non-history) with other communities, with whom the link is still becoming apparent today. Our place is the Antilles' (Glissant, 1981, p. 139). To 'return to the place', to the point of entanglement, is truly to remain where you are, finally to connect with such a land that has always been foreign, instead of looking for an elsewhere in order to resist oppression.

Bibliography

Britton, C. (1999) *Édouard Glissant and Postcolonial Theory: Strategies of Language and Resistance* (Charlottesville, VA: University of Virginia Press).

Césaire, A. (1956) 'Culture et colonisation', *Présence Africaine*, 8: 190–205.

— (2001) *Discourse on Colonialism* (New York: Monthly Review Press).

— (2010) 'Culture and colonization', *Social Text*, 28: 127–44, https://doi.org/10.1215/01642472-2009-071 [accessed 5 April 2019].

— (2013) *The Original 1939 Notebook of a Return to the Native Land: Bilingual Edition*, ed. A.J. Arnold and C. Eshleman (Middletown, CT: Wesleyan University Press).

Coulthard, G.S. (2014) *Red Skin, White Masks: Rejecting the Colonial Politics of Recognition* (Minneapolis, MN: University of Minnesota Press).

Drabinski, J.E. (2015) 'Aesthetics and the abyss. Between Césaire and Lamming', in J. E. Drabinski and M. Parham (eds.), *Theorizing Glissant: Sites and Citations* (London: Rowman & Littlefield), pp. 139–64.

Fanon, F. (1952) *Peau noire, masques blancs* (Paris: Édition du Seuil).

— (1961) *Les damnés de la terre* (Paris: La Découverte).

— (2001) *Black Skin, White Masks*, trans. by R. Philcox (New York: Grove).

— (2010) *The Wretched of the Earth*, trans. by R. Philcox (New York: Grove Press).

Glissant, É. (1990) *Poétique de la Relation* (Paris: Gallimard).

— (1997) *Poetics of Relation*, trans. by B. Wing (Ann Arbor, MI: University of Michigan Press).

— (1997 [1981]) *Discours Antillais* (Paris: Gallimard).

— (1999) *Caribbean Discourse: Selected Essays* (Charlottesville: University of Virginia Press).

Gualdrón Ramírez, M. (forthcoming, 2019) 'Transversality as disruption and connection: on the possibilities and limits of using the framework of trauma in Glissant's philosophy of Caribbean history', in *Philosophy in Colombia* (special issue of *Philosophical Readings*, 11).

Kincaid, J. (1988) *A Small Place* (New York: Farrar, Straus and Giroux).

Laforgue, P. (2012) 'Le Cahier d'un retour au pays natal de 1939 à 1947 (de l'édition Volontés à l'édition Bordas): Étude de génétique césairienne', *Études françaises* 48: 131–79, https://doi.org/10.7202/1012898ar [accessed 5 April 2019].

Yountae, A. (2017) *The Decolonial Abyss: Mysticism and Cosmopolitics from the Ruins* (New York: Fordham University Press).

10. Finding the Anancyesque in Shakespeare's *Julius Caesar* and the decolonisation project in Jamaica from 1938 to the present

Ruth Minott Egglestone

Decolonisation is a long, slow, multilayered, nuanced and selective process which should privilege agency, self-knowledge and respect. It is a rich palette from which our experience and imagination can choose and combine fresh colour combinations alongside the tried and tested ones. This chapter explores an allegorical connection between *The Tragedy of Julius Caesar* and the transition towards decolonisation from the Jamaica of 1938 to the present. The central argument has three strands: the idea of Cassius as a heroic figure; the role of Sir Alexander Bustamante as catalyst in the Jamaican movement for independence; and the model of a redeemed Anancy as a positive expression of the Jamaican self for the future.

An important component of the enduring popularity of Shakespeare's *Julius Caesar* – from schools and universities in the Asian subcontinent to global symbolism on stage in Central Park under the presidency of Donald Trump – is that this play has built-in resonance (Marks, 2017). For generations the values of honour, dignity, equality and civic duty have been rekindled through its rhetoric within an imperial educational mould, recognisable across the Commonwealth. Moreover, *Julius Caesar* still describes the dynamic of contemporary history. The dilemma of the Roman conspirators becomes a trope which allows for consideration of some of the tensions that underlie the closing phase of Tudor rule. Beyond that, we ask ourselves whether the debate that led to Caesar's demise and its consequences is also germane to the politics of the end of empire, still at play time and time again in Britain and abroad.

My career as a secondary-school teacher of English language and literature began in January 1982 at Manchester School in rural Jamaica. I was going to learn to be a good teacher on the job. The first Shakespeare play I taught was *Macbeth* but I was always only a few scenes ahead of the class. I had hoped to do better the second time around, but that would be in Kingston at Campion College and with another unfamiliar Shakespeare play: *Julius Caesar*. I was 23

R.M. Egglestone, 'Finding the Anancyesque in Shakespeare's Julius Caesar and the decolonisation project in Jamaica from 1938 to the present', in J.D. Webb, R. Westmaas, M. del Pilar Kaladeen and W. Tantam (eds.), *Memory, migration and (de)colonisation in the Caribbean and beyond* (London: University of London Press, 2019), pp. 153–71. License: CC-BY-NC-ND 4.0.

years old and burdened with the thought of preparing the play over Christmas to be ready for a spirited, co-education class of very bright 13-year-olds at the beginning of the new term. Again, I taught that tragedy only once and yet the play's dogged pursuit of the freedom *to be* has encouraged me ever since on those occasions when I have found it necessary to swim against the current and then hold my ground on a point of principle. I have always felt that a life based on mutual respect is an essential framework for relating to ourselves and others.

I knew that Brutus was the hero of the play for my West Indian father's generation, with the fault line being the betrayal of friendship in favour of patriotism. But when I first read *Julius Caesar* my attention was riveted by the voice of Cassius – that 'hungry' thinker[1] – with its emphasis on self-respect and a notion of dignity that values each person equally. Contrary to the view that presents him as a spin doctor solely intent on the manipulation of truth for his own ends, I found to my surprise that I identified with this overt dissenter because he is so earnest. I believed his statement that:

> Well, honour is the subject of my story.
> I cannot tell what you and other men
> Think of this life; but, for my single self,
> I had lief not be as live to be
> In awe of such a thing as I myself. (I. 2. 92–6)

To start with, I agreed with the reasonableness of his assertion in lines 95–6, with its affirmation of sovereignty. I easily identified with the concept of agency inherent in statements such as: 'Cassius from bondage will deliver Cassius' (I. 3. 90). Cassius is prepared to resist the oppression that he sees Caesar – who 'doth bestride the narrow world | Like a Colossus' (I. 2. 135–6) – threatening; and he feels justified in doing so because the point of a republic is that the leader is one among equals. So strongly does Cassius feel about all of them being bullied by Caesar, and so great a threat to the Roman way of life does this possibility seem to him, that he feels compelled to do something about the dilemma.

I was 12 years old when Michael Manley, the trade unionist with a 'passionate commitment to equality and justice', became Jamaica's fourth prime minister after winning the elections for the People's National Party (PNP) on 29 February 1972 (Franklyn, 2014). So, my adolescence was shaped by the process of becoming a very happy product of the – not only turbulent but also very inspiring – experiment in democratic socialism of the 1970s. This happened in tandem with a heightened public awareness of Jamaica's global voice in Third World affairs and the ascendancy of reggae music as a cultural

---

1   The Shakespearean line most commonly associated with Cassius in the Caribbean context comes from Caesar's first reference to him in the play: "Yond Cassius has a lean and hungry look, / He thinks too much: such men are dangerous" (1.2.194–5). In Jamaica, it is not unusual for the epithet to be misquoted as 'mean and hungry', which supports a negative perception of the character as an untrustworthy figure.

force. I was as much of an idealist as Cassius and during my teenage years democracy in action had been a defining principle for me at home, at school and in the wider society. Furthermore, my West Indian education had pivoted on the value of original thinking. How, then, could Cassius be condemned at the outset because he thought too deeply about the dynamics of his society?

Thematically, the play's flirtation with the dynamic of one-upmanship provides much scope for application to the importance of dignity as embodied by the Jamaican folk hero Anancy. This unapologetic go-getter finds a sense of worth in managing to make the most of his disadvantages, and especially the hardship he has experienced, but usually at a great cost to others. Louise Bennett, storyteller par excellence, sums up Jamaica's most powerful metaphorical figure in these terms: 'Anancy, the trickify little spider man who speaks with a lisp and lives by his wits, is both comic and sinister, both hero and villain of Jamaican folk stories' (1979, p. xi). He has great respect for the power that words have to give shape to reality, not only in their capacity for presenting the element of risk incumbent in the choice to be made in the crossroads experiences in life, but also as a tool for the pursuit of an aim which finds expression in the alluring and masking potential of rhetoric.

Anancy, whose reputation has been created by the folktales that bear his name, is the ultimate opportunist, who does his best to take advantage of the gullibility of others. The Anancy story is, however, a morality tale centred on the ironic truth that what goes around comes around and, therefore, in the cycle of life Anancy will inevitably become a victim of his own scheming. *Julius Caesar*, like the folk stories that belong to the trickster Anancy, illustrates the negative aspects of both naivety and one-upmanship. The action centres on an obsession with power which usurps any sense of fulfilment found in public-spiritedness. Caesar, the great republican conqueror of the enemies of Rome, is unable to keep his own ego in check, acquiring pre-eminence, at first as a reluctant wolf among sheep and then, in the words of Cassius:

> Most like this dreadful night,
> That thunders, lightens, opens up graves, and roars
> As doth the lion in the Capitol –
> A man no mightier than thyself, or me,
> In personal action, yet prodigious grown
> And fearful, as these strange eruptions are. (I. 3. 73–8)

The citizenry naively behave like deer as they exultantly seek to crown Caesar for his victory over Rome's erstwhile hero Pompey; by so doing, they create a lion in their midst.

Showing unselfish interest in public welfare, motivated by genuine devotion to the general good, does not come naturally to Anancy, who, like Caesar, has few friends. According to Montesquieu (read through the eyes of Isaiah Berlin), the principle which causes a republic to flourish is *virtue* – as expressed in a disposition to act with energy for the public interest or advantage and a willingness to sacrifice private interest for the public good.² In my reading of the play, these traits apply to Cassius and Brutus as they individually explain their rationale for joining the conspiracy against Caesar. However, they jostle each other in their devotion to a cause which admits gamesmanship as they exploit each other's foibles in the interests of progress. This deficit in trust ultimately surfaces as 'some grudge' (IV. 1. 125) that seriously tests the bond between them. As much as it discusses the excesses of power, this Shakespearean play is a study of the course of friendship in difficult times. It is, therefore, in the danger to the continuing relationship between Cassius and Brutus that the tragedy lies, rather than in the assassination of Julius Caesar.

Looking through the lens of enlightened self-interest, Cassius has little to gain by standing in opposition to Caesar (except, perhaps, self-respect) and much to lose. The man Julius Caesar was a consummate politician, an exceptionally good leader and an effective writer. His *Conquest of Gaul* was taught for centuries as a Latin reader in schools and his demise at the hands of his compatriots resounds as a warning to all political leaders, who must inevitably spar with hubris as they try to rise above the temptations of power. 'Liberty! Freedom! Tyranny is dead!', cries Cinna, the conspirator, as Caesar falls (III. 1. 78). In his tragedy about this Roman hero's untimely death, William Shakespeare plays sport with ambiguity, using stress and elasticity, smoothness and resilience to create a nuanced dramatic structure that has the tensile strength, but gossamer quality and complexity of a spider's web.

As a young teacher in the early 1980s, I felt that Cassius's point of view was more relevant to my world than that of Brutus because it accommodates status anxiety as a driver of ambition, in tandem with noble respectability, and therefore presents a much more nuanced analysis of an emergent West Indian discourse on national sovereignty. Packaged in a dialectic which he calls 'crab antics', the anthropologist Peter Wilson's analysis of the role of the hero within the West Indian value system pivots on a code of honour centred on ambition fuelled by the principle of either 'respectability' or conversely 'reputation' (1969).³

2   Berlin says of Montesquieu: 'According to him each type of society possesses an inner structure, an inner dynamic principle or force, which makes it function as it does – and this "inner" force differs from type to type. Whatever strengthens the "inner" principle causes the organism to flourish, whatever impairs it causes it to decay. His catalogue of these forces is very famous; monarchy rests on the principle of honour, aristocracy on that of moderation, the republican regime on that of virtue (that is, public spirit, *civisme*, almost team spirit) and despotism on that of terror. Montesquieu conceives of social organisms in the manner of Aristotle as teleological – purposive – wholes, as entelechies. The model is biological, not chemical. The inner spring of these societies is conceived by him as that which causes them to fulfil themselves by moving towards an inner goal, in terms of which alone they can be understood' (1981, p. 140).

3   See Wilson (1969) *Crab Antics*, first published in 1973. 'Crab antics' is an anthropological model in relation to Caribbean men distilled by Wilson through his observations of life and culture on the island of Providencia. The term refers to the behaviour of crabs (caught

My own research, based on cultural patterns within the Little Theatre Movement's National Pantomime tradition in Jamaica, makes the case that the 'crab antics' model is a good match for masculinity within the Jamaican context.[4] For this male-dominated play, however, Jean Besson's summary of Wilson's framework is most helpful. The idea of respectability, she says, 'is based on class, colour, wealth and Eurocentric culture, life style and education'. Then she points out that '[r]eputation, by contrast, is an indigenous counter-culture based on the ethos of equality and rooted in personal, as opposed to social worth' (1993, p. 16). In these terms, the question of integrity in *Julius Caesar* is a tussle between the reputation-based approach of Cassius, Caesar's childhood competitor, and the respectability of Brutus, Caesar's protégé, whose ancestor Lucius Junius Brutus founded the Roman republic.

Julius Caesar is the embodiment of honour in every sense of the word except that of nobility of spirit, for, like Macbeth, he is possessed of an 'o'er vaulting ambition'.[5] He is a patrician of the Julian clan, but also very much a self-made man and his fame lies not in his inherited 'respectability' but rather in his military prowess and therefore his 'reputation'. His flaw is that he is not satisfied, despite seeming to have as much as it is reasonable for any highly successful man to have. His ambition is beyond measure and he is prepared to overstep any boundary to fulfil it. Excess is the undoing of equality and the state of social equilibrium. Excess is also the opposite of unity. Caesar has to be contained because he cannot contain himself.

Jean Besson adds: 'Reputation is also based on verbal skills and anti-establishment activities' (1993, p. 16). In this context Cassius, the great persuader and initiator of the counter-insurgency, emerges as the first Anancy-type figure. Cassius is the most complex character in the play because he is an earnest and effective subversive whose purpose is not hidden. Caesar knows and articulates the threat that this kind of senator poses. Cassius is perceptive, well-educated, principled and 'he thinks too much; such men are dangerous' (I. 2. 195). It is also true, as Caesar puts it, that Cassius is one of those men who can never be 'at heart's ease | Whiles they behold a greater than themselves' (I. 2. 208–9), for he believes firmly in the republican principle that *all* citizens should be equal, claiming, 'I was born free as Caesar' (I. 2. 106).

Then, somewhat unexpectedly, as a fully fledged exemplar of a carefully cultivated, organic and potent spirit of Jamaicanness, I migrated to the United

---

in a bucket), which pull each other down as they try to get out and is used to explain a social dynamic of non-productive self interest, within Wilson's analysis. However, J. Besson's anthropological riposte to Wilson's model from the Afro-Caribbean peasant woman's perspective is also highly important and should be considered in tandem in future research.

4   R. Minott Egglestone, '"A place with no style of its own": a dialectic of dominance in the pantomime', unpublished lecture given to the Caribbean Team, Department of Education at the University of Sheffield, 23 May 2011.

5   This was Macbeth's fatal flaw: 'I have no spur | To prick the sides of my intent, but only | Vaulting ambition, which o'er-leaps itself | And falls on the other' (*Macbeth*, I. 7. 27–30).

Kingdom in 1986 to continue teaching and then go on to postgraduate studies. What were to be six years have now become more than thirty, but during this time Cassius's statement, 'I'd lief not be as live to be in awe of such a thing as I myself' (I. 2. 95–6), has become an oft-repeated assertion in both my professional and personal life. I learnt from Cassius that when we have to accommodate the menace of wolves or lions in our midst, it is the sheepish behaviour of the collective in the past that has brought this threat into being.

For this reason there is always the danger of inscribing Caesar within the action. Cassius's commitment to the cause of freedom is total. Casca recognises this in his acknowledgement that 'every bondman in his own hand bears | The power to cancel his captivity' (I. 3. 101–2) if he is willing to die for freedom, for there is merit in considering the angle that Caesar 'would not be a wolf, | But that he sees the Romans are but sheep: | He were no lion, were not Romans hinds' (I. 3. 104–6). The question is, how serious are we about guarding our freedom? In an essay on the fall of the Roman Republic for the BBC History website, Cambridge professor of classics Mary Beard speaks of 'the carefully regulated system of "power sharing" that characterised traditional Republican politics' (2011). We need to ask ourselves why within our democracies we behave like sheep. It seems like the easy option at first; only that we then feel, too late, the iron fist within the velvet glove as the wolves we have created terrorise the collective. In turn the following question could be asked: 'Why can't the Jamaican people see through their politicians?' The answer would probably be: 'Because the successful ones are so reminiscent of Anancy'.

For me, Cassius emerged as a tragic hero but I realise now, as I reflect on my ensuing journey through life with Shakespeare's Roman play, that teaching *Julius Caesar* in this way in 1983 was an exercise in what Sylvia Wynter would have called decolonial 'intellectual disobedience'.[6] My reading would make Brutus a foil to Cassius, for, by allowing the tone in which his lines are spoken to be honest rather than conniving, the voice of Cassius as freedom-fighter emerges from Shakespeare's text. Such an attitude is one that a Jamaican theatre-going public would respect, for as the esteemed sociolinguist Mervyn Alleyne says at the end of a long career of cultural engagement: 'Jamaicans won't put up with foolishness: they rebel at anything that looks like discrimination'.[7]

---

6 The phrase comes from Mignolo (2015, p.107). The full quotation underscores the attitude of this chapter: 'It is across both neurobiological cognition and decolonial practices that Sylvia Wynter's work and her intellectual disobedience emerge. Wynter suggests that if we accept that epistemology gives us the *principles and rules of knowing* through which the Human and Humanity are understood, we are trapped in a knowledge system that fails to notice that the stories of what it means to be Human – specifically origin stories that explain who/what we are – are, in fact, narratively constructed'.

7 'The interdisciplinary scholarship of a Caribbeanist: a tribute to Dr. Mervyn Alleyne' was a discussion panel organised by the Institute of Caribbean Studies, which was held on 20 Oct. 2011 at University of Puerto Rico-Río Piedras.

My thinking here also rests on the fact that in 2013 Liam Martin published *De Tragedy au Julias Ceazaa*/*Julius Caesar in Jamaican English*, a translation of Shakespeare's play into two versions of Jamaican 'nation language' – *A Patwa Vosian* (a Jamaica Creole version) and *A Rastafarian Vosian* (a Dread Talk version) (2013).[8] The translation of *Julius Caesar* into Jamaican nation language gives Shakespeare's play the intimacy of an Anancy story, while the confluence of the Great and the Little Traditions is an echo in itself of the dialectic of respectability and reputation that sits at the heart of a male value system that privileges the idea of honour over virtue, for indeed both Cassius and Brutus are honourable men.

Something of the distinction that can be made between the linguistic register of the two *vosians* [versions] is given in the helpful summary of their relationship alongside Standard Jamaican English (the language of this chapter) by the linguist and educator Velma Pollard in her book *Dread Talk: The Language of Rastafari*:

> The official language of Jamaica is Standard Jamaican English (SJE). It is the language of the formal motions of society and of education. Jamaica Creole (JC), the speech of the man in the street and the language of informal interaction in the society, is a creole of English lexicon; the code of Rastafari is an adjustment of the lexicon of either of the languages, to satisfy certain requirements of speakers sympathetic to the philosophy of Rasta. All language within the Jamaican speech community may be described as 'English related'. The significance of this fact is that writers are able to include usage and meaning from within the conventions of Rasta, while writing either in English or in Jamaican Creole (1994, p. 60).

As a result of the 1970s, contemporary Jamaica prides itself on being a socially mobile society. Nonetheless, Jamaican Standard English is the language of the establishment and *patwa* carries the indigenous countercultural stamp. Liam Martin's double translation in *De Tragedy au Julias Ceazaa* presents a synchronicity between his two versions but this is not surprising because during the second half of the 20th century, and especially in the late 1970s, Dread Talk became part of that code shifting, linguistic continuum of everyday language in Jamaica, which also includes reference to frequent (mis)quotations in 16th-century English from the King James Bible and Shakespeare's oeuvre. Rastafarian/Dread Talk is also the language of reggae music and, as Velma Pollard points out, despite the continued disapproval of classroom teachers, 'the youth who in earlier years spoke Patwa (JC) for peer group acceptance with or without their parents' assent, speaks today the same language but deeply laced with DT (*Dread Talk*) phrases and lexical items, and this in a most effortless fashion' (1994, p. 10).[9]

---

8 'Nation language' is the term that K. Brathwaite (1984) uses to refer to the Creole languages of the Caribbean.

9 Originally published in 1980; reprinted as ch. 1 in Pollard (1994).

It is only in sharing his plans with Brutus in Act 1 that Cassius becomes vulnerable, for his safety rests entirely on their bond of friendship. In response Brutus affirms that he is talking to a kindred spirit for theirs is a relationship of mutual trust: 'That you do love me, I am nothing jealous' (I. 2. 162). It is interesting to see how the Rasta translation of these words conveys the sincerity of Brutus's confidence in this friendship with Cassius. It reads: 'Dhat de-I lov I, I-man no dae suspicious at all' (Martin, 2013, p. 122) and means: 'I know without the shadow of a doubt that you love me'. Uttered by a Ras Tafari whose distinctively grounded identity represents the understatedly comfortable masculinity of a lion, these intimate words come across as a noble affirmation, a straightforward encapsulation of an easily understood truth.

A decolonial reading ultimately gives scope for analysing the play in response to the question that Walter Mignolo associates with Sylvia Wynter: What does it mean to be human? This involves imagining 'the "right" or "noble" or "moral" characteristics of Human' (2015, p. 108). The Rastafarian voice is that of 'the man at the bottom of the social ladder, the suffering Jamaican' (Pollard, 1994, p. 60) but the language of Rastafari privileges the individual as subject not object (always using 'I' not 'me'); asserts membership of a royal priesthood as part of the identity of the ordinary man; establishes a personal identification with the lion as a symbol of African power, courage and nobility; employs vocabulary that carries the severity of the Old Testament prophets; and transforms words so that they reflect a commitment to the elevation of dignity and freedom over the lure of materialism symbolised by 'Babylon' (that is, the culture of the industrialised west).

One has to remember, too, that the wordsmith – the teller of tales – has played a significant part in the decolonial story. Brother Man, the eponymous character created by anti-imperialist journalist and novelist Roger Mais, who is the hero of his novel of the same name (1954), a philosophical 'Rasta cobbler with a gift for healing' (Paul, 2004) would fit comfortably into the opening scene of Liam Martin's *Julias Ceazaa*. Furthermore, to follow on at another social level, the conversation of 'dhat magga tincka' Cassius and his associates in the second scene of the play easily resonates with the culture, accent and beat of contemporary parliamentarians in Jamaica, engaging in a political discourse built on foundations laid down by the country's 20th-century national heroes: William Alexander Bustamante, Marcus Mosiah Garvey and Norman Washington Manley.

For the most part, however, the founding fathers would have articulated their decolonial visions in Jamaican Standard English, as illustrated in an extract from a 1932 speech by Marcus Garvey which the governor general used to inspire Jamaicans at home and abroad on Independence Day in 2003. His Excellency the Most Honourable Sir Howard Felix Hanlan Cooke ON, GCMG, GCVO, CD, referred in his message to rhetoric that stirred the early days of the island's struggle for sovereignty but which was still applicable:

Marcus Garvey said in his 'Building the New Jamaica' speech in 1932
– Those of us who love our country cannot but interest ourselves in this
desire to see our country taking a place and standing second to none in
the world. When I say second to none, I mean it only in a limited sense,
because our country is small. I mean it from an economical, industrial,
social, educational point of view . . . There is no reason why we should
not do everything for the development of our country to make Jamaicans
the happiest people in the world . . . Satisfied and contented. Nature has
blessed us with everything conducive to this . . . Arise Jamaicans and do!
(cited in Cooke, 2003).

Interestingly, the label 'small island' could also be applied to Great Britain with respect to its physical size in proportion to its impact on the global stage. The reality of the enduring legacy of empire shows that it is not the size of the country that matters so much as the imagination and ambition of its people. Not dissimilar to the dynamic of the early Roman republic but in a more osmotic way, the Jamaican nation is characteristically spirited and resilient, gritty and resolute and punches well above its weight in terms of the soft power of cultural influence. On the international stage of the 21st century, phrases like 'What a gwaan?' [What's going on?] have moved from London street talk to hip banter among intellectuals on BBC Radio 4 in response to President Barack Obama's use of the term on a state visit to Jamaica in 2015 (Gloudon, 2015).

Alongside this, though, the Jamaican 'national' story – which could easily be cast as a series of power struggles – arises out of a continuing substratum of internecine conflict.[10] Consequently, within the landscape of that small, tropical island at the heart of the Caribbean Basin, as in so many other postcolonial societies, there rages a politics of violence encouraged by 'de ambitious Ceazaa dem' which enmeshes the citizenry in latent, as well as blatant, aggression. Analysing the dynamics of Shakespeare's text also presents the challenge of subjecting our own matrices of empowerment to scrutiny in evaluating the 'crab antics' of political leadership in a decolonisation project that intensified in 1938 and – it is to be hoped – continues with vigour in the present. Freedom

---

10   Some key dates in the island's 'national' story: 1494, 1655, 1831–2, 1865 ('Jamaican history: 10 facts: things you need to know about the country you love', *The Voice*, posted 6 Aug. 2012, http://www.voice-online.co.uk/article/jamaican-history-10-facts [accessed 9 Feb. 2016]). The arrival of Christopher Columbus in 1494 secured the island for Spain and heralded the ultimate destruction of its indigenous Taino inhabitants. In 1655, Cromwell's expeditionary force seized the island from the Spanish and ushered in over 300 years of British colonial rule. These were punctuated by various slave revolts like the 1831–2 Christmas rebellion, led by the Baptist deacon Sam Sharpe, who was convinced that the entitlement of freedom for the enslaved was being withheld by the plantocracy. The 1865 Morant Bay rebellion grew out of protest marches by the freed peasantry against mounting social and economic injustice. This seditious behaviour was savagely repressed under martial law with the resultant imposition of Crown Colony status on the island, indefinitely placed under the sole control of the colonial governor.

is fragile and its durability is dependent on the power of equality, which has to be guarded by checks and balances.

Ironically, the values of honour, dignity, equality and civic duty are prized qualities within an island social structure still influenced by a nuanced skin-tone continuum of shades of brown as a measure of individual worth; also of an education system which privileges mastery of Jamaican Standard English (ostensibly the language of the head) over Jamaica Creole/Patwa (purported to be the language of the heart). The process of counteracting the British government's colonial, racist policy, which maintained – 'a carefully nurtured sense of inferiority in the governed' – is a battle that has to be fought in the mind.[11] This was the strength of Marcus Garvey's contribution to the world of 20th-century politics. Historically, social stratification in Jamaica has been closely aligned to gradations in skin tone and even in the 21st century the phenomenon of 'shadeism', a Jamaican form of racial prejudice, remains a social reality. Therefore, a significant challenge for Jamaica as an independent country has been a sovereignty of the imagination which might truly conceive of all human beings as equal in terms of intrinsic worth. Almost eight decades since the death of Marcus Garvey, who did so much to promote the idea that 'Black is Beautiful',[12] the island nation is still trying to emancipate itself from the mental slavery of institutionalised racism.

The key players in establishing architecture of decolonisation in Jamaica were Norman Washington Manley, the distinguished barrister, and his cousin William Alexander Bustamante, 'one of the four principal usurers in Kingston' (Hart, 1999, p. xiii). They were in opposition to His Excellency Sir Arthur Richards, GCMG, the authoritarian governor of Jamaica from 1938 to 1943 and then to each other. Professor Edward Seaga, the country's fifth prime minister, makes this observation about the two political heavyweights (as they were when he met them in the 1950s): 'In a crowd, it was easy to recognise that the handsome features of the two cousins, Bustamante and Manley, had been chiselled from the same stone, Manley being the darker, brown-skin version of the two. Bustamante stood out visually as a figure and personality: Manley had to be engaged in conversation for his outstanding mind to be appreciated. Both men were attractive and respected leaders in the true sense of the word' (Seaga, 2009, p. 90).

11 This phrase from Commander R. C. Bodilly, a retired English naval officer who was a resident magistrate in Jamaica in the early 1930s, is cited in Hart (1999, pp. 147–8 and p. 149, n. 15). The full quotation is: 'Our rule exists in the last resort on a carefully nurtured sense of inferiority in the governed. As soon as we lessen that we lessen the security of our laws' (p. 148).
12 *The Oxford Dictionary of Modern Quotations* (5.20) lists this phrase as an anonymous slogan of civil rights campaigners in the mid 1960s, cited in Newsweek, 11 July 1966. The political phrase gained international currency from the 1960s but the idea comes out of the Harlem Renaissance of the 1920s and was promoted in the 1950s and 1960s through the work of Brooklyn photographer Kwame Brathwaite, who was inspired by Marcus Garvey.

In a sense Norman Manley and Alexander Bustamante could have been Brutus and Cassius versus the Caesar-like representative of imperial Britain. As he tries to explain some of the dynastic intricacies at the heart of Jamaican politics, Adam Kuper makes the point in his anthropological study *Changing Jamaica* that 'both parties are regarded as the expression of the personalities of their founders' (1976, p. 120). The contrasting characters of the 'noble patrician' Norman Manley and the 'daringly flamboyant' Alexander Bustamante presented a choice between 'the man who thought too much' like Cassius (1.2.195) or 'the man who loved the name of honour more than he feared death' like Brutus (1.2.88–9). The choice between 'the intellectual' or 'the entrepreneur', the prophet or the trickster, can be equated to that between Manley, the statesman whose strategic vision was to build the bakery and Bustamante, the vote-winning politician who promised to give the people bread. Caesar, the oppositional figure, was represented by Prime Minister Winston Churchill in the mother country but locally by the governor Sir Arthur Richards. Captain R. W. Thompson, a British naval intelligence officer posted to Jamaica in late October 1942, refers to the island situation in his account *Black Caribbean* (1946) in these terms: 'It was clear at the outset that Great Britain had a considerable headache thumping away in the Caribbean, and only the voice of the Old Warrior, baying his faith to resound to the ends of the earth, showed that there was nothing amiss with the spirit: . . . I did not become the King's first minister to preside at the liquidation of the British Empire!' (p. 60).

When, as an 82-year-old historian, the trade unionist and *griot*, Richard Hart (1917–2013) mapped in *Towards Decolonisation* (1999) his first-hand account of the political, labour and economic development in Jamaica between 1938 and 1945, he presented a story in which one man – like Alexander Bustamante – could in fact play many parts: Cassius, Antony and Caesar. In his early 20s, Hart himself was a major player among that cast of types – patriots, statesmen, rogues and opportunists – who developed the Jamaican nationalist framework in the 20th century. He trained to be a solicitor and became 'a trouble-making journalist and a key trade union organiser ... detained ... twice [by the colonial government] as a subversive during the second world war' (Drayton, 2014). He had been a founder member of the PNP in 1938 at the age of 21 but was expelled for being too radical in 1952. Yet it was Hart who took on the role of historian as *griot*, deliberately eschewing autobiography in favour of 'an objective history' of the Jamaican struggle for nationhood. Rupert Lewis, professor of political thought at the University of the West Indies (Mona), saw Richard Hart as 'a symbol of the nationalist awakening and the twentieth century struggle for decolonization in Jamaica and the Caribbean' (2012). During the course of a long life, Richard Hart was also a good example of the Jamaican character's propensity to stand against oppression and fight to the very end. Like Cassius, he never stopped being a 'magga tincka'.

As Hart was the main archivist for that period, however, it is his collection of primary source material which underpins much of the history of the time as it continues to be written. Very honourably, however, he strove to bring to our attention the potential dominance of his *version* – he would say 'understanding' – of events as the evidence is all provided from the same source.[13] At his death, Ken Jones dubbed Hart 'a giant of a man' for his service to the national story in the 20th century and also pointed out that 'as far as his monumental work in the interest of Jamaica's trade union and political development is concerned, further respect may still be due' (2013).

The road to Jamaican independence gathered pace in 1938 following the return of Alexander Bustamante to the island in 1934. In 1905, at the age of 21, he had left Jamaica 'to work and live abroad, and did so for thirty years in Central America and the United States' (Seaga, 2009, p. 36). Bustamante had some of the qualities of Anancy, who 'can change himself into whatever and whoever he wishes at certain times, and his stories make it quite plain that he is able to get away with tricks which ordinary mortals can't' (Bennett, 1979, p. xi). Richard Hart says of him: 'There are so many conflicting stories about his early life that it is difficult to distinguish fact from fiction. One of the more fanciful and improbable stories which he himself contributed, was that he had changed his name from Clarke to Bustamante on being adopted by a Spanish general and that he had seen active service with the Spanish army' (1999, p. xii).

When the PNP was founded in 1938 it was the brainchild of O. T. Fairclough (1904–70), a black accountant whose experience of class prejudice in Jamaica prompted him to look for political solutions to the problem of inequality, which went in tandem with shadeism.[14] Fairclough invited the distinguished lawyer Norman Washington Manley to be co-founder, and eventually persuaded him to become leader, of the party.[15] The Bustamante Industrial Trade Union (BITU) and the PNP were established in the same year (1938) and the original intention was that there would be one union and one party trying to set the

---

13 As the trade union scholar Jeffrey Harrod points out, Hart, as a centrally involved participant, is himself all too often the common source of unattributed documents from the period 'relating to the nature of Jamaican trade unions, regional trade union organisations, trade union education and history' (1972, as cited in Hart, 1999, pp. xix–xx and n.10).

14 A. Bertram (historian, teacher, journalist, former politician) explains the basis of the phenomenon of shadeism: 'Plantation slavery, the greatest wealth producing system of the 18th century, systematically created and legalised a racist society in Jamaica, which separated whites at the top, browns in the middle and blacks at the base' (2005).

15 '"The People's National Party (PNP) was founded by Norman Manley in 1938." Not quite, he was a co-founder, and he said so himself. If there is any one man who is to be credited with the founding of the PNP it is O.T. Fairclough, who also founded the *Public Opinion* newspaper. Fairclough it was who invited Manley to be the leader of the party.' E. Walters of Carlton University submitted this comment (as a point of clarification) to Fact 6 in this online newspaper article: 'Jamaican history: 10 facts: things you need to know about the country you love', *The Voice*, 6 Aug. 2012.

stage for the vision of the New Jamaica. Edward Seaga notes: 'The PNP was founded on the principles of Fabian socialism, named after the Roman general Quintus Fabius Maximus who believed in gradual rather than revolutionary change' (2009, p. 41). However, the 'heroics' of Bustamante during World War Two meant that he was jailed for 17 months for allegedly violating the Defence of the Realm Act. He emerged a hero from detention at Up Park Camp and, by consolidating his power base in his trade union, set himself up as a rival to Norman Manley, forming the Jamaica Labour Party (JLP) in 1943.

In the role of leader, Bustamante ruthlessly dealt with rivals for his position as chief. He was courageous and could control the mob, but he was also a potential Caesar and highly skilled in the tricks of politics. Consequently, in the tussle over who would be Jamaica's first prime minister, it was the maverick moneylender who had also begun 'to take a personal interest in the problems which affected the ordinary man' (ibid., p. 36) who came out on top. Bustamante 'was not learned in an academic sense and never pretended to be, although he came to prominence through incessant letter-writing. He was street smart and understood, as only a few others did, the nuances of the life of working-class and rural people' (ibid., p. 37). He was principally an oppositional (anti-authoritarian) figure who lived by his wits but, as Edward Seaga adds, 'knew the language of the people and what key references to draw from their lifestyle for impact' (ibid.).

Hart reports: 'The PNP was an organised expression of Jamaica's nationalist aspirations' (1999, p. 261). Norman Manley's campaign in 1944 was based on a carefully worked-out plan for self-government within five years. However, Bustamante won the elections for the JLP by discrediting the PNP in the eyes of the masses by adopting the slogan 'self-government means brown man rule' in his campaign. Richard Hart tells us that 'the black masses were only too conscious of the contemptuous attitude towards them of many members of the brown middle class. "Brown man rule" was the last thing the majority of black people wished to see in Jamaica . . . For the 1944 election, the first to be held under full adult suffrage, the slogan effectively served its purpose' (1999, p. 253).

By 1958 the dream of a West Indian Federation had begun to take shape as a serious postcolonial option for Jamaica. However, Bustamante in opposition allied himself with the business sector, which had been unsettled by the presence of PNP radicals (like Richard Hart) in the leadership of the unions. In a referendum in 1961 the Jamaican public voted in favour of national sovereignty as an independent island state. Bustamante's role as agitator might have made him seem like a Cassius, but as 'a demagogic orator' (Seaga, 2009, p. 37) he was much more of an Antony and his rhetoric only enhanced his popularity. Consequently, it was he, as the first prime minister of the new Jamaica, who welcomed Princess Margaret on the runway of Palisadoes Airport

(Kingston) when she arrived to represent Queen Elizabeth II at the declaration of independence in August 1962.

Julius Caesar certainly occupies a valid space as a postcolonial text because it maps the destruction of the 'dream', the specific set of ideals which once held the republic together and gave it strength. This 'problem play' (Schanzer, 1963; Maquerlot, 1995, pp. 72–86) presents the strain and kinaesthetic dynamic of a centre that cannot hold because it is beset by the sort of internecine rivalry that triggered and fuelled the two world wars in the 20th century and, indeed, the battle between Hilary Clinton and Donald Trump in the 2016 American election, during which truth became the most significant casualty. The danger of conflicts in which the public is divided between its gratitude to a Pompey and its love for a Caesar is that clever people and thinking heads become 'blocks . . . stones . . . worse than senseless things'[16] – as dense as wood – when baited with the short-term satisfaction of greed and can so easily be tempted to sell their birthright for a mess of pottage (Genesis 25.29–34).

There is significance in the lyrical sweep of the action in *Julius Caesar* from a triumphal display of sovereignty to nothing. We see the tragic consequences of the freedom struggle in the ensuing violence. As Tom Holland describes it, 'everywhere, what had once been scenes of luxury were converted to the needs of war' (2011, Kindle edition, 70%, Loc 5468 of 7487). The 'problem' that is unpacked in the second half of Shakespeare's play is that despite their best efforts to the contrary the conspirators manage to destroy the Rome they know when they try to save it. How could they have guessed that by assassinating Julius Caesar and prompting a change of regime the people would exchange 'black dog fi monkey' in the ascension of Octavius, Caesar's great-nephew and heir, to the role of 'first citizen of the state' for life – Augustus Caesar, Rome's autocratic first emperor.

In the Royal Shakespeare Company's production of *Julius Caesar* under the direction of Angus Jackson in 2017, the dialogue is crystal-clear and so Shakespeare's words are given the opportunity to speak above the action. As the audience engages with the nuances of relationships, the characters do not come across as types but rather as individual personalities reacting to a collective crisis. Within this context, the friendship between Brutus and Cassius occupies the centre stage of our imagination, and the humanity of all the participants in the story is underscored.

The play *Julius Caesar* is a tragedy. The outcome is dire for Brutus and Cassius, whose death tips the balance in favour of Antony and Octavius. The classical historian Tom Holland says: 'Octavian was the man whom those defeated at Philippi chiefly reviled as the murderer of liberty' (2011, Kindle edition, 70%, Loc 5454 of 7487). The importance of the second half of Shakespeare's play

---

16 The tribune Murellus, infuriated by their fickle nature, refers to the Roman tradesmen as 'You blocks, you stones, you worse than senseless things!' as they capriciously shift their loyalty from Pompey to Caesar at the start of the play (I. 1. 34).

is captured by Kamau Brathwaite's rejoinder: 'so let me sing | nothing | now' (1973, p. 13). This is what Anancy does. He endures the storm of conflict and begins to spin and enact his stories of freedom again.

Over the years tragedians have plied their wares with trepidation on the Jamaican stage because the less sophisticated in the audience can be guaranteed to respond to the most distressing scene with uproariously disruptive laughter. I have written and spoken elsewhere (2004) on the redemptive approach to the figure of Anancy within Jamaica's Little Theatre Movement and the new nationalist drama of the LTM Pantomime tradition as a showcase of decolonial identity.[17] The Jamaican Pantomime is an example of nationalism producing a progressive cultural practice based on the importance of unity.

To signpost is the ultimate purpose of this experiment in indigenous theatre, which organically supported the exercise of nation-building from 1941, and found that, as it became translated into something else, it could not shed the name 'pantomime'. Furthermore, this label guaranteed that the Christmas show would be a comedy and so no matter how strong the compulsion to tackle serious issues, the treatment would be undertaken in a spirit of joviality and conclude with a happy ending and, always, hope. Within the LTM National Pantomime process, therefore, the figure of Anancy has to be redeemed.

In order to be true to ourselves as Jamaicans, we need to acknowledge the Anancyesque as an 'inner spring' in the decolonisation process.[18] Adaptability is a quality which seems to be reinforced in the Anancy stories, which 'record the stupidities of the less quickly assimilative in meeting new conditions of life' (Beckwith, 1929, p. 221). Traditionally, where Anancy comes a cropper is in his motives, for he is supremely, even cruelly, selfish. The folk tales warn us about so many of the other animals in the forest (Anancy frequently assumes the shape of a spider) who 'are too easily trusting . . . [who] seem almost to want to be deceived', says Mervyn Morris as he responds to the work of the virtuoso storyteller Louise Bennett. Morris adds that perhaps 'now is as good a time as any to re-read Anancy stories as a warning against credulity' (1979, p. x).

Despite his appeal, in the folk tales Anancy is an anti-hero from whom the Jamaican student can learn much about the kind of negativity that ultimately leads to violence, tragedy and social destruction. The importance of the biblical warning 'humble yourself' (Luke 18:14) is firmly integrated into our trickster stories, for as the proverb says, 'di more monkey climb, di more im expose'.[19] However, within the comedic framework of the Jamaican National Pantomime

---

17 There is an earlier version of this chapter online: Minott Egglestone (2001). See also Minott Egglestone (2010). For access to a spoken account, see Minott Egglestone (2014).
18 See I. Berlin's observations on Montesquieu in note 1.
19 In English rather than *patwa*, this proverb reads: 'The higher the monkey climbs, the more he shows his tail'. This means: 'The further an unsuitable person is promoted, the more obvious his inadequacies become' (Simpson and Speake, 2015, p. 151).

tradition, Anancy sees the error of his ways and is redeemed through the love and forgiveness of others; and his cleverness is put to good use to save the day for the embattled community. Consequently, in order to maintain this heroic status and to consolidate his reputation with respectability, Anancy on stage has to shift his default position from selfishness to altruism.

William Shakespeare's *Julius Caesar* is an exercise in reasoning around the impact of political power on the human condition which remains uncannily current across geographical space and historical time. Liam Martin's two adaptations of *Julius Caesar* in Jamaican English, if used in staging the play, would provide Jamaican audiences with the opportunity to engage so seamlessly with the uncomfortable political questions posed by Shakespeare's drama that it would be really difficult to shirk responsibility for truly thinking in 'new' terms, maybe even with a response *from the heart*, about the island's problems. A 'new Jamaican' audience should be charged to watch its political leadership closely and wisely. That this challenge could be delivered in Patwa, the nation language, with full access to the catharsis of tragedy showing that Shakespeare can speak his truths just as comfortably in a Jamaican accent, is in itself a reminder to the audience that we as human beings – on a global, as well as on a national, level – should be relating as equals.

Bibliography

Anon. (2012) 'Jamaican history: 10 facts: things you need to know about the country you love', *The Voice*, 6 August 2012, http://www.voice-online. co.uk/article/jamaican-history-10-facts [accessed 9 Feb. 2016].

Alleyne, M. (2011) 'The interdisciplinary scholarship of a Caribbeanist: a tribute to Dr. Mervyn Alleyne', audio recording by the Institute of Caribbean Studies, 20 Oct. 2011, at the University of Puerto Rico, http:// www.scl-online.net/membership/profiles/mervyn-alleyne.htm [accessed 7 April 2019].

Augarde, T. (ed.) (1991) *The Oxford Dictionary of Modern Quotations* (Oxford: Oxford University Press).

Beard, M. (2011) 'The fall of the Roman Republic', BBC History, http:// www.bbc.co.uk/history/ancient/romans/fallofromanrepublic_article_01. shtml [accessed 7 April 2019].

Beckwith, M.W. (1929) *Black Roadways: A Study of Jamaican Folk Life* (Chapel Hill, NC: University of North Carolina Press).

Bennett, L. (1979) *Anancy and Miss Lou* (Kingston: Sangster's Book Stores).

Berlin, I. (1981) *Against the Current: Essays in the History of Ideas* (Oxford: Oxford University Press).

Bertram, A. (2005) 'Overcoming racial oppression and political violence', *Jamaica Gleaner*, 24 April, p. G2, http://www.jamaica-gleaner.com/gleaner/20050424/focus/focus2.html [accessed 7 April 2019].

Besson, J. (1993) 'Reputation and respectability reconsidered: a new perspective on Afro-Caribbean peasant women', in J.H. Momsen (ed.), *Women and Change in the Caribbean: A Pan Caribbean Perspective* (London: Currey), pp. 15–37.

Brathwaite, E. (1973) *The Arrivants: A New World Trilogy* (Oxford and New York: Oxford University Press).

Campbell, H. (2011) 'Richard Hart: activist in the shadows', *The Gleaner*, 16 Oct., http://jamaica-gleaner.com/gleaner/20111016/arts/arts1.html [accessed 7 April 2019].

Cooke, H. (2003) 'Independence Day 2003 Message from His Excellency the Most Honourable Sir Howard Felix Hanlan Cooke, ON, GCMG, GCVO, CD, on August 6, 2003', published online by the Jamaica Information Service 2003, http://www.jis.gov.jm/special_sections/Independence/GGIndependenceMessage.html [accessed 6 Jan. 2004, no longer active (digital version available from R Minott Egglestone's personal archive)].

Drayton, R. (2014) 'Richard Hart obituary', *The Guardian*, 20 Feb., https://www.theguardian.com/society/2014/feb/20/richard-hart-obituary [accessed 7 April 2019].

Franklyn, D. (2014) 'Michael Manley – the visionary who will never be', *Jamaica Observer*, 13 Dec. 2014, http://www.jamaicaobserver.com/news/Michael-Manley---the-visionary-who-will-never-be [accessed 7 April 2019].

Gloudon, B. (2015) 'Big up massive! What a gwaan?', *The Jamaica Observer*, 24 April, http://www.jamaicaobserver.com/columns/Big-up-massive--What-a-gwaan-_18811066 [accessed 7 April 2019].

Harrod, J. (1972) *Trade Union Foreign Policy: A Study of British and American Trade Union Activities in Jamaica (1936–1939)* (London: Macmillan).

Hart, R. (1999) *Towards Decolonisation: Political, Labour and Economic Development in Jamaica 1938–1945* (Kingston: Canoe).

Holland, T. (2003) *Rubicon: The Triumph and Tragedy of the Roman Republic* (London: Abacus).

Jones, K. (2013) 'A giant of a man – Richard Hart', *Jamaica Gleaner*, 31 Dec., http://jamaica-gleaner.com/gleaner/20131231/lead/lead71.html [accessed 7 April 2019].

Kamau Brathwaite, E. (1984) *History of the Voice: The Development of Nation Language in Anglophone Caribbean Poetry* (London and Port of Spain: New Beacon).

Kuper, A. (1976) *Changing Jamaica* (London and Boston: Routledge & Kegan Paul).

Lewis, R. (2012) 'Introduction: Richard Hart's evaluation of early modern Jamaican politics', in R. Lewis (ed), *Richard Hart: Caribbean Political Activism* (Kingston: Ian Randle).

Marks, P. (2017) 'When "Julius Caesar" was given a Trumpian makeover, people lost it. But is it any good?', *The Washington Post*, 16 June 2017, https://www.washingtonpost.com/news/arts-and-entertainment/wp/2017/06/16/calpurnia-as-melania-octavius-as-jared-the-public-theater-goes-full-trump-with-julius-caesar-in-central-park/?utm_term=.ed4bf548e1e6 [accessed 7 April 2019].

Maquerlot, J.-P. (1995) *Shakespeare and the Mannerist Tradition: A Reading of Five Problem Plays* (Cambridge: Cambridge University Press).

Martin, L. (trans.) (2013) *De Tragedy au Julias Ceazaa /Julius Caesar in Jamaican English: Two Patois Versions of Shakespeare's Play* (Washington, DC: Island).

Mignolo, W. D. (2015) 'Sylvia Wynter: what does it mean to be human?', in K. McKittrick (ed.), *Sylvia Wynter: On Being Human as Praxis* (Durham, NC: Duke University Press), pp. 106–23.

Minott Egglestone, R. (2001) 'Anancyism: a philosophy of survival', in S. Courtman (ed.), *The Society for Caribbean Studies Annual Conference Papers*, vol. 2, http://community-languages.org.uk/SCS-Papers/olv2p5.pdf [accessed 7 April 2019].

— (2004) 'Anancyism: a philosophy of survival', in S. Courtman (ed.), *Beyond the Blood, the Beach and the Banana* (Kingston: Ian Randle), pp. 335–53, digital copy of earlier version of this paper available at http://community-languages.org.uk/SCS-Papers/olv2p5.pdf.

— (2010) 'Encountering discovery and the politics of sorry in Jamaican pantomime', in S. Courtman (ed.), *Society for Caribbean Studies (UK) Annual Conference Papers*, vol. 11, http://www.caribbeanstudies.org.uk/papers/2010/Egglestone_2010.pdf and http://community-languages.org.uk/SCS-Papers/Egglestone2010.pdf [accessed 7 April 2019].

— (2014) 'Tek serious ting mek joke: justice, truth & pantomime . . . Jamaica, land we love', lecture given at the Jamaican Cultural Conference, Art Department, University of Reading, 17 May, https://www.youtube.com/watch?v=FGg3OMvXuoE [accessed 7 April 2019].

Morris, M. (1979) 'Introduction', in L. Bennett, *Anancy and Miss Lou* (Kingston: Sangster's Book Stores), pp. vii–x.

Paul, A. (2004) 'Rastaman vibration: Roger Mais', *Caribbean Beat*, https://www.caribbean-beat.com/online-exclusives/rastaman-vibration-roger-mais [accessed 7 April 2019], originally published in *The Caribbean Review of Books,* Aug. 2004.

Pollard, V. (1980), 'Dread talk: the speech of the Rastafari in Jamaica', *Caribbean Quarterly*, 26 (4): 32–41.

— (1994) *Dread Talk: The Language of Rastafari* (Kingston: Canoe Press).

Schanzer, E. (1963) *The Problem Plays of Shakespeare* (London: Routledge & Kegan Paul).

Seaga, E. (2010) *My Life and Leadership*, I, *Clash of Ideologies 1930–1980* (2 vols., Oxford: Macmillan).

Shakespeare, W. (2014) *Julius Caesar* (Cambridge: Cambridge University Press).

Simpson, J. and J. Speake (2015) *The Oxford Dictionary of Proverbs*, 5th edn (Oxford: Oxford University Press).

Thompson, R.W. (1946) *Black Caribbean* (London: Macdonald).

Wilson, P.J. (1969) 'Reputation and respectability: a suggestion for Caribbean ethnology', *Man*, 4: 70–84.

11. Maybe one day I'll go home

Rod Westmaas

This chapter explores the experiences of two people who migrated from British Guiana (Guyana) to Britain during the Windrush era (1948–64), Eric Huntley and Joyce Trotman. These stories were told during a panel session at the conference 'Memory, Migration, and Decolonisation in the Caribbean and Beyond' and to me in oral interview. In their very particular ways the stories related here illustrate the ways in which Caribbean migrants came to Britain, fought against discrimination and contributed to British culture, while longing to return 'home'.

Due to being part of a political movement in Guyana seeking independence, Eric Huntley was incarcerated for one year in a prison in which his father worked as a warden. He knew, once released, that he needed to lie low and take care of his family. According to Huntley, the love for his country made his departure all the more painful. 'England', he said, 'was my only solution'. His wife, Jessica (now late), reassured him, as they stood on the wharf prior to his boarding the ship to the UK, that he should never stop thinking that, 'One day I will go home'. When in Britain, however, Huntley continued to campaign for decolonisation and to fight the severe racial discrimination he regularly faced by establishing the radical publisher and bookshop, Bogle-L'Ouverture Publications.

As a teacher in London's East End, Joyce Trotman demonstrated her resilience to racial abuse and her steadfastness in providing her students with the very best education the system would allow. Taking advantage of the many learning opportunities in the UK, Trotman did return home armed with a BA (1956) in Latin, English and history from Durham University and an MLit (1958) in linguistics from the University of Lancaster. She went back to Guyana, taught at the Government Training Centre, wrote a highly praised book on Guyanese proverbs and retired in London, where she continues to be a beacon of authority with regard to educating Guyanese.

Eric Huntley's fondest memories as a boy were of the harvest festivals held at the Smith Memorial Church. Its members would bring crops harvested from their farms along with baked goods. The church would be filled with sugar cane, corn, yams, plantain, sugar apples and golden apples as well as delicious

R. Westmaas, 'Maybe one day I'll go home', in J.D. Webb, R. Westmaas, M. del Pilar Kaladeen and W. Tantam (eds.), *Memory, migration and (de)colonisation in the Caribbean and beyond* (London: University of London Press, 2019), pp. 173–81. License: CC-BY-NC-ND 4.0.

Figure 1. Eric Lindbergh Huntley (born in Kitty, British Guiana, 25 September 1929).

plaited breads and other baked goods. On the streets of Georgetown he saw and interacted with persons of Indian and African descent. These were happy days. He observed that each appeared to be drawn towards different persuasions. Indians were stereotyped as being good gardeners and the Africans were mainly clerical workers. His school teachers were all African and strict disciplinarians. He remembers fondly Miss Leitch from the Smith Memorial Church School, who placed young Eric on the front row of the classroom because he was regarded as a clever and attentive student. He and his friends would often play in churchyards and their cemeteries. He can recall reading a faded sign in one church saying, 'Dogs and slaves not allowed', an impression, he thought, that was very similar to the 'No Coloured, No Irish, No Dog' sign he would encounter in London several years later. The congregation of his church, St Sidwell's, in the 1930s comprised mainly well-to-do black churchgoers, almost a *Who's Who* of British Guiana's African citizens.

His first job after leaving school was working for the New Amsterdam, Berbice Post Office as a messenger. He eventually moved (back) to Kitty, a suburb of Georgetown, as a 19-year-old post-office worker. He became aware that the postmasters, who were usually older men, treated younger postal workers with respect, often encouraging them to seek higher education. This, he observed, was the exception in British Guiana, as typical workers did not enjoy this type of relationship with their managers. He joined the Post Office

Workers trade union, becoming its assistant secretary, and published a bulletin for the post-office workers countering the pro-colonial literature taught in the majority of British Guianese schools. The bulletin became an important source of information, giving its sole author, Eric Huntley, nationwide notoriety.

Demands for better working conditions in British Guiana in the late 1940s and 1950s led to mounting tension in British Guiana with the ruling British. An East Indian-led political party, the People's Progressive Party (PPP), along with public- and private-sector unions, were becoming increasingly agitated and asserting their role in British Guiana. Eric felt compelled to join in the struggle. He believed in the fair distribution of wealth to allow everyone to fulfil his or her potential and contribute to society to the best of his or her ability. He had found his calling. As his political awareness increased he developed links with the World Federation of Labour and the World Federation of Trade Unions. He joined the World Peace Council (WPC), promoting peace and nuclear disarmament. The love of his life, Jessica Elleisse Carroll, whom he married in 1950, shared many of Eric's convictions with regard to equality, justice, world peace and fair representation for all.

In 1953 the PPP, under the leadership of Cheddi Jagan, an Indo-Guianese, hard-line Marxist, won the country's first general election based on universal adult suffrage. Fearing a potential communist takeover of the government, the British government suspended the constitution and declared a state of emergency. British troops were brought in to maintain law and order. Eric, in describing how the British Guianese situation was different from the other colonial governments, said they were told: '"You behave yourself, you're a good boy, you play our game." We did not. Or at least, they [the British government] didn't give us time to play the game, I think that's more like it. We protested against the conviction of the Rosenbergs, we didn't send a representative to the Queen's Coronation'.[1]

With the suspension of the constitution came a state of emergency in the country. It was illegal for more than three people to congregate on the streets. Travel within the country was prohibited unless permission was granted by the police, emergency government or army. Cautioned not to leave his home, Eric, now working in Soesdyke, did so without seeking permission and was subsequently arrested. He was incarcerated for one year from 1954 to 1955 in the Georgetown prison, where, ironically, his father Frank Huntley was working as a prison warder. Given his occupation, Warder Huntley did not differentiate between convicted felon and political prisoner. Eric, insensitive at the time of his incarceration, reflected many years later what 'mental torture' it must have been for his father to have a son in prison.

Upon being released from prison, his first priority was to find work to support his young family. He had difficulty in securing permanent employment. With

---

1   Julius and Ethel Rosenberg were American citizens who spied on behalf of the Soviet Union and were tried, convicted and executed by the federal government of the United States.

the political situation between the PPP and the mainly Afro-Guianese party the People's National Congress (PNC) creating an unstable climate, Eric and Jessica decided it was time for him to leave the country and study overseas. In December 1956 he left British Guiana on a Bookers Ship for Trinidad, where he then boarded the SS Columbia for Southampton, England.

After completing all the necessary formalities at the Port of Southampton, Eric and his fellow passengers boarded a train to London. It was damp, grey and foggy. The wintry temperatures of January 1957 quickly made him realise the inadequacy of his best, 'wedding' suit. Donning a warm military jacket and coat given to him by his friend, Rory Westmaas, he then became more prepared for the elements. People were growing used to purchasing essential foodstuffs without the wartime ration cards. His friend and former PPP treasurer, Lionel Jeffrey, took him under his wing and gave him a crash course in how to keep warm, shopping and travelling around London.

Eric missed his wife Jessica and two sons, Karl and Chauncey, tremendously, writing home sometimes several times a week, 'Dear wife', 'Darling Jessica', 'My dear Sica'; and to his sons, 'My two Musketeers, I MISS YOU'. His first job was with British Rail, working at the Stonebridge Park Depot as a shunter. It paid him £12 a week, of which £5 was sent home for Jessica to save towards the passage for her and the two boys. He eventually found a job working for the largest Royal Mail sorting office in London at Mount Pleasant. Not enjoying his job, he viewed it as a way to allow him to make ends meet. He was able to work extremely demanding schedules as well as attend night classes. In April 1958 his wife joined him in London, with the boys following, accompanied by Jessica's mother, in 1962. With the family together their new life in the UK began in earnest.

Eric and Jessica did not find it easy securing adequate rental accommodation. Eric recalled the tobacconist shop window that would display vacant rental homes. He would check it on Fridays and Saturdays. He says: 'Invariably I would call and they would say come on and have a look and the moment I arrive, they see me and it had gone'. Additionally, they were up against the aforementioned 'No coloured, no Irish and no dog' sign found frequently on property windows. It happened so often that Eric no longer considered it an impingement. They viewed it like 'water off a duck's back'. They eventually managed to borrow money privately to purchase their first house. Unfortunately, their living expenses and mortgage became overwhelming, forcing them to surrender the house to the bank.

With regard to employment, Jessica had it worse than Eric. She had several 'work-related race issues', one of which led to her being sacked by a regional manager who oversaw one of the shipping-agency offices she worked for. He was unaware there was someone 'coloured' working for the company and she was released shortly after he paid her a visit. Eric's sons were often stopped by the police for no apparent reason. Victims of the Stop and Search Law (SUS), they accepted it as the norm and often failed to tell their parents. Accabre, Eric and Jessica's only daughter, who was born in London, was a child of the 1970s and by then things were changing for the better.

The loss of their first home forced Eric and Jessica to rent accommodation in the north London home of their Trinidadian friends, John and Irma La Rose. The La Rose household was abuzz with left-wing discussions described by Eric as a 'university'. British politics fascinated Eric, in particular the discussions that centred on Britain's relationship with its African and Caribbean subjects. The 'student Eric' ended prematurely, with him finding it hard to concentrate on his studies amidst all the politically charged intercourse at the house. Admitting that it was a bad decision to drop his educational plans, personally, politically and intellectually it was a tremendous opportunity for him to grow in other ways.

The historian and Guyanese political activist Walter Rodney partook in many a discussion at the La Rose home while he pursued his postgraduate studies at London University's School of Oriental and African Studies. Eric's having met Rodney changed the Huntleys' whole future. Living in London in the late 1960s was extremely toxic. In spite of the many challenges, racial and otherwise, the Huntley family remained resilient, strong and unified. By embracing the community they were assured that a friend was always close at hand. From the gatherings at the Commonwealth Institute and the many meetings at the West Indian Student Centre in Earl's Court, they knew that change would only come if the diaspora were to remain together and spoke with one voice. They just happened to be two of the loudest.

Describing himself as a socialist and internationalist, Eric's life was entwined with that of his wife, Jessica. The legacy of the Huntleys has been permanently stamped on the social-activism map of the UK. From the establishment of their publishing company, Bogle L'Ouventure Publishing, to the opening of the Walter Rodney Bookstore, the community and West Indian diaspora as a whole were so much richer because Eric and Jessica cared. Preserved in the London Metropolitan Archives, the invaluable Huntley Collection is available for anyone wishing to research and refer to it.

When Eric (and Jessica) came to the UK in the 1950s, like countless other black people who arrived with their British passports they were largely focused on earning a living, working hard in the face of discrimination, which they ignored, and on returning home. Eric's plan was to absorb and use his studies and return home to take care of his family. The Huntleys were among a small group of Black activists who were prepared to set aside their own self-development in exchange for offering support to the community against the racism that was, at that time, so prevalent and vicious in the UK. Going home was no longer an option.

Figure 2. Estelle Joyce Trotman (born in Stanleytown Village, British Guiana, 22 October 1927).

As a child Joyce grew up in Georgetown in religious surroundings, crediting her mother, Diana Elizabeth a.k.a Gertrude Petrie, for teaching both her and her sister Christian love and Christian loyalty. Considering herself a child of the empire, Joyce sang, 'Land of Hope and Glory' with passion and much gusto every year on 24 May, Queen Victoria's birthday. She and her fellow school friends would stream into a local Georgetown cinema, weeks before, rehearsing for the big day. The chorus was her favourite:

> Land of Hope and Glory, Mother of the Free,
> How shall we extol thee, who are born of thee?
> Wider still and wider shall thy bounds be set;

God, who made thee mighty, make thee mightier yet,
God, who made thee mighty, make thee mightier yet.[2]

She attended the Kingston Methodist School in Georgetown, where she regularly saw (indentured) Indians assembling at a compound adjacent to the school, awaiting passage back to India or to be given a piece of land as an enticement to stay. The adjoining property to this compound was, in later years, turned into a woman's dormitory for trainee teachers. Although the accommodations were not 'the best', this was a significant step forward for the training college as they were now able to attract potential teachers from throughout the country. Joyce was instrumental in establishing this facility. Aspiring to become a teacher, Joyce was offered her initial training at the Government Training College which subsequently led to her being given a Commonwealth (teaching) bursary at the University of Durham in the UK.

In 1955 Joyce and two others from the Government Training College set sail for England from Barbados. 'A horrible ship', she said, 'It took 12 long days'. With regard to the weather, Joyce said that it was extremely cold: 'I just didn't realise it could be so cold'. This was the first time she had experienced actual shivering. Greeted at Waterloo Station in London by her friend Viola Burnham (the wife of the future president Forbes Burnham), Joyce was overjoyed to see a familiar face. After spending a few days in the Notting Hill area of London she was Newcastle-bound. On her way there, she recalled on the train journey a man sitting opposite her admiring the way she held a knife and fork. He said to Joyce in a matter of fact way, 'I didn't expect people like you to know how to use a knife and fork'. She almost slapped him.

The academic year of 1955 to 1956 began with a wonderful summer. Joyce wore sandals until the end of September. Eventually the weather changed. The east winds kicked in. It was the worst winter since 1947. On several occasions Joyce found herself saying, 'What the hell am I doing in this country?'. Everyone kept calling her 'pet'. Often she would hear the locals say, 'Lovely morning, pet!'. She would look at the overcast sky and say, 'What's lovely about it?'. Newcastle was friendly and receptive to Joyce. Their mayor even invited the foreign students to have tea.

Staying at the Methodist International House in Newcastle, she found herself in the middle of an uncomfortable situation. A young, white, English girl staying at the house was ill and had several visitors, one of whom was her black boyfriend from one of the African countries. The manager of the house accused the young English girl of sullying the sanctity of English womanhood. She was told that she had to leave the house, illness notwithstanding. Outraged by this seemingly racist act, Joyce petitioned the fellow residents to have this decision reversed. She was successful, proclaiming that as a Methodist house it was unconscionable for it to act in this way. Joyce believes that they relented

---

2   'Land of Hope and Glory' (1902), music by Edward Elgar; lyrics by A. C. Benson.

because she confronted them by pointing out that if they held fast to that 'unchristian-like' principle, the word 'international' should be removed from their name.

A New Year ritual of having a 'dark person' enter your home to ensure prosperity was attempted while Joyce was in Newcastle. A British family had approached the Methodist International House to see if they could 'spare' an African chap to cross their threshold. Needless to say, this request was denied. As a teacher-in-training Joyce was once approached by a five-year-old and asked if she was 'black all over like a golliwog?'. He wanted to know if she needed to bathe but Joyce assured the youngster that she did bathe and very often.

As a black woman teaching at an all-boys comprehensive school in East London throughout the 1970s and 1980s, Joyce endured much racial abuse, taunting and workplace discrimination. Christmas time was particularly challenging at the school. She would often hear the pupils singing in the corridor when she was in earshot: 'I'm dreaming of a white Christmas, just like the ones before the niggers came'. Once being the recipient of the vilest expletives in the midst of a class, Joyce took it in her stride. She tells the story that years later the offending student would say, 'Miss Trotman was the best teacher I ever had'. Her demeanour and character were often equated to that of Sidney Poitier in the acclaimed 1960s film, *To Sir With Love*. Joyce took all this in her stride. These were teenagers whom she chose to treat as adults. Never asking for an apology, she adhered to her Christian side by showing them kindness and understanding.

Once her initial training had ended in 1958, Joyce returned to British Guiana to take up a teaching role at an infants' school. She then taught English at the country's foremost girls' school, Bishops' High School. Joyce and her friend Yvonne Stevenson established the first library at the teacher training college. From the shelves and books to the index cards, this was a major accomplishment. Eventually returning to the UK to further her education and settling in South London, teaching became her life. Along with her Quaker faith she became an integral part of the Guyanese diaspora in London. Her love of words led to the publication in 2006 of the book *The Proverbs of Guyana Explained*, which is cited as a significant history of the language of Guyana because it exemplifies and preserves the syntactic structure as well as the powerful imagery of Guyanese Creole.

Joyce had always felt she needed to return to Guyana. Returning after her initial training in Newcastle, then going on to Leicester, she always had the desire to 'give back'. Her completion of a degree at the University of Guyana gave her and her family immense pride.

Family members have played a significant role in Joyce's life. Nieces, nephews, sister and brother have all looked out for Joyce's welfare. When a health issue arose and Joyce needed medical attention, her siblings encouraged her to return to the UK. She made a full recovery. She reflected that in the UK she no longer had to worry about locking her gate and staying indoors all the time, as she had to do in Guyana. This was not the life she wanted to live. She felt she had to leave Guyana for good, declaring that she is a Guyanese, British and both, but first and foremost a child of God.

Index

Activism, 102, 107
African descendants, 139, 141
African heritage, 63–4
    and musical cultures, 66
Africanness as a source of liberation, 144
Age of revolutions, 117
Aluminium Company of Canada, 88, 90 94 95
Anancy, 155
Antigua, 113, 143
AntipodeFoundation, 102
archipelago as metaphor, 139
archival practice, 102
archival silence, 4, 50
archives in the Caribbean, 38
authenticity, 72

Bahamas
    colonial history, 39
    communities, 38
        Eleuthera Arts and Cultural Centre, 49
    trade, 39–42
    foreign investment, 44
    House of Assembly, 45
    intangible heritage, 51
    living heritage, 38, 47, 49
    memory, 38, 39, 47, 51
    personal memories, 39–44, 46, 48
    Progressive Liberal Party, 45
    Tarpum Bay, 37–52
    Tarpum Bay Historical and Heritage Society, 52

United Bahamian Party Black Power, 46
Bauxite, 91, 94, 96, 99, 100
Beach as metaphor, 139
Bishop's High School (Guyana), 109, 180
Black aesthetics, 68
Black Atlantic, 57
Black British youth, 58, 63, 63, 74; the raising of, 176
Black cultural knowledge, 66
Black exploitation and responses to, 63
Black History Month, 100
Black Power in Guyana, 108
Bogle-L'Ouverture Publications, 7, 176
Booker's Company, 109
Botswana, 84
Bourbon reforms, 122
Brexit, 111
Bronze Woman, the, 34
Brutus of *Julius Caesar*, 154
Burnham, Forbes, 109
Bustamente, Alexander, 153
    and Anancy, 164
    and Caesar, 165
    and Jamaican independence, 164

Caesar of *Julius Caesar*, 155, 157
Canada, colonial status, 98
Caribbean federation, 88
Caribbean immigration to Britain, 31, 108
    experiences of racism, 6, 108, 173

resistance against racism, 7, 173
first impressions, 34, 80 81
finding employment, xii, 32, 33
finding housing, 33
and decolonisation, 7, 8
Caribbean War Memorial, Brixton, 79
Cassius of *Julius Caesar*
   and social equality, 154
   and Anancy, 157
   and democracy, 157
Césaire, Aimé, 137, 140, 141
Central Intelligence Agency
   interventions in Guyana, 112
   whistleblowing, 112
community knowledge, 11
Congress of Vienna, 122
consuls
   citizenship, 118
   information exchange, 118
   the political geography of, 123
   relation to surveillance, 118
counter-culture, 61
Creole culture, 136
Creole language,136
Creolisation, 144

dancehall culture, 58, 74
De Tragedy au Julias Ceazaa/Julius Caesar in Jamaican English, 159
Decolonial gestures, 140
Decolonisation
   of the academy, 9–13
   in the Caribbean, 107
   and the creation of a new history, 144
   (de)colonisation, 1
   and the everyday, 2
   histories of, 1
   in Jamaica, 153
   and open access, 11
decolonising memory, 87
deejay, 57, 74

demystification, 143
development studies, 107
diasporic dialect, 70
displacement within the Caribbean, 100
dread talk, 160

Earl's Court West Indian Students' Centre, 109
Education, 110
   in the colonial Caribbean
   and the military, 81
   in the commonwealth, 153
enslavement, 99, 136
Eurocentrism: resistance against, 71

Fanon, Frantz, 2, 137, 141
   on decolonisation, 142–3
free trade, 122

Garvey, Marcus, 136
   contribution to global politics, 162
Garveyism, 59, 63, 64
Georgetown (Guyana), 174
Glissant, Édouard, 136, 140, 141
Glocal
   language, 67
   experience, 75
Government Training College (Guyana), 179
Griot, 60
Guyana
   and Britishness, 7
   and colonialism, 9
   Dutch Guyana, 3, 32
   emigration from xi, 80, 107
   Guyana Freedom Association, 6
   and independence, 107, 108
Guyanese High Commission, 109

Haisla, 91, 94, 95, 101
Haiti

and 'exceptionalism', 124
and exclusion from the consular Caribbean, 124
and imperialism, 111
and independence, 4
Haitian Revolution, 3, 85
Hart, Richard, 164, 165
Henaksiala, 91
Hudson Bay Company, 90
Huntley Collection, 177
Huntley, Eric, 6, 175–78
Huntley, Jessica, 6
  migration to Britain, 176
hybridity
  cultural, 68
  linguistic, 69

Indigeneity, 88
Indigenous
  struggles, 97, 98
  studies, 99, 102
  scholars, 102
Institute for Indigenous Government and Langara College, 98
island talk, 69

Jagan, Cheddi, 108
Jamaica
  child welfare, 21
  coat of arms, 87
  and colonialism, 9
  colonisers, 88
  and emigration, 20–1, 24–6, 97, 157–8
  English invasion of, 3
  farming communities, 95
  impact on British popular culture, 160
  independence day celebrations, 19–20
  national identity, 22
  national memory, 88
  neighbourhood clearances, 24
  post-colonial government, 22
  return migration, 27
  social unrest, 24
  student protests, 28
  sovereignty, 162
  on world stage, 88, 154
  and youth, 19
People's National Party, 23
  origins of, 165
Jamaican Labour Party, 165
Jamaican Sound Systems, 58
Jonestown Massacre, 110

Kincaid, Jamaica, 133, 137, 138
Kingston Methodist School, 179
Kitimat, 91, 93, 94, 97

La Rose, Irma, 177
La Rose, John, 177
Little Theatre Movement Pantomime (Jamaica), 166
London Metropolitan Archives, 177
Lyricism, 60, 64, 68, 71

Macbeth, 157
Mackenzie, Charles, 128
Mais, Roger, 29
Manichean world view, 142, 143, 144
Martinique, 139
Mercantilism, 117
Manley, Michael, 28, 29, 154
Manley, Norman, 22, 25, 27
  in relation to Brutus, 163
Middle Passage, 135
mining, 90, 91, 96
  catastrophes, 113
  Canadian ownership of, 113
multiracialism, 84

Nandy, Ashis, 2
Napoleon Bonaparte, 125
Napoleonic Wars, 128

National Archives (Kew), 111
National sovereignty (Caribbean), 119
Négritude, 135
Neo-colonialism, 109
National Health Service, 81
   Caribbean staff, 80
   equal opportunity, 80
   and ethnic minority staff, 82
Nobrega, Cecil, 34

Oral testimony, 5, 6
outernational, 71

Padmore, George, 136
Pakistan, 84
Patwa, 66, 71, 159
People's National Party, 154
People's Progressive Party, 108
plantocracy, 99
pollution by multinational corporations, 113
Post Office Workers Union (Guyana), 174
post-Windrush migrants, 107
postcolonial studies, 98
poverty, conditions of, 138
Puerto Rico, 120

Queen's College (Guyana), 109
Queen Elizabeth, loyalty to, 81

Race Relations Act, 81
Rastafari, 23, 27, 29, 59, 61
   and language, 160
reggae music, 61, 63, 74, 154, 159
   its listeners, 66
   as transcendental, 67
religion of Caribbean migrants, 80
reparations, 98, 110, 111
Return to Africa, 135
Rhodes Must Fall, 9

Rodney, Walter, 28, 177
   assassination of, 110, 112
Royal Air Force, 81
Royal Shakespeare Company, 166

Saint-Domingue (Haiti), 120
   relations with the Spanish Empire, 125
schooling in England, 35
self-emancipation, 110
shadeism, 162
   and political inequality in Jamaica, 164
Shakespeare, William, 156
silencing, 37, 46, 50, 74, 97
Sir Arthur Lewis Institute for Social and Economic Studies, 91, 94, 95
Smith Memorial Church School, 174
Spanish American revolutions, 121
Spanish Empire, 120
   relations with the US, 121
spatiality, 140
Stop and Search Law, 176

Tanzania, 84
Territorial contest, 124
The Tragedy of Julius Caesar
   as a postcolonial text, 166
   relation to Jamaican national sovereignty, 156
Thomas Jefferson, 125
tourism, 133
transcendentalism, 68
Treaty of San Lorenzo, 119
Trotman, Joyce, 7, 1, 21, 73, 179–80

University of the West Indies, 88
US Constitution, 118

Vancouver, 89, 90
   and mining, 100

West Indian Federation, 165
West Indian Student's Centre, 177
white supremacy, 61
whiteness, 58
Windrush
   generation xii, 2, 7, 31
   impact on British society, 84
   scandal, 111
   teachers and educators, 8
Working People's Alliance Support
   Group, 110, 111
World Peace Council, 175
World War Two, contribution of
   Caribbean personnel, 79

Founded in 1965, the Institute of Latin American Studies (ILAS) forms part of the University of London's School of Advanced Study, based in Senate House, London.

ILAS occupies a unique position at the core of academic study of the region in the UK. Internationally recognised as a centre of excellence for research facilitation, it serves the wider community through organising academic events, providing online research resources, publishing scholarly writings and hosting visiting fellows. It possesses a world-class library dedicated to the study of Latin America and is the administrative home of the highly respected *Journal of Latin American Studies*. The Institute supports scholarship across a wide range of subject fields in the humanities and cognate social sciences and actively maintains and builds ties with cultural, diplomatic and business organisations with interests in Latin America, including the Caribbean.

As an integral part of the School of Advanced Study, ILAS has a mission to foster scholarly initiatives and develop networks of Latin Americanists and Caribbeanists at a national level, as well as to promote the participation of UK scholars in the international study of Latin America.

The Institute currently publishes in the disciplines of history, politics, economics, sociology, anthropology, geography and environment, development, culture and literature, and on the countries and regions of Latin America and the Caribbean. Since autumn 2019, the Institute's books, together with those of the other institutes of the School, have been published under the name University of London Press.

Full details about the Institute's publications, events, postgraduate courses and other activities are available online at http://ilas.sas.ac.uk.

Institute of Latin American Studies
School of Advanced Study, University of London
Senate House, Malet Street, London WC1E 7HU

Tel 020 7862 8844, Email ilas@sas.ac.uk
http://ilas.sas.ac.uk

Recent and forthcoming titles published by the Institute of Latin American Studies:

Rethinking Past and Present: Essays in memory of Alistair Hennessy (2018)
edited by Antoni Kapcia

Shaping Migration between Europe and Latin America: New Approaches and Challenges (2018)
edited by Ana Margheritis

Brazil: Essays on History and Politics (2018)
Leslie Bethell

Creative Spaces: Urban Culture and Marginality in Latin America (2019)
edited by Niall H.D. Geraghty and Adriana Laura Massidda

Cultures of Anti-Racism in Latin America and the Caribbean (2019)
edited by Peter Wade, James Scorer and Ignacio Aguiló

A Nicaraguan Exceptionalism? Debating the Legacy of the Sandinista Revolution (2020)
edited by Hilary Francis

Cultural Worlds of the Jesuits in Colonial Latin America (2020)
edited by Linda Newson

Lightning Source UK Ltd.
Milton Keynes UK
UKHW020413070220
358286UK00008B/67